U0589187

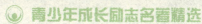

青少年成长励志名著精选

The Chosen Inspirational Classics on Youth's Growth

·中英对照·

〔英〕拉迪亚德·吉卜林 著　　文美惠 译

丛林故事

中国国际广播出版社

总序

　　成长是一个美好而动人的话题。因为成长，我们从天真烂漫的孩童变成至情至性的青年；从不谙世事到看透世间百态；从懵懂无知到肩负起家庭和社会的重任。在成长中，我们一点点长大，心智慢慢成熟，我们的理想和抱负也逐渐成形。而成长中的少年和青年，如朝阳，如晨露，如春前之草，充满了活力与生机。少年和青年时期是人生中最宝贵、最关键的阶段，也是进步最快的阶段，在这个阶段里，我们有迷茫，有困惑，有失落，也有梦想，有憧憬，有抱负。在得到与失去中，在成功与失败中，在欢喜与哀愁中，我们一天天地长大，一天天地读懂什么是"成长"。

　　列夫·托尔斯泰说过，人类被赋予了一种工作，那就是精神的成长。在成长过程中，我们渴望知识，渴望精神的充实，渴望灵魂的完善。为此，我们特地选编了世界文学宝库中八本不朽的名著，《小王子》、《长腿叔叔》、《秘密花园》、《彼得·潘》、《水孩子》、《绿野仙踪》、《丛林故事》和《成长》。它们都是有关成长、有关爱的著作，并深深地影响和感染了一代代读者。《小王子》是一部脍炙人口的儿童文学作品，被称为是仅次于《圣经》的经典读物。同时它也是一部写给成年人的，关于生命、热诚和爱的哲理童话。作品表现出来的想象力、智慧和情感，使各个年龄的读者都能从中找到乐趣，并且随时能够发现新的精神财富；《长腿叔叔》是简·韦伯斯特最负盛名的代表作，已成为世界少女的成长必读书。它讲述了孤女朱蒂受到一个理事的资助完成学业，并与之相恋的美好故事。作品中流露出来的温馨、亲切和真爱让我们感知到世间的真善美；《秘密花园》是弗朗西丝·伯内特最著名、最成功的作品，被公认为是一部无年龄界限的佳作。自私专横的小姑娘玛莉在姑父家发现了秘密花园，她不仅使荒芜的花园重现生机，自己也变成一个礼貌善良、有爱心的小姑娘；《彼得·潘》是詹姆斯·巴里影响最大的作品，也是迈克尔·杰克逊生前最喜欢的童话。彼得·潘是生活在永无岛上的永远也长不大的男孩，在海岛上他和别的小伙伴经历了许多有趣的事情；《水孩子》查尔斯·金斯利的代表作，讲述了一个扫烟囱的孩子汤姆如何变成水孩子的故事；《丛林故事》是 1907 年诺贝尔文学奖得主拉迪亚德·吉卜林的作品，讲述了印度少年莫格里狼群中成长为一个勇武聪慧的少年的故事。作者超凡的语言和杰出的叙事才能描绘了大自然的美妙画面，动物之间温暖的友谊和他们充满生趣的冒险；《绿野仙踪》是美国著名作家及剧作家莱曼·弗兰克·鲍姆最受读者欢迎的一部作品。小姑娘多萝西和没有脑子的稻草人、没有心脏的铁皮人和胆小的狮子齐心协力，完成了各自的心愿；《成长》是美国知名作家詹妮·M·德林克沃特的作品。爱讲故事的孤女小朱迪在失去双亲后顽强、倔强地成长，并最终收获美满的爱情。作品内容时而欢快，时而忧伤，将朱迪不平凡的成长经历展现在我们眼前。

塞缪尔·斯麦尔曾经说过，"最优秀的书是一种由高贵的语言和闪光的思想构成的财富，为人类所铭记、所珍惜，是我们永恒的伴侣和慰藉……书籍把我们介绍给良师益友，是我们认识迄今为止人类最伟大的灵魂。"该套丛书精选名家名作，阅读该套丛书，我们可以通过主人公的经历感受其中的真爱与温馨，鼓舞与感动，不仅可以滋养我们的心灵，提高我们的文学修养，还可以给我们人生的启迪。相信本套丛书必定会给您别样的体验，如同一泓清泉，滋润您的心田。

编者

译者序

拉迪亚德·吉卜林（1865~1936）是二十世纪英国享有盛誉的重要作家之一。他的创作十分丰富，有长篇小说、短篇小说、诗歌、游记、儿童文学、随笔、回忆录等等。其中尤以短篇小说的成就最为突出。他的以在狼群中长大的印度少年莫格里为主人公的一组丛林动物故事，更是他创作中的瑰宝。吉卜林的《丛林之书》里的动物故事，已被译成数十种语言，传遍全世界。它不仅博得无数青少年的喜爱，同时也使成年读者得到了无穷的乐趣，把他们带回了童年时代金色的美妙幻想世界。正像美国著名作家马克·吐温说的那样："我了解吉卜林的书……它们对于我从来不会变得苍白，它们保持着缤纷的色彩，它们永远是新鲜的。"

拉迪亚德·吉卜林的父亲约翰·洛克伍德·吉卜林出生在约克郡，是一位陶瓷雕塑工艺设计师，曾在南坎辛登博物馆任职。母亲艾丽斯·麦唐纳出生于牧师家庭，是位很有艺术修养的妇女。1865年，约翰·洛克伍德·吉卜林接到印度孟买艺术学校的聘书，当年三月，这对新婚夫妇便远渡重洋，来到孟买。约翰在孟买艺术学校任建筑雕塑学教授，后又迁居拉合尔，任拉合尔博物馆馆长。吉卜林出生在孟买。

1871年，不满六岁的吉卜林和三岁的妹妹一同被送回英国受教育。他们被托养在一位退休海军军官家里。这家主妇和她的儿子对吉卜林肆意侮辱虐待，给他幼小的心灵上留下了抹不掉的伤痕。吉卜林在十二岁时被送入德文郡的联合服务学院上学，这是一所培养家境贫寒的海外军人子弟的中学。校长普赖斯是吉卜林父母的老友，他发现吉卜林有文学才能，便委托他编辑校刊。吉卜林在校刊上发表了一些诗歌。1881年，他的母亲把他写的诗歌收集起来，在拉合尔自费出版，名为《学童的抒情诗》。这是他的第一部诗集。

1882年吉卜林中学毕业了。他离开英国，回到印度，当上了拉合尔《军民报》的副编辑，立即投入了繁忙的采访和报道中。这段生活大大丰富了吉卜林的经验，使他熟悉了印度社会，接触到了社会上各个阶层的人物。他尤其同情和了解英国驻印度的士兵和印度下层的穷苦人民，后来在他的作品中出色地描写了他们的形象。从1884年起，吉卜林开始为《军民报》写些诗歌和短篇小说。1886年，他出版了诗集《机关打油诗》，获得好评。1888年，吉卜林出版了他的第一部短篇小说集《山里的故事》。同年，他又以"印度铁路丛书"小册子的形式，出版了另外六个短篇小说集。这些以印度生活为题材的小说，一方面用神奇壮丽的色彩揭示了古老印度的不为人知的广阔世界，使读者耳目一新；另一方面，它又以严峻的现实主义笔法告诉人们：印度这片丰饶美丽的殖民地，由于征服者贪婪掠夺和连年的战火灾患，已经满目疮痍，印度人民已经被投入到深重的苦难中。吉卜林用他做新闻记者时练就的简洁明快的笔法，讲述了一个又一个的故事，写出了生活在这片土地上的形形色色的人物：从殖民地军官，到被人蔑称为"汤米"的英国士兵和终日辛劳的英国小职员；从天真的印度姑娘，到处流浪的土著水手，到城市骗子、"占星家"和神庙里的祭司。他讲述的是充满神秘色彩的仇杀、爱情、复仇和死亡，他讲述的还有英国大兵在印度那些诙谐幽默的冒险故事。通过这些故事，人们看到了印度的现实：奴役、战争、屠杀、灾荒、饥馑、宗教迷信、落后习俗……吉卜林不仅是个讲故事的能手，他还是个具有深刻观察力和强烈同情心的作家，因此，他笔下那些小人物的欢乐和悲哀，追求和幻灭，都写得那么真实感人，发人深思，以致在读者心里留下了难以磨灭的印象。

吉卜林的小说集很快就传到英国。几乎是一夜之间，吉卜林在英国文坛成了知名人物，受到各大文学杂志的赞扬。吉卜林小说中充满雄浑粗犷的男子汉的阳刚气概，给世纪末英国文坛上充斥着的萎靡文风吹进了一股清新的空气，也使看腻了老一套维多利亚时期小说的读者产生了迥然相异的新鲜印象。1889年，这个年仅二十四岁的作家经过长途旅行，踏上家乡英国的土地时，他发现自己俨然已是一位引人注目的"文坛新秀"。

吉卜林没有使读者失望，他在几年内陆续写出了《营房歌谣》、小说《消失的光芒》和他的著名短篇小说集《生命的阻力》。1892年吉卜林和美国女子卡罗琳·贝利斯蒂尔结婚，婚后定居于美国的弗蒙特。这是吉卜林的一段幸福而多产的日子，在这个时期，他写出了不少重要作品，如短篇小说集《许多发明》、冒险小说《大宝石》。也就是在这时，他创作并出版了他最为著名的动物故事集《丛林之书》（1894）和《丛林之书续篇》（1895）。这两部故事集一共包括十五篇，它们成了吉卜林最有影响和最受读者欢迎的作品。

二十世纪初期，英布战争爆发，吉卜林由于支持政府的扩张政策，声誉大大下降，于是他隐居于英国乡村。这个时期他创作了几部儿童文学作品，受到重视和好评，如《供儿童阅读的平常故事》、历史故事集《普克山的帕克》和《奖赏和仙女》。值得一提的还有吉卜林的长篇小说《基姆》。它被公认为他最重要的长篇小说。由于吉卜林主要以短篇小说见长，没有写多少部长篇小说，因此，英国小说家威·亨·赫德逊认为，在吉卜林的长篇小说中"只有这一部足以和他的短篇小说媲美"。

在晚年，由于儿子在战场上阵亡，吉卜林自己又疾病缠身，他的创作内容多涉及战争创伤、病态心理、神秘主义、疯狂和死亡的题材。这个时期的创作有短篇小说集《各种各样的人》、《借方和贷方》、《限期和展期》等。评论家在推崇他的前期作品时，有的认为他后期的创作技巧更臻成熟。但是不可否认，他的前期作品，尤其是印度题材的作品和他的《丛林之书》，仍是他最为出色的代表作品。

吉卜林生前受到尊崇，获得过多种荣誉。1907年，他因为"观察的能力、新颖的想象、雄浑的思想和杰出的叙事才能"而被瑞典学院授予当年的诺贝尔文学奖金，他是英国作家中获此奖金的第一位。

1936年1月，吉卜林因病去世。他的骨灰被隆重地安葬在威斯敏斯特教堂的诗人角，就在狄更斯和哈代两位伟大英国作家的墓地旁边。

《丛林之书》和《丛林之书续篇》共有十五篇故事，在我们编的这本《丛林故事》里，共收入了五篇，其中有《丛林之书》中的三篇，接下来的一篇选自《丛林之书续篇》。最后一篇《在丛林里》则选自短篇小说集《许多发明》。

《丛林之书》和它的续篇所包括的十五篇故事中，七篇是互不相关的动物故事，如《白海豹》就属于这一类。另外八篇则是以少年莫格里为中心人物的系列动物故事。莫格里是印度樵夫的儿子。当他还是个婴儿时，在森林里受到老虎谢尔汗追逐，父母逃散，他误入狼穴，被母狼收养，成为狼群中的一员。他长成了一个勇武而又聪慧的少年。他的朋友有慈祥的狼妈妈，忠诚的狼兄弟，以及足智多谋的黑豹巴希拉，憨厚的老熊巴卢，正直的狼群头领阿克拉，孔武有力的蟒蛇卡阿等等。他们在莫格里周围形成了一个温暖的集体，教给他生活的智慧和谋生的本领，教给他丛林动物必须遵守的"丛林法律"。老虎谢尔汗仍然不时前来捣乱。莫格里具有人类的智慧，学会了使用火。他从附近的村子里取来了动物们称之为"红花"的火，帮助阿克拉平息了狼群的叛乱，把煽动叛乱的老虎烧得焦头烂额，落荒而逃。后来，莫格里被村子里一位失去儿子的村妇收养，当了放牧牛群的牧童。但是老虎谢尔汗跟踪而来，要加害于他。莫格里和狼兄弟们定下计策，利用牛群设下埋伏，谢尔汗陷进牛群的包围，被牛蹄践踏而死。但莫格里也因冒犯村里的巫师而被村民用石子驱赶出来，回到了丛林。在本书中还可以读到莫格里的不少冒险故事。而《在丛林里》这篇故事则讲述了莫格里故事的大结局——他离开了兽群，回到人类中间，结了婚，当上了看林人，帮助林务官保护森林。从出版时间上说，这个故事比《丛林之书》早一年出版，吉卜林对朋友解释说，"这个故事是莫格里故事里最先写出的，不过它讲的是他的事业的最后章节……时间估计在他最终和丛林里的朋友们分手两三年之后。"这个故事显然比他后来写的那些神奇的莫格里故事要逊色些，试想一个能震慑森林里凶猛野兽的天神般的少年莫格里，竟然降格为英国文官制度下一名小职员，并且期望将来能领到一份退休金，这实在有点儿"煞风景"。不过我们应该记住，吉卜林的灵感和才华在这最初一篇里只是刚刚被启发出来，而在后来的故事里得到了充分的发挥。由于这是莫格里故事里有独特地位的一篇，我们在这里把它也选了进来。

吉卜林讲述的其他动物故事也同样充满活力和生趣。《白海豹》描写了一头有一身与众不同的白皮毛的海豹。为了帮助同类免遭捕猎者的残杀，他历经千辛万苦，到处搜寻，终于找到了一片人迹不至的海滩，并且带领同伴迁居到那片乐土上。

吉卜林的这些有趣的动物故事不仅把儿童引进了一个新奇的想象中的天地，而且通过莫格里和动物们的冒险活动，教会了他们生活的哲理：要团结友爱，互相帮助，形成一个温暖的集体，同时，每个人都应该充分发挥自己的智慧和勇气，不屈不挠地克服困难，和邪恶势力进行不屈不挠的斗争。

吉卜林为了阐述他心目中理想的社会秩序，在《丛林之书》里还创造了一套动物们都必须遵守的"丛林法律"。对这套"丛林法律"，不同的评论家往往有不同的看法。有的认为吉卜林在鼓吹"弱肉强食"的强权统治，有的认为吉卜林是在为帝国主义的掠夺政策做辩护。那么，吉卜林在小说里又是怎样说明他的"丛林法律"的呢？书中对这条法律所作的描写是这样的：首先，"丛林法律"要求动物有"无声无息的脚步，明察秋毫的锐利目光，识别风向的耳朵和尖锐的白牙"，这显然是动物为了维护自己的生存所必须具备的条件。这使他们不但可以避开危险，还可以进行厮杀和捕猎食物。其次，"丛林法律"还规定母兽和幼兽必须受到保护，这样，动物们繁衍后代才能得到保证。在《莫格里的兄弟们》里，每个月圆之夜，狼群都要举行大会，让狼群成员认识每一头新生的狼崽，并规定他们"不能用任何借口杀死一头狼崽"，否则"立即处死"。狼群正是用这条法律制止恃强凌弱的行为。除此以外，"丛林法律"里还有一些有利于弱小动物生存的特殊规定。比如，禁止动物吃人的法律，因为一旦猛兽吃了人，便会招来人类的报复，长牙、枪弹会不分青红皂白地射杀丛林里的兽类，"森林里每一个子民都得遭殃"。遇到干旱威胁丛林生物时，这条丛林法律又规定：只要丛林里那唯一的大河的河水下降到露出了河床中央的大石头时，这条唯一的水源便成了动物的"禁猎"区。不管是凶猛的老虎，还是狡猾的豺狼，都不得在饮水的地方捕杀麋鹿和山羊。这说明，"丛林法律"的核心是要求动物们遵守一定的秩序，服从法律，以达到生存和繁衍后代的目的。老虎谢尔汗，正是因为不服从法律，犯了"不许吃人"的罪行，才遭到声讨和谴责的。

吉卜林对一位评论家解释过，他是如何构思出莫格里的故事的。他说："在我发现了'丛林法律'之后，其余的一切便十分顺利地随之诞生了。"显然，在动物故事里他是企图用丛林中的法律来鼓吹他的社会理想。他认为人类社会和动物世界一样，人和人的利益是相互制约、相互依存的。因此为了人类的生存和繁荣，人人都要遵守一定的社会法规。更进一步说，吉卜林十分强调实干家的奋斗精神。瑞典学院的常务秘书威尔森在向吉卜林颁发诺贝尔文学奖时，在授奖词中也谈到了对"丛林法律"的看法。他认为："丛林的法则，也就是宇宙的法则。如果我们要问这些法则的主旨是什么，就会得到以下简洁的回答：'奋斗、尽责和服从。'所以吉卜林鼓吹的是勇气、自我牺牲和忠诚，他最恨的是缺乏丈夫气概和缺乏自我克制力。"

威尔森的这种观点和他对"丛林法律"的解释，着眼点在于个人对集体、对社会的责任，因此他所强调的，正是吉卜林所推崇的实干家的责任感。这也可以说是对"丛林法律"的又一种解释。

不过，《丛林之书》里最吸引读者的，不是关于"丛林法律"的宣扬，而是那美妙的大自然画面，那动物之间温暖的友谊和他们充满生趣的冒险。意大利共产党创始人葛兰西对这部作品曾经给予极高的评价。1933年，他在身陷法西斯监狱的时候，还从狱中写信给他的妻子，建议他们的小儿子德里奥读一读这部作品。他是这样写的：

"如果德里奥能够阅读拉迪亚德·吉卜林（1865～1936）的两部《丛林之书》，我将感到高兴。这部作品中就有他提到的那些故事：白海豹成功地援助海豹摆脱其他居民的侵害；獴战胜印度人花园里的群蛇；从小由母狼喂养长大的狼孩莫格里的种种经历。这些故事中荡漾着一种奋发的精神和意志力，这正同'汤姆叔叔'相对立，我以为这是需要让德里奥和任何一个孩子领会的，如果我们希望这些孩子赋有坚强的性格和昂扬奋发的活力的话。"

葛兰西的信在七十年后的今天，读起来仍那么亲切有力。让我们的青少年以及成年人，也都来读读吉卜林的丛林故事吧。

文美惠

CONTENTS

目录

The Jungle Book

丛林故事

充满生趣的冒险故事

人与自然的和谐篇章

Mowgli's Brothers

莫格里的兄弟们

*Now Rann the **Kite** brings home the night*
That Mang the Bat sets free—
*The herds are shut in **byre** and hut*
For loosed till dawn are we.
This is the hour of pride and power,
***Talon** and **tush** and claw.*
Oh, hear the call! —Good hunting all
*That keep **the Jungle Law**!*

—Night-Song in the Jungle

It was seven o'clock of a very warm evening in the Seeonee hills when Father Wolf woke up from his day's rest, **scratched** himself, **yawned**, and spread out his paws one after the other to get rid of the sleepy feeling in their tips. Mother Wolf lay with her big gray nose dropped across her four **tumbling, squealing cubs**, and the moon shone into the mouth of the cave where they all lived. "Augrh!" said Father Wolf. "It is time to hunt again." He was going to spring down hill when a little shadow with a bushy tail crossed the **threshold** and whined: "Good luck go with you, O Chief of the Wolves. And good luck and strong white teeth go with noble children that they may never forget the hungry in this world."

It was the jackal—Tabaqui, the Dish-licker—and the

kite

[kaɪt]

n. 鸢鹰

byre

['baɪə(r)]

n. 牛棚

talon

['tælən]

n. 魔爪

tush

[tʌʃ]

n. 尖牙

the Jungle Law

丛林法则，弱肉强食的原则

scratch

[skrætʃ]

v. 搔；挠，抓

yawn

[jɔːn]

v. 打哈欠

tumble

['tʌmb(ə)l]

v. 翻滚，翻筋斗

squeal

[skwiːl]

v. 长声尖叫

cub

[kʌb]

n. 幼兽，小崽

threshold

['θreʃhəʊld]

n. 入口，门口

蝙蝠蒙释放了黑夜，

　于是鸢鹰朗恩把它带了回来——

牛群都被关进了牛棚和茅屋，

　因为我们要恣意放纵直到黎明。

这是耀武扬威的时刻，

　尖牙利爪巨钳一齐进攻。

哦，听那呼唤声——祝大家狩猎成功，

　遵守丛林法律的全体生物！

——《丛林夜歌》

　　这是西奥尼山里一个非常暖和的夜晚，狼爸爸睡了一天，醒来已经七点钟了。他搔了搔痒，打了个呵欠，把爪子一只接一只舒展开来，好赶掉爪子尖上的睡意。狼妈妈还躺在那儿，她那灰色的大鼻子埋在她的四只滚来滚去叽叽尖叫的狼崽子身上。月亮的光辉倾泻进了他们一家居住的山洞。"噢呜！"狼爸爸说，"又该去打猎了。"他正要纵身跳下山去，一个长着蓬松的大尾巴的小个子身影遮住了洞口，用乞怜的声音说道："祝您走好运，狼大王，愿您的高贵的孩子们走好运，长一副结实的白牙，好让他们一辈子也不会忘记这世界上还有挨饿的。"

　　他是那只豺——专门舔吃残羹剩饭的塔巴克。

wolves of India despise Tabaqui because he runs about making mischief, and telling tales, and eating rags and pieces of leather from the village rubbish-heaps. But they are afraid of him too, because Tabaqui, more than anyone else in the jungle, is apt to go mad, and then he forgets that he was ever afraid of anyone, and runs through the forest biting everything in his way. Even the tiger runs and hides when little Tabaqui goes mad, for madness is the most disgraceful thing that can overtake a wild creature. We call it **hydrophobia**, but they call it dewanee—the madness—and run.

"Enter, then, and look," said Father Wolf stiffly, "but there is no food here."

"For a wolf, no," said Tabaqui, "but for so mean a person as myself a dry bone is a good feast. Who are we, the Gidur-log [the jackal people], to pick and choose?" He **scuttled** to the back of the cave, where he found the bone of a buck with some meat on it, and sat **cracking** the end merrily.

"All thanks for this good meal," he said, licking his lips. "How beautiful are the noble children! How large are their eyes! And so young too! Indeed, indeed, I might have remembered that the children of kings are men from the beginning."

Now, Tabaqui knew as well as anyone else that there is nothing so unlucky as to **compliment** children to their faces. It pleased him to see Mother and Father Wolf look uncomfortable.

Tabaqui sat still, **rejoicing** in the mischief that he had made, and then he said **spitefully**:

"Shere Khan, the Big One, has shifted his hunting grounds. He will hunt among these hills for the next moon, so he has told me."

印度的狼都看不起塔巴克，因为他到处耍奸计，搬弄是非，在村里垃圾堆上找破布和烂皮子吃。但是他们也怕他。因为塔巴克比起丛林里任何一个生物来，都更容易犯疯病，他一犯病，就忘了他过去曾经那么害怕别人，他会在森林里横冲直撞，遇见谁就咬谁。就连老虎遇上小个子塔巴克犯疯病的时候，也连忙逃开躲起来，因为野兽们觉得最丢脸的事儿，就是犯疯病。我们管这种病叫"狂犬病"，可是动物们管它叫"狄沃尼"——也就是"疯病"，遇上了便赶紧逃开。

hydrophobia
['haidrəu'fəubjə]
n. 狂犬病，恐水病

"好吧，进来瞧吧，"狼爸爸板着脸说，"可是这儿什么吃的也没有。"

"在一头狼看来，的确是没有什么可吃的，"塔巴克说，"但是对于像我这么一个微不足道的家伙，一根干骨头就是一顿盛宴了。我们这伙豺民，还有什么好挑剔的？"他一溜烟儿钻进洞的深处，在那里找到一块上面带点肉的公鹿骨头，便坐下来美滋滋地啃起了残骨。

scuttle
['skʌt(ə)l]
v. 急促地跑
crack
[kræk]
v. 啃，大口咀嚼

"多谢这顿美餐，"他舔着嘴唇说，"您家的高贵孩子们长得多漂亮呀，他们的眼睛多大呀！而且，这么年轻，就出落得这么英俊！说真的，说真的，我早该知道，大王家的孩子，打小时候起就像男子汉。"

compliment
['kɔmplimənt]
v. 恭维，赞美
rejoice
[ri'dʒɔis]
v. 高兴

其实，塔巴克完全明白，当面恭维别人的孩子是最犯忌讳的事。他看见狼爸爸和狼妈妈一副不自在的样儿，心里可得意啦。

塔巴克一动不动地坐在那里，为他干的坏事而高兴，接着他又不怀好意地说：

spitefully
['spaitfuli]
adv. 不怀好意地，恶意地

"大头领谢尔汗把狩猎场挪了个地方。从下个月起他就要在这附近的山里打猎了。这是他告诉我的。"

Shere Khan was the tiger who lived near the Waingunga River, twenty miles away.

"He has no right!" Father Wolf began angrily, "By the Law of the Jungle he has no right to change his quarters without due warning. He will frighten every head of **game** within ten miles, and I...I have to kill for two, these days."

"His mother did not call him Lungri [the Lame One] for nothing," said Mother Wolf quietly. "He has been **lame** in one foot from his birth. That is why he has only killed cattle. Now the villagers of the Waingunga are angry with him, and he has come here to make our villagers angry. They will **scour** the jungle for him when he is far away, and we and our children must run when the grass is set alight. Indeed, we are very grateful to Shere Khan!"

"Shall I tell him of your **gratitude**?" said Tabaqui.

"Out!" **snapped** Father Wolf. "Out and hunt with thy master. **Thou hast** done harm enough for one night."

"I go," said Tabaqui quietly. "Ye can hear Shere Khan below in the **thickets**. I might have saved myself the message."

Father Wolf listened, and below in the valley that ran down to a little river he heard the dry, angry, **snarly**, singsong whine of a tiger who has caught nothing and does not care if all the jungle knows it.

"The fool!" said Father Wolf. "To begin a night's work with that noise! Does he think that our buck are like his fat Waingunga bullocks?"

"H'sh. It is neither bullock nor buck he hunts to-night," said Mother Wolf. "It is Man." The whine had changed to a sort of humming purr that seemed to come from every quarter

game
[geim]
n. 猎物
lame
[leim]
adj. 瘸的
scour
['skauə(r)]
v. 搜索，仔细或彻底地查看
gratitude
['grætitju:d]
n. 感激
snap
[snæp]
v. 呵斥
thou
[ðau]
pron. 你
hast
[hæst,həst]
v. have 的第二人称单数现在式
thicket
['θikit]
n. 灌木丛
snarly
['snɑ:li]
adj. 脾气坏的，善于叫嚣的

谢尔汗就是住在二十英里外韦根加河畔的那只老虎。

"他没有那个权利！"狼爸爸气呼呼地开了口，"按照'丛林法律'，他不预先通知是没有权利改换场地的。他会惊动方圆十英里之内的所有猎物的。可是我……我最近一个人还得猎取双份的吃食呢。"

"他的母亲管他叫'瘸腿'，不是没有缘故的，"狼妈妈从容不迫地说道，"他打生下来就瘸了一条腿。所以他一向都只猎杀耕牛。现在韦根加河一带村子里的老百姓都被他惹得冒火了，他又到这儿来惹我们这里的村民冒火。他倒好，等他走得远远的，他们准会到丛林里来搜捕他，还会点火烧着茅草，害得我们和我们的孩子无处藏身，只好离开这儿。哼，我们真得感谢谢尔汗！"

"要我向他转达你们的感激吗？"塔巴克说道。

"滚出去！"狼爸爸怒喝道，"滚去和你的主子一块儿打猎吧！这一晚你干的坏事已经够多了。"

"我就走，"塔巴克不慌不忙地说，"你们可以听见，谢尔汗这会儿正在下面林子里走动。其实我用不着给你们捎信来。"

狼爸爸侧耳细听，他听见下面通往一条小河的河谷里有只气冲冲的老虎在发出单调粗鲁的哼哼声。这只老虎什么也没有逮着，而且，哪怕全丛林都知道这一点，他也不在乎。

"傻瓜！"狼爸爸说，"刚开始干活就那么吵吵嚷嚷的！难道他以为我们这儿的公鹿都像他那些养得肥肥的韦根加小公牛一样蠢吗？"

"嘘！他今晚捕猎的不是小公牛，也不是公鹿，"狼妈妈说，"他捕猎的是人。"哼哼声变成了低沉震

of the **compass**. It was the noise that **bewilders** woodcutters and gypsies sleeping in the open, and makes them run sometimes into the very mouth of the tiger.

"Man!" said Father Wolf, showing all his white teeth. "Faugh! Are there not enough beetles and frogs in the **tanks** that he must eat Man, and on our ground too!"

The Law of the Jungle, which never orders anything without a reason, forbids every beast to eat Man except when he is killing to show his children how to kill, and then he must hunt outside the hunting grounds of his **pack** or tribe. The real reason for this is that man-killing means, sooner or later, the arrival of white men on elephants, with guns, and hundreds of brown men with **gongs** and rockets and **torches**. Then everybody in the jungle suffers. The reason the beasts give among themselves is that Man is the weakest and most defenseless of all living things, and it is unsportsmanlike to touch him. They say too—and it is true—that man-eaters become **mangy**, and lose their teeth.

The purr grew louder, and ended in the full-throated "Aaarh!" of the tiger's charge.

Then there was a howl—an untigerish howl—from Shere Khan. "He has missed," said Mother Wolf. "What is it?"

Father Wolf ran out a few paces and heard Shere Khan **muttering** and **mumbling** savagely as he tumbled about in the **scrub**.

"The fool has had no more sense than to jump at a woodcutter's campfire, and has burned his feet," said Father Wolf with a grunt. "Tabaqui is with him."

"Something is coming uphill," said Mother Wolf, **twitching** one ear. "Get ready."

颤的呜呜声,仿佛来自四面八方。这种吼声常常会把露宿的樵夫和吉卜赛人吓得晕头转向,有时候会使他们自己跑进老虎嘴里。

"人!"狼爸爸龇着满口大白牙说,"嘿!难道池塘里的甲壳虫和青蛙还不够他吃的,他非要吃人不可?——而且还要在我们这块地盘上?"

"丛林法律"的每条规定都是有一定原因的,"丛林法律"禁止任何一头野兽吃人,除非他是在教他的孩子如何捕杀猎物,而且即使那样,他也必须在自己这个兽群或是部落的捕猎场地以外的地方去捕猎。这条规定的真实原因在于:杀了人就意味着迟早会招来骑着大象、带着枪支的白人,和几百个手持铜锣、火箭和火把的棕褐色皮肤的人。那时住在丛林里的兽类全部得遭殃。而兽类自己对这条规定是这样解释的:因为人是生物中最软弱和最缺乏自卫能力的,所以去碰他是不公正的。他们还说——说得一点儿也不假——吃人的野兽的毛皮会长癞痢,他们的牙齿会脱落。

呜呜声愈来愈响,后来变成了老虎扑食时一声洪亮的吼叫:"噢呜!"

接着是谢尔汗发出的一声哀号,一声很缺乏虎气的哀号。"他没有抓住,"狼妈妈说道,"怎么搞的?"

狼爸爸跑出去几步远,听见谢尔汗在矮树丛里跌来撞去,嘴里怒气冲冲地嘟囔个不停。

"这傻瓜竟然蠢得跳到一个樵夫的篝火堆上,把脚烫伤了,"狼爸爸哼了一声说,"塔巴克跟他在一起。"

"有什么东西上山来了,"狼妈妈的一只耳朵抽搐了一下,说道,"准备好。"

The bushes **rustled** a little in the thicket, and Father Wolf dropped with his **haunches** under him, ready for his leap. Then, if you had been watching, you would have seen the most wonderful thing in the world—the wolf checked in mid-spring. He made his bound before he saw what it was he was jumping at, and then he tried to stop himself. The result was that he shot up straight into the air for four or five feet, landing almost where he left ground.

"Man!" he snapped. "A man's cub. Look!"

Directly in front of him, holding on by a low branch, stood a naked brown baby who could just walk—as soft and as **dimpled** a little atom as ever came to a wolf's cave at night. He looked up into Father Wolf's face, and laughed.

"Is that a man's cub?" said Mother Wolf. "I have never seen one. Bring it here."

A Wolf accustomed to moving his own cubs can, if necessary, mouth an egg without breaking it, and though Father Wolf's jaws closed right on the child's back not a tooth even scratched the skin as he laid it down among the cubs.

"How little! How naked, and how bold!" said Mother Wolf softly. The baby was pushing his way between the cubs to get close to the warm hide. "Ahai! He is taking his meal with the others. And so this is a man's cub. Now, was there ever a wolf that could boast of a man's cub among her children?"

"I have heard now and again of such a thing, but never in our Pack or in my time," said Father Wolf. "He is altogether without hair, and I could kill him with a touch of my foot. But see, he looks up and is not afraid."

rustle
['rʌs(ə)l]
v. 沙沙作响

haunch
[hɔːntʃ]
n. 腰腿

dimple
['dɪmp(ə)l]
v. (微笑)露出酒窝

树丛的枝条簌簌响了起来，狼爸爸蹲下身子，准备往上跳。接着，你要是注意瞧他的话，你就可以看见世界上最了不起的事——狼在向空中一跃时，半路上收住了脚。原来他还没有看清他要扑的目标就跳了起来，接着，他又设法止住自己。其结果是，他跳到四五尺高的空中，几乎又落在他原来起跳的地方。

"人！"他猛地说道，"是人的小娃娃，瞧呀！"

一个刚学会走路的小娃娃，全身赤裸，棕色皮肤，抓着一根低矮的枝条，正站在他面前。从来还没有一个这么娇嫩而露出笑靥的小生命，在夜晚的时候来到狼窝。他抬头望着狼爸爸的脸笑了。

"那是人的小娃娃吗？"狼妈妈问道，"我还从来没有见过呢。把他叼过来吧。"

狼是习惯于用嘴叼他自己的小狼崽子的。如果需要的话，他可以嘴里叼一只蛋而不会把它咬碎。因此，尽管狼爸爸咬住小娃娃的背部，当他把娃娃放在狼崽中间的时候，他的牙连一点娃娃的皮都没有擦破。

"多小呀！多光溜溜呀，啊，多大胆呀！"狼妈妈柔声说道。小娃娃正往狼崽中间挤过去，好靠近暖和的狼皮。"哎！他跟他们一块儿吃起来了。原来这就是人的娃娃。谁听说过一头狼的小崽子们中间会有个小娃娃呢？"

"我们有时听说过这样的事，可要说是发生在我们的狼群里，或是在我这一辈子里，那倒从没有听说过。"狼爸爸说道，"他身上没有一根毛，我用脚一碰就能把他踢死。可是你瞧，他抬头望着，一点儿也不怕。"

The moonlight was **blocked** out of the mouth of the cave, for Shere Khan's great square head and shoulders were thrust into the entrance. Tabaqui, behind him, was **squeaking**: "My lord, my lord, it went in here!"

"Shere Khan does us great honor," said Father Wolf, but his eyes were very angry. "What does Shere Khan need?"

"My **quarry**. A man's cub went this way," said Shere Khan. "Its parents have run off. Give it to me."

Shere Khan had jumped at a woodcutter's campfire, as Father Wolf had said, and was furious from the pain of his burned feet. But Father Wolf knew that the mouth of the cave was too narrow for a tiger to come in by. Even where he was, Shere Khan's shoulders and forepaws were **cramped** for want of room, as a man's would be if he tried to fight in a barrel.

"The Wolves are a free people," said Father Wolf. "They take orders from the Head of the Pack, and not from any striped cattle-killer. The man's cub is ours—to kill if we choose."

"Ye choose and ye do not choose! What talk is this of choosing? By the bull that I killed, am I to stand nosing into your dog's den for my fair dues? It is I, Shere Khan, who speak!"

The tiger's roar filled the cave with thunder. Mother Wolf shook herself clear of the cubs and **sprang** forward, her eyes, like two green moons in the darkness, facing the **blazing** eyes of Shere Khan.

"And it is I, Raksha [The Demon], who answers. The man's cub is mine, Lungri—mine to me! He shall not be killed. He shall live to run with the Pack and to hunt with the Pack; and in the end, look you, hunter of little naked cubs,

block
[blɔk]
v. 遮住,挡住

squeak
[skwi:k]
v. 发出尖叫声

quarry
['kwɔri]
n. 猎物

cramp
[kræmp]
v. 关住,卡住,被…
箍住

spring
[spriŋ]
v. 突然跳出,跳起

blazing
['bleiziŋ]
adj. 炽烧的,闪耀
的,强烈的

洞口的月光被挡住了,因为谢尔汗的方方的大脑袋和宽肩膀塞进了洞口。塔巴克跟在他身后尖声尖气地叫嚷道:"我的老爷,我的老爷,他是打这儿进去的。"

"多承谢尔汗赏脸光临,"狼爸爸说,可是他的眼睛里充满了怒气。"谢尔汗想要什么吗?"

"我要我的猎物。有一个人娃娃冲这儿来了,"谢尔汗说,"他的爹妈都跑掉了。把他给我吧。"

正像狼爸爸说的那样,刚才谢尔汗跳到了一个樵夫的篝火堆上,把脚烧伤了,痛得他怒不可遏。但是狼爸爸知道洞口很窄,老虎进不来。就在这会儿,谢尔汗的肩膀和前爪已挤得没法动弹,一个人要是想在一只木桶里打架,就会尝到这种滋味。

"狼是自由的动物,"狼爸爸说道,"他们只听狼群头领的命令,不听随便哪个身上带条纹的、专宰杀牲口的家伙的话。这个人娃娃是我们的——要是我们愿意杀它,我们自己会杀的。"

"什么你们愿意不愿意!这是什么话?凭我杀死的公牛起誓,难道真要我把鼻子伸进你们的狗窝来找回应该属于我的东西吗?听着,这是我谢尔汗在说话!"

老虎的咆哮声像雷鸣一般,震动了整个山洞。狼妈妈抛下了崽子们跳上前来,她的眼睛在黑暗里像两个绿莹莹的月亮,直冲着谢尔汗闪闪发亮的眼睛。

"这是我,是拉克夏(魔鬼)在回答。这个人娃娃是我的,瘸鬼——他是我的!谁也不许杀死他。我要让他活下来,跟狼群一起奔跑,跟狼群一起猎食。瞧着吧,你这个猎取赤裸裸的小娃娃的家伙,你这个吃青蛙的家伙,杀鱼的家伙,总有一天,他

frog-eater, fish-killer, he shall hunt thee! Now get hence, or by the Sambur that I killed (I eat no starved cattle), back thou **goest** to thy mother, burned beast of the jungle, lamer than ever thou camest into the world! Go!"

Father Wolf looked on amazed. He had almost forgotten the days when he won Mother Wolf in fair fight from five other wolves, when she ran in the Pack and was not called The Demon for compliment's sake. Shere Khan might have faced Father Wolf, but he could not stand up against Mother Wolf, for he knew that where he was she had all the advantage of the ground, and would fight to the death. So he backed out of the cave mouth **growling**, and when he was clear he shouted:

"Each dog barks in his own yard! We will see what the Pack will say to this **fostering** of man-cubs. The cub is mine, and to my teeth he will come in the end, O bush-tailed thieves!"

Mother Wolf threw herself down **panting** among the cubs, and Father Wolf said to her gravely:

"Shere Khan speaks this much truth. The cub must be shown to the Pack. Wilt thou still keep him, Mother?"

"Keep him!" she **gasped**. "He came naked, by night, alone and very hungry; yet he was not afraid! Look, he has pushed one of my babes to one side already. And that lame butcher would have killed him and would have run off to the Waingunga while the villagers here hunted through all our lairs in revenge! Keep him? **Assuredly** I will keep him. Lie still, little frog. O thou Mowgli —for Mowgli the Frog I will call thee— the time will come when thou wilt hunt Shere Khan as he has hunted thee."

"But what will our Pack say?" said Father Wolf.

goest

['gəuist]

〈古〉go 的第二人称
单数现在式

会来捕猎你的！你现在马上给我滚开，否则凭我杀
掉的大公鹿起誓（我可不吃挨饿的牲口），我可要
让你比你出世时瘸得更厉害地滚回你妈那儿去，你
这丛林里挨火烧的野兽！滚开！"

狼爸爸惊异地呆呆望着。他几乎已经忘记了过
去的时光，那时他和五头狼决斗之后才得到了狼妈
妈。她那时在狼群里被称作"魔鬼"，那可完全不是
随便的恭维话。谢尔汗也许能和狼爸爸对着干，然
而他可没法对付狼妈妈。他很明白，在这儿狼妈妈
占据了有利的地形，而且一旦打起来，就定要和他
拼个你死我活。于是他低声咆哮着，退出了洞口，
到了洞外，他大声嚷嚷道：

growl

[graul]

v. 咆哮

foster

['fɔstə(r)]

v. 收养，养育

pant

[pænt]

v. 气喘吁吁

"每条狗都会在自己院子里汪汪叫，我们等着
瞧狼群对于收养人娃娃怎么说吧。这个娃娃是我
的，总有一天他会落进我的牙缝里来的，哼，蓬松
尾巴的贼！"

狼妈妈气喘吁吁地躺倒在崽子们中间。狼爸爸
认真地对她说：

"谢尔汗说的倒是实话。小娃娃一定得带去让
狼群看看。你还是打算收留他吗，妈妈？"

gasp

[gɑ:sp]

v. 气喘吁吁地说

"收留他！"她气喘吁吁地说，"他是在黑夜里光
着身子、饿着肚子、孤零零一个人来的；可是他一点
儿不害怕！瞧，他已经把我的一个小崽子挤到一边去
了。那个瘸腿的屠夫会杀了他，然后逃到韦根加，而
村里的人就会来报仇，把我们的窝都搜遍的！收留
他？我当然收留他！好好躺着，不要动，小青蛙。

assuredly

[ə'ʃuəridli]

adv. 确信地

噢，你这个莫格里——我要叫你青蛙莫格里。现在谢
尔汗捕猎你，将来有一天会是你捕猎谢尔汗。"

"可是我们的狼群会怎么说呢？"狼爸爸问道。

The Law of the Jungle lays down very clearly that any wolf may, when he marries, withdraw from the Pack he belongs to. But as soon as his cubs are old enough to stand on their feet he must bring them to the Pack Council, which is generally held once a month at full moon, in order that the other wolves may identify them. After that **inspection** the cubs are free to run where they please, and until they have killed their first buck no excuse is accepted if a grown wolf of the Pack kills one of them. The punishment is death where the murderer can be found; and if you think for a minute you will see that this must be so.

Father Wolf waited till his cubs could run a little, and then on the night of the Pack Meeting took them and Mowgli and Mother Wolf to the Council Rock—a hilltop covered with stones and **boulders** where a hundred wolves could hide. Akela, the great gray Lone Wolf, who led all the Pack by strength and cunning, lay out at full length on his rock, and below him sat forty or more wolves of every size and color, from **badger**-colored **veterans** who could handle a buck alone to young black three-year-olds who thought they could. The Lone Wolf had led them for a year now. He had fallen twice into a wolf trap in his youth, and once he had been beaten and left for dead; so he knew the manners and customs of men. There was very little talking at the Rock. The cubs tumbled over each other in the center of the circle where their mothers and fathers sat, and now and again a senior wolf would go quietly up to a cub, look at him carefully, and return to his place on noiseless feet. Sometimes a mother would push her cub far out into the moonlight to be sure that he had not been overlooked.

"丛林法律"十分明确地规定,任何一头狼结婚的时候,都可以退出他从属的狼群;但是一旦他的崽子长大到能够站立起来的时候,他就必须把他们带到狼群大会上去,让别的狼认识他们。这样的大会一般是在每个月月亮圆的那一天举行。经过检阅之后,崽子们就可以自由自在地到处奔跑。在崽子们第一次杀死一头公鹿以前,狼群里的成年狼绝不能用任何借口杀死一只狼崽。只要抓到凶手,就立即把他处死。你只要略加思索,就会明白必须这么做的道理。

狼爸爸等到他的狼崽子们稍稍能跑点路的时候,就在举行狼群大会的晚上,带上他们,以及莫格里,还有狼妈妈,一同来到会议岩。那是一个铺满了大大小小的石块和巨岩的小山头,在那里连一百头狼也藏得下。独身大灰狼阿克拉,不论是力气还是智谋,都算得上是全狼群的首领。这会儿他正直挺挺地躺在他的岩石上。在他下面蹲着四十多头有大有小、毛皮不同的狼,有能单独杀死一只公鹿的、长着獾色毛皮的老狼,还有自以为也能杀死公鹿的三岁年轻黑狼。孤狼率领他们已有一年了。他在年轻时期曾经两次掉进捕狼的陷阱,还有一次他被人狠揍了一顿,被当作死狼扔在一边;所以他很了解人们的风俗习惯。在会议岩上大家都很少吭声。狼崽们在他们父母围坐的圈子中间互相打闹,滚来滚去。时常有一头老狼静悄悄地走到一头狼崽跟前,仔细地打量打量他,然后轻手轻脚走回自己的座位。有时有个狼妈妈把她的崽子往前推到月光下面,免得他被漏掉了。阿克拉在他那块岩石上喊

Akela from his rock would cry: "Ye know the Law—ye know the Law. Look well, O Wolves!" And the anxious mothers would take up the call: "Look—look well, O Wolves!"

At last—and Mother Wolf's neck **bristles** lifted as the time came—Father Wolf pushed "Mowgli the Frog," as they called him, into the center, where he sat laughing and playing with some **pebbles** that **glistened** in the moonlight.

Akela never raised his head from his paws, but went on with the **monotonous** cry: "Look well!" A **muffled** roar came up from behind the rocks—the voice of Shere Khan crying: "The cub is mine. Give him to me. What have the Free People to do with a man's cub?" Akela never even twitched his ears. All he said was: "Look well, O Wolves! What have the Free People to do with the orders of any save the Free People? Look well!"

There was a **chorus** of deep growls, and a young wolf in his fourth year **flung** back Shere Khan's question to Akela: "What have the Free People to do with a man's cub?" Now, the Law of the Jungle lays down that if there is any dispute as to the right of a cub to be accepted by the Pack, he must be spoken for by at least two members of the Pack who are not his father and mother.

"Who speaks for this cub?" said Akela. "Among the Free People who speaks?" There was no answer and Mother Wolf got ready for what she knew would be her last fight, if things came to fighting.

Then the only other creature who is allowed at the Pack Council—Baloo, the sleepy brown bear who teaches the wolf cubs the Law of the Jungle: old Baloo, who can come and go where he pleases because he eats only nuts and roots and

道："大家都知道咱们的法律——大家都知道咱们的法律。好好瞧瞧吧，狼群诸君！"那些焦急的妈妈们也急忙跟着叫嚷："仔细瞧瞧啊——仔细瞧瞧，狼群诸君！"

最后，时候到了，狼妈妈脖颈上的鬃毛直竖了起来，狼爸爸把"青蛙莫格里"——他和狼妈妈是这样叫他的——推到圈子中间。莫格里坐到那里，一边笑着，一边玩着几颗在月光下闪烁发亮的鹅卵石。

阿克拉一直没有把头从爪子上抬起来，他只是不停地喊着那句单调的话："好好瞧瞧吧！"岩石后面响起了一声瓮声瓮气的咆哮，那是谢尔汗在叫嚷："那崽子是我的。把他还给我。自由的兽民要一个人娃娃干什么？"阿克拉连耳朵也没有抖动一下，只是说："好好瞧瞧吧，狼群诸君！自由的兽民只听自由的兽民的命令，别的什么命令都不听。好好瞧瞧吧！"

响起了一片低沉的嗥叫声，一头四岁的年轻狼用谢尔汗提出过的问题责问阿克拉："自由的兽民要一个人娃娃干什么？""丛林法律"规定：如果狼群对于某个崽子被接纳的权利发生了争议，那么，除了他的爸爸妈妈，至少得有狼群的其他两个成员为他说话，他才能被接纳入狼群。

"谁来替这个娃娃说话？"阿克拉说，"自由的兽民里有谁出来说话？"没有人回答。狼妈妈做好了战斗的准备，她知道，如果事情发展到非得搏斗一场的话，这将是她这辈子最后一次战斗。

这时，唯一被允许参加狼群大会的异类动物巴卢用后脚直立起来，咕哝着说话了。他是只老是打瞌睡的褐熊，专门教小狼崽们"丛林法律"。老巴卢

bristle

['brisl]

n. 鬃毛

pebble

['peb(ə)l]

n. 小圆石，鹅卵石

glisten

['glisn]

v. 闪光

monotonous

[mə'nɒtənəs]

adj. 单调的，无变化的

muffle

['mʌfl]

v. (用东西蒙住或包扎住)使声音降低

chorus

['kɔːrəs]

n. 合唱，齐声

fling

[fliŋ]

过去式为 flnng

v. 猛地做出某种举动

honey—rose upon his **hind quarters** and grunted.

"The man's cub—the man's cub?" he said. "I speak for the man's cub. There is no harm in a man's cub. I have no gift of words, but I speak the truth. Let him run with the Pack, and be entered with the others. I myself will teach him."

"We need yet another," said Akela. "Baloo has spoken, and he is our teacher for the young cubs. Who speaks besides Baloo?"

A black shadow dropped down into the circle. It was Bagheera the Black **Panther**, inky black all over, but with the panther markings showing up in certain lights like the pattern of watered silk. Everybody knew Bagheera, and nobody cared to cross his path; for he was as cunning as Tabaqui, as bold as the wild buffalo, and as reckless as the wounded elephant. But he had a voice as soft as wild honey dripping from a tree, and a skin softer than down.

"O Akela, and **ye** the Free People," he purred, "I have no right in your **assembly**, but the Law of the Jungle says that if there is a doubt which is not a killing matter in regard to a new cub, the life of that cub may be bought at a price. And the Law does not say who may or may not pay that price. Am I right?"

"Good! Good!" said the young wolves, who are always hungry. "Listen to Bagheera. The cub can be bought for a price. It is the Law."

"Knowing that I have no right to speak here, I ask your leave."

"Speak then," cried twenty voices.

"To kill a naked cub is shame. Besides, he may make better sport for you when he is grown. Baloo has spoken in his

可以随意自由来去，因为他只吃坚果、植物块根和蜂蜜。

"人娃娃——人娃娃？"他说道，"我来替人娃娃说话。人娃娃不会伤害谁。我笨嘴拙舌，不会说话，但是我说的是实话。让他跟狼群一起奔跑好了，让他跟其他狼崽子一块儿参加狼群。我自己来教他。"

一条黑影跳进圈子里，这是黑豹巴希拉，他浑身的皮毛是黑的，可是在亮光下面就显出波纹绸一般的豹斑。大伙都认识巴希拉，谁都不愿意招惹他。因为他像塔巴克一样狡猾，像野水牛一样凶猛，像受伤的大象那样不顾死活。可是他的嗓音却像树上滴下的野蜂蜜那么甜润，他的皮毛比绒毛还要柔软。

"噢，阿克拉，还有诸位自由的兽民，"他愉快地柔声说道，"我没有权利参加你们的大会，但是'丛林法律'规定，如果对于处理一个新的崽子有了疑问，可还不到把他杀死的地步，那么这个崽子的性命是可以用一笔价钱买下来的。法律并没有规定谁有权买，谁无权买。我的话对吗？"

"好哇！好哇！"那些经常饿肚子的年轻狼喊道，"让巴希拉说吧。这崽子是可以赎买的。这是法律。"

"我知道我在这儿没有发言权，所以我请求你们准许我说说。"

"说吧，"二十条嗓子一齐喊了起来。

"杀死一个赤裸裸的娃娃是可耻的。何况他长大了也许会给你们捕猎更多的猎物。巴卢已经为他说了话。现在，除了巴卢的话，我准备再加上一头

behalf. Now to Baloo's word I will add one bull, and a fat one, newly killed, not half a mile from here, if ye will accept the man's cub according to the Law. Is it difficult?"

There was a **clamor** of scores of voices, saying: "What matter? He will die in the winter rains. He will **scorch** in the sun. What harm can a naked frog do us? Let him run with the Pack. Where is the bull, Bagheera? Let him be accepted." And then came Akela's deep **bay**, crying: "Look well—look well, O Wolves!"

Mowgli was still deeply interested in the pebbles, and he did not notice when the wolves came and looked at him one by one. At last they all went down the hill for the dead bull, and only Akela, Bagheera, Baloo, and Mowgli's own wolves were left. Shere Khan roared still in the night, for he was very angry that Mowgli had not been handed over to him.

"Ay, roar well," said Bagheera, under his whiskers, "for the time will come when this naked thing will make **thee** roar to another tune, or I know nothing of man."

"It was well done," said Akela. "Men and their cubs are very wise. He may be a help in time."

"Truly, a help in time of need; for none can hope to lead the Pack forever," said Bagheera.

Akela said nothing. He was thinking of the time that comes to every leader of every pack when his strength goes from him and he gets feebler and feebler, till at last he is killed by the wolves and a new leader comes up—to be killed in his turn.

"Take him away," he said to Father Wolf, "and train him as **befits** one of the Free People."

And that is how Mowgli was entered into the Seeonee Wolf Pack for the price of a bull and on Baloo's good word.

clamor
['klæmə(r)]
n. 喧闹,叫嚷
scorch
[skɔːtʃ]
v. 烧焦,烤焦
bay
[bei]
n. 吠叫声,咆哮声

thee
[ðiː]
pron. (古)(thou 的宾格)你

befit
[bi'fit]
v. 适合,适应

公牛，一头刚刚杀死的肥肥的大公牛，就在离这儿不到半英里的地方，只要你们按法律规定接受这个人娃娃。怎么样，这事难办吗?"

几十条嗓子乱哄哄地嚷嚷道："有什么关系?他会被冬天的雨淋死，他会被太阳烤焦的。一只光身子的青蛙能给我们带来什么损害呢?让他跟狼群一起奔跑吧。公牛在哪里，巴希拉?我们接纳他吧。"接着响起了阿克拉低沉的喊声："好好瞧瞧吧——好好瞧瞧，狼群诸君!"

莫格里还在一心一意地玩鹅卵石，他一点儿也没留意到一只接着一只的狼跑过来仔细端详他。后来，他们全都下山去找那头死公牛去了，只剩下阿克拉、巴希拉、巴卢和莫格里自己家的狼。谢尔汗仍然在黑夜里不停地咆哮。他十分恼怒，因为没有把莫格里交给他。

"哼，就让你吼个痛快吧，"巴希拉在胡子掩盖下低声说道，"总有一天，这个赤裸的家伙会让你换一个调门嚎叫的，否则就算我对人的事情一窍不通。"

"这件事办得不错，"阿克拉说道，"人和他们的崽子是很聪明的。到时候他很可能成为我们的帮手。"

"不错，到急需的时候，他真能成个帮手。因为谁都不能永远当狼群的头领。"巴希拉说。

阿克拉没有回答。他在想，每个兽群的领袖都有年老体衰的时候，他会愈来愈衰弱，直到最后被狼群杀死，于是会出现一个新的头领。然后，又轮到这新的头领被杀死。

"带他回去吧，"他对狼爸爸说，"把他训练成一个合格的自由兽民。"

于是，莫格里就这样凭着一头公牛的代价和巴卢的话被接纳进了西奥尼的狼群。

Now you must be content to skip ten or eleven whole years, and only guess at all the wonderful life that Mowgli led among the wolves, because if it were written out it would fill ever so many books. He grew up with the cubs, though they, of course, were grown wolves almost before he was a child. And Father Wolf taught him his business, and the meaning of things in the jungle, till every rustle in the grass, every breath of the warm night air, every note of the owls above his head, every scratch of a bat's claws as it **roosted** for a while in a tree, and every **splash** of every little fish jumping in a pool meant just as much to him as the work of his office means to a business man. When he was not learning he sat out in the sun and slept, and ate and went to sleep again. When he felt dirty or hot he swam in the forest pools; and when he wanted honey (Baloo told him that honey and nuts were just as pleasant to eat as raw meat) he climbed up for it, and that Bagheera showed him how to do. Bagheera would lie out on a branch and call, "Come along, Little Brother," and at first Mowgli would cling like the **sloth,** but afterward he would fling himself through the branches almost as boldly as the gray **ape.** He took his place at the Council Rock, too, when the Pack met, and there he discovered that if he stared hard at any wolf, the wolf would be forced to drop his eyes, and so he used to stare for fun. At other times he would pick the long **thorns** out of the pads of his friends, for wolves suffer terribly from thorns and **burs** in their coats. He would go down the hillside into the cultivated lands by night, and look very curiously at the villagers in their huts, but he had a mistrust of men because Bagheera showed him a square box with a drop gate so cunningly hidden in the jungle that he nearly walked

roost
[ruːst]
v. 栖息,歇息

splash
[splæʃ]
n. 溅,飞溅

sloth
[sləuθ]
n. 树獭

ape
[eip]
n. 猿

thorn
[θɔːn]
n. 刺,荆棘

bur
[bəː]
n. (多)刺果,(刺果般的)粘附物

现在我要请你跳过整整十年或者十一年的时间,自己去猜想一下这些年里莫格里在狼群中度过的美好生活。因为要是把这段生活写出来,那得写好几本书。他是和狼崽们一块儿成长起来的,当然,在他还是孩子时,他们就已经是成年的狼了。狼爸爸教给他各种本领,让他熟悉丛林里一切事物的含义,直到草儿的每一声响动,夜间的每一股温暖的风,头顶上猫头鹰的每一声啼叫,在树上暂时栖息片刻的蝙蝠脚爪的抓搔声,和一条小鱼在池塘里跳跃发出的溅水声,他都能明明白白地分辨清楚,就像商人对他办公室里的事务一样熟悉。他在不学习本领的时候,就待在阳光下睡觉,吃饭,吃完又睡。当他觉得身上脏了或者热了的时候,他就跳进森林里的池塘去游泳。他想吃蜂蜜的时候(巴卢告诉他,蜂蜜和坚果跟生肉一样美味可口),他就爬上树去取。他是从巴希拉那里学会怎么取蜜的。巴希拉会躺在一根树枝上,叫道:"来吧,小兄弟。"起初,莫格里像只懒熊一样死死搂住树枝不放,但是到后来,他已经能在树枝间攀缘跳跃,像灰人猿一样大胆。狼群开大会的时候,他也参加。他发现如果他死死地盯着某一头狼看,那头狼就会被迫垂下眼睛,所以他常常紧盯着他们,借以取乐。有时候他又帮他的朋友们从他们脚掌心里拔出长长的刺,因为扎在狼的毛皮里的刺和尖石头硌使他们非常痛苦。黑夜里他就下山走进耕地,非常好奇地看着小屋里的村民们。但是他不信任人,因为有次巴希拉指给他看一个在丛林里隐蔽得非常巧妙的装着活门的方闸子,他差点儿走了进去。巴希拉说,

into it, and told him that it was a trap. He loved better than anything else to go with Bagheera into the dark warm heart of the forest, to sleep all through the **drowsy** day, and at night see how Bagheera did his killing. Bagheera killed right and left as he felt hungry, and so did Mowgli—with one exception. As soon as he was old enough to understand things, Bagheera told him that he must never touch cattle because he had been bought into the Pack at the price of a bull's life. "All the jungle is **thine**," said Bagheera, "and thou canst kill everything that thou **art** strong enough to kill; but **for the sake of** the bull that bought thee thou must never kill or eat any cattle young or old. That is the Law of the Jungle." Mowgli obeyed faithfully.

And he grew and grew strong as a boy must grow who does not know that he is learning many lessons, and who has nothing in the world to think of except things to eat.

Mother Wolf told him once or twice that Shere Khan was not a creature to be trusted, and that some day he must kill Shere Khan. But though a young wolf would have remembered that advice every hour, Mowgli forgot it because he was only a boy—though he would have called himself a wolf if he had been able to speak in any human tongue.

Shere Khan was always crossing his path in the jungle, for as Akela grew older and feebler the lame tiger had come to be great friends with the younger wolves of the Pack, who followed him for **scraps**, a thing Akela would never have allowed if he had dared to push his authority to the proper **bounds**. Then Shere Khan would **flatter** them and wonder that such fine young hunters were content to be led by a dying wolf and a man's cub. "They tell me," Shere Khan would say, "that at Council ye dare not look him between the

drowsy
['drauzi]
adj. 昏昏欲睡的

thine
[ðain]
pron. 你的东西，
你的
art
[ɑ:t]
be 的第二人称单数，
现在陈述语气动词
for the sake of
为了…好处，为
了…的缘故

scrap
[skræp]
n. 残余物，剩下的
东西
bound
[baund]
n. 范围，限度
flatter
['flætə(r)]
v. 吹捧，奉承

那是陷阱。他最喜欢和巴希拉一块儿进入幽暗温暖的丛林深处，懒洋洋地睡上一整天，晚上看巴希拉怎么捕猎。巴希拉饿了的时候，见猎物便杀，莫格里也和他一样，但只有一种猎物他们是不杀的。莫格里刚刚懂事的时候，巴希拉就告诉他，永远不要去碰牛，因为他是用一头公牛为代价加入狼群的。"整个丛林都是你的，"巴希拉说，"只要你有气力，爱杀什么都可以，不过看在那头赎买过你的公牛分上，你绝对不能杀死或吃掉任何一头牛，不管是小牛还是老牛。这是'丛林法律'。"莫格里也就诚心实意地服从了。

于是莫格里像别的男孩一样壮实地长大了，他不知道他正在学很多东西。他活在世上，除了吃的东西以外，不用为别的事操心。

有一两回狼妈妈曾经对他说，一定要提防谢尔汗这家伙；她还对他说，有一天他一定得杀死谢尔汗；但是，尽管一只年轻的狼会时时刻刻记住这个忠告，莫格里却把它忘了，因为他毕竟只是个小男孩。不过，要是他会说任何一种人的语言的话，他会把自己叫作狼的。

他在丛林里常常遇见谢尔汗。因为随着阿克拉愈来愈年老体衰，瘸腿老虎就和狼群里那些年轻的狼交上了好朋友，他们跟在他后面，吃他剩下的食物。如果阿克拉敢于严格地执行他的职权的话，他是绝不会允许他们这么做的。而且，谢尔汗还吹捧他们，说他感到奇怪，为什么这么出色的年轻猎手会甘心情愿让一只垂死的狼和一个人娃娃来领导他们。谢尔汗还说："我听说你们在大会上都不敢正眼看

eyes." And the young wolves would growl and bristle.

Bagheera, who had eyes and ears everywhere, knew something of this, and once or twice he told Mowgli in so many words that Shere Khan would kill him some day. Mowgli would laugh and answer: "I have the Pack and I have thee; and Baloo, though he is so lazy, might strike a blow or two for my sake. Why should I be afraid?"

It was one very warm day that a new **notion** came to Bagheera—born of something that he had heard. Perhaps Ikki the **Porcupine** had told him; but he said to Mowgli when they were deep in the jungle, as the boy lay with his head on Bagheera's beautiful black skin, "Little Brother, how often have I told thee that Shere Khan is thy enemy?"

"As many times as there are nuts on that palm," said Mowgli, who, naturally, could not count. "What of it? I am sleepy, Bagheera, and Shere Khan is all long tail and loud talk—like Mao, the **Peacock**."

"But this is no time for sleeping. Baloo knows it; I know it; the Pack know it; and even the foolish, foolish deer know. Tabaqui has told thee too."

"Ho! ho!" said Mowgli. "Tabaqui came to me not long ago with some rude talk that I was a naked man's cub and not fit to dig pig-nuts. But I caught Tabaqui by the tail and **swung** him twice against a palm-tree to teach him better manners."

"That was foolishness, for though Tabaqui is a **mischief-maker**, he would have told thee of something that concerned thee closely. Open those eyes, Little Brother. Shere Khan dare not kill thee in the jungle. But remember, Akela is very old, and soon the day comes when he cannot kill his buck,

他。"年轻的狼听了都气得皮毛竖立，咆哮起来。

巴希拉的消息十分灵通，这件事他也知道一些。有一两回他十分明确地告诉莫格里说，总有一天谢尔汗会杀死他的。莫格里听了总是笑笑，回答说："我有狼群，有你；还有巴卢，虽说他懒得很，但也会为我助一臂之力的。我有什么可以害怕的呢？"

在一个非常暖和的日子里，巴希拉有了一个新的想法，这是从他听到的一件事想起的，也许是豪猪伊基告诉他的。当他和莫格里来到丛林深处，莫格里头枕巴希拉漂亮的黑豹皮躺在那里的时候，他对莫格里说："小兄弟，我对你说谢尔汗是你的敌人，说过多少次了？"

"你说过的次数跟那棵棕榈树上的硬果一样多，"莫格里回答道，他当然是不会数数的。"什么事啊？我困了，巴希拉。谢尔汗不就是尾巴长、爱吹牛，跟孔雀莫奥一个样吗？"

"可现在不是睡大觉的时候。这事儿巴卢知道，我知道，狼群知道，就连那傻得要命的鹿也知道。塔巴克也告诉过你了。"

"哈哈！"莫格里说，"前不久塔巴克来找我，他毫无礼貌地说我是个赤身露体的人娃娃，不配去挖花生。可是我一把拎起塔巴克的尾巴，朝棕榈树上甩了两下，好教训他放规矩点。"

"你干了蠢事。塔巴克虽说是个捣鬼的家伙，但是他能告诉你一些和你有很大关系的事。把眼睛睁大些吧，小兄弟。谢尔汗是不敢在森林里杀死你的。但是要记住，阿克拉已经太老了，他没法杀死公鹿的日子很快就要到了。那时他就当不成头领

notion
['nəuʃ(ə)n]
n. 想法，观念

porcupine
['pɔ:kjupain]
n. 豪猪，箭猪

peacock
['pi:kɔk]
n. 孔雀

swing
[swiŋ]
v. 摇摆，旋转

mischief-maker
['mistʃif-meikə(r)]
n. 挑拨离间的人，搬弄是非的人

and then he will be leader no more. Many of the wolves that looked thee over when thou **wast** brought to the Council first are old too, and the young wolves believe, as Shere Khan has taught them, that a man-cub has no place with the Pack. In a little time thou **wilt** be a man."

"And what is a man that he should not run with his brothers?" said Mowgli. "I was born in the jungle. I have obeyed the Law of the Jungle, and there is no wolf of ours from whose paws I have not pulled a thorn. Surely they are my brothers!"

Bagheera **stretched** himself at full length and half shut his eyes. "Little Brother," said he, "feel under my jaw."

Mowgli put up his strong brown hand, and just under Bagheera's silky chin, where the giant rolling muscles were all hid by the **glossy** hair, he came upon a little **bald** spot.

"There is no one in the jungle that knows that I, Bagheera, carry that mark—the mark of the collar; and yet, Little Brother, I was born among men, and it was among men that my mother died—in the cages of the king's palace at Oodeypore. It was because of this that I paid the price for thee at the Council when thou wast a little naked cub. Yes, I too was born among men. I had never seen the jungle. They fed me behind **bars** from an iron pan till one night I felt that I was Bagheera—the Panther—and no man's plaything, and I broke the silly lock with one blow of my paw and came away. And because I had learned the ways of men, I became more terrible in the jungle than Shere Khan. Is it not so?"

"Yes," said Mowgli, "all the jungle fear Bagheera—all except Mowgli."

"Oh, thou art a man's cub," said the Black Panther very

了。在你第一次被带到大会上的时候那些仔细端详过你的狼也都老了。而那帮年轻的狼听了谢尔汗的话，都认为狼群里是没有人娃娃的地位的。很快，你就该长大成人了。"

"长大成人又怎么啦，难道长大了就不该和兄弟们一块儿奔跑吗？"莫格里说，"我生在丛林，我一向遵守'丛林法律'。我们狼群里不管哪只狼，我都帮他拔出过爪子上的刺。他们当然都是我的兄弟啦！"

巴希拉伸直了身体，眯上了眼睛。"小兄弟，"他说，"摸摸我的下巴颏儿。"

莫格里伸出他强壮的棕色的手。在巴希拉光滑的下巴底下，在遮住几大片肌肉的厚厚毛皮那里，有一小块光秃秃的地方。

"丛林里谁也不知道我巴希拉身上有这个记号——戴过颈圈的记号。小兄弟，我是在人群中间出生的，我的母亲也死在人群中间，死在奥德普尔王宫的笼子里。就是为了这个缘故，当你还是一个赤身露体的小崽子的时候，我在大会上为你付出了那笔价钱。是的，我也是在人群中间出生的。我那时从来没有见过森林。他们把我关在铁栏杆后面，用一只铁盘子喂我。直到有天晚上，我觉我是黑豹巴希拉，不是什么人的玩物。我用爪子一下子砸开了那把没用的锁，就离开了那儿。正因为我懂得人的那一套，所以我在森林中比谢尔汗更加可怕。你说是不是？"

"是的，"莫格里说，"森林里谁都怕你。只有莫格里不怕。"

"咳，你呀，你是人的小娃娃，"黑豹温柔地说，

---

wast
[wɔst]
be 的第二人称单数过去式

wilt
[wilt]
will 的第二人称单数现在时

stretch
[stretʃ]
v. 伸展, 伸长

glossy
['glɔsi]
adj. 平滑的

bald
[bɔːld]
adj. 光秃的

bar
[bɑː(r)]
n. 栅, 横木

033

tenderly. "And even as I returned to my jungle, so thou must go back to men at last—to the men who are thy brothers—if thou art not killed in the Council."

"But why—but why should any wish to kill me?" said Mowgli.

"Look at me," said Bagheera. And Mowgli looked at him steadily between the eyes. The big panther turned his head away in half a minute.

"That is why," he said, shifting his paw on the leaves. "Not even I can look thee between the eyes, and I was born among men, and I love thee, Little Brother. The others hate thee because their eyes cannot meet thine; because thou art wise; because thou hast pulled out thorns from their feet—because thou art a man."

"I did not know these things," said Mowgli sullenly, and he frowned under his heavy black eyebrows.

"What is the Law of the Jungle? Strike first and then give tongue. By thy very carelessness they know that thou art a man. But be wise. It is in my heart that when Akela misses his next kill—and at each hunt it costs him more to pin the buck—the Pack will turn against him and against thee. They will hold a Jungle Council at the Rock, and then—and then—I have it!" said Bagheera, leaping up. "Go thou down quickly to the men's huts in the valley, and take some of the Red Flower which they grow there, so that when the time comes thou mayest have even a stronger friend than I or Baloo or those of the Pack that love thee. Get the Red Flower."

By Red Flower Bagheera meant fire, only no creature in the jungle will call fire by its proper name. Every beast lives in deadly fear of it, and invents a hundred ways of describing it.

tenderly

['tendə(r)li]

adv. 温柔地

"就像我终归回到森林来一样。如果你在大会上没有被杀死，你最后也一定会回到人那儿去，回到你的兄弟们那儿去的。"

"可是为什么，为什么他们想杀死我?"莫格里问道。

"望着我，"巴希拉说。莫格里死死地盯住了他的眼睛。只过了半分钟，大黑豹就把头掉开了。

"原因就在这里，"他挪动着踩在树叶上的爪子说，"就连我也没法用眼正面瞧你，我还是在人们中间出生，而且我还是爱你的呢，小兄弟。别的动物恨你，因为他们的眼睛不敢正面瞧着你的眼睛，因为你聪明，因为你替他们挑出脚上的刺，因为你是人。"

sullenly

['sʌlənli]

adv. 阴沉地,郁郁不乐地

mayest

['meiist]

〈古〉may 的第二人称单数现在时（仅与 thou 连用）

"我以前一点儿也不懂得这些事情。"莫格里紧锁起两道浓黑的眉毛，愠怒地说。

"什么是'丛林法律'? 先动手再出声儿。他们就是因为你大大咧咧，才看出你是个人。你可得聪明点儿啊。我心里有数，如果下一次阿克拉没有逮住猎物——现在每一次打猎他都要费更大的劲才能逮住一头公鹿了——狼群就会起来反对他和反对你了。他们就会在会议岩那儿召开丛林大会，那时……那时……有了!"巴希拉跳起来说道，"你快下山到山谷里人住的小屋里，取一点儿他们种在那儿的红花来，那样，到时候你就会有一个比我、比巴卢、比狼群里爱你的那些伙伴们都更有力量的朋友了。去取来红花吧!"

proper name

专有名称

巴希拉所说的红花，指的是火。不过丛林里的动物都不知道它的名字叫火。所有的动物都怕火怕得要命，他们创造了上百种方式来描绘它。

"The Red Flower?" said Mowgli. "That grows outside their huts in the **twilight**. I will get some."

"There speaks the man's cub," said Bagheera proudly. "Remember that it grows in little pots. Get one swiftly, and keep it by thee for time of need."

"Good!" said Mowgli. "I go. But art thou sure, O my Bagheera" —he slipped his arm around the splendid neck and looked deep into the big eyes—"art thou sure that all this is Shere Khan's doing?"

"By the Broken Lock that freed me, I am sure, Little Brother."

"Then, by the Bull that bought me, I will pay Shere Khan full tale for this, and it may be a little over," said Mowgli, and he **bounded away**.

"That is a man. That is all a man," said Bagheera to himself, lying down again. "Oh, Shere Khan, never was a blacker hunting than that frog-hunt of thine ten years ago!"

Mowgli was far and far through the forest, running hard, and his heart was hot in him. He came to the cave as the evening **mist** rose, and drew breath, and looked down the valley. The cubs were out, but Mother Wolf, at the back of the cave, knew by his breathing that something was troubling her frog.

"What is it, Son?" she said.

"Some bat's chatter of Shere Khan," he called back. "I hunt among the plowed fields tonight," and he **plunged** downward through the bushes, to the stream at the bottom of the valley. There he checked, for he heard the **yell** of the Pack hunting, heard the **bellow** of a hunted Sambur, and the **snort** as the buck turned at bay. Then there were wicked, bitter

twilight
['twailait]
n. 傍晚

bound away
跳走了,跳开了

mist
[mist]
n. 薄雾

plunge
[plʌndʒ]
v. 冲入

yell
[jel]
n. 大叫,呼喊

bellow
['beləu]
n. (牛,象等)吼叫

snort
[snɔ:t]
n. 喷鼻声,呼哧声

"红花?"莫格里说, "那不是傍晚时候在他们的小屋外面开的花吗? 我去取一点回来。"

"这才像人娃娃说的话,"巴希拉骄傲地说, "它是种在小盆盆里的。快去拿一盆来, 放在你身边, 好在需要的时候用它。"

"好!"莫格里说, "我这就去。不过, 你有把握吗? 呵, 我的巴希拉,"他伸出胳膊抱住巴希拉漂亮的脖子, 深深地盯着他的眼睛, "你敢肯定这一切全都是谢尔汗挑动起来的吗?"

"凭着使我得到自由的那把砸开的锁起誓, 我敢肯定是他干的, 小兄弟。"

"好吧, 凭着赎买我的那头公牛发誓, 我一定要为这个跟谢尔汗算总账, 或者还要多算一点儿呢,"莫格里说。于是他蹦蹦跳跳地跑开了。

"这才是人呢, 完完全全是个大人了,"巴希拉自言自语地说, 又躺了下来。"哼, 谢尔汗呀, 从来没有哪次打猎, 比你在十年前捕猎青蛙那回更不吉利的了!"

莫格里已经远远地穿过了森林。他飞快地奔跑着, 他的心情是急切的。傍晚的薄雾升起时, 他已来到了狼穴。他喘了口气, 向山谷下面望去。狼崽们都出去了, 可是狼妈妈待在山洞顶里面。一听喘气声她就知道她的青蛙在为什么事儿发愁。

"怎么啦, 儿子?"

"是谢尔汗胡扯了些蠢话,"他回头喊道, "我今晚要到耕地那儿去打猎。"于是他穿过灌木丛, 跳到下面山谷底的一条河边。他在那里停住了脚步, 因为他听见狼群狩猎的喊叫声, 听见一头被追赶的大公鹿的吼叫和他陷入困境后的喘息。然后就

howls from the young wolves: "Akela! Akela! Let the Lone Wolf show his strength. Room for the leader of the Pack! Spring, Akela!"

The Lone Wolf must have sprung and missed his hold, for Mowgli heard the snap of his teeth and then a **yelp** as the Sambur knocked him over with his forefoot.

He did not wait for anything more, but dashed on; and the yells grew fainter behind him as he ran into the croplands where the villagers lived.

"Bagheera spoke truth," he panted, as he **nestled down** in some cattle **fodder** by the window of a hut. "To-morrow is one day both for Akela and for me."

Then he pressed his face close to the window and watched the fire on the **hearth**. He saw the **husbandman**'s wife get up and feed it in the night with black **lumps**. And when the morning came and the mists were all white and cold, he saw the man's child pick up a wicker pot **plastered** inside with earth, fill it with lumps of red-hot **charcoal**, put it under his blanket, and go out to tend the cows in the byre.

"Is that all?" said Mowgli. "If a cub can do it, there is nothing to fear." So he **strode** round the corner and met the boy, took the pot from his hand, and disappeared into the mist while the boy howled with fear.

"They are very like me," said Mowgli, blowing into the pot as he had seen the woman do. "This thing will die if I do not give it things to eat"; and he dropped twigs and dried bark on the red stuff. Halfway up the hill he met Bagheera with the morning dew shining like moonstones on his coat.

"Akela has missed," said the Panther. "They would have

是一群年轻狼发出的不怀好意的刻薄嚎叫声："阿克拉！阿克拉！让孤狼来显显威风，给狼群的头领让开道！跳吧，阿克拉！"

孤狼准是跳了，但却没有逮住猎物，因为莫格里听见他的牙齿咬了一个空，然后是大公鹿用前蹄把他蹬翻在地时他发出的一声疼痛的叫唤。

他不再听下去了，只顾向前赶路。当他跑到村民居住的耕地那儿时，背后的叫喊声渐渐听不清了。

"巴希拉说对了，"他在一间小屋窗外堆的饲草上舒舒服服地躺下，喘了口气说，"明天，对于阿克拉和我都是个重要的日子。"

然后他把脸紧紧贴近窗子，瞅着炉子里的火。他看见农夫的妻子夜里起来往火里添上一块块黑黑的东西。到了早晨，降着白茫茫的大雾，寒气逼人，他又看见那个男人的孩子拿起一个里面抹了泥的柳条罐儿，往里面添上烧得通红的木炭，把它塞在自己身上披的毯子下面，就出去照顾牛栏里的母牛去了。

"原来是这么简单！"莫格里说，"如果一个小崽子都能捣鼓这东西，那又有什么可怕的呢。"于是他迈开大步转过屋角，冲着男孩子走过去，从他手里夺过罐儿。当男孩儿吓得大哭起来的时候，他已经消失在雾中。

"他们长得倒挺像我，"莫格里一面像刚才他看见女人做的样子吹着火，一面说，"要是我不喂点东西给它吃，这玩意儿就会死的。"于是他在这火红的东西上面扔了些树枝和干树皮。他在半山腰上遇见了巴希拉，清晨的露珠像月牙石似的在他的皮毛上闪闪发光。

"阿克拉没有抓住猎物，"黑豹说，"他们本想

yelp
[jelp]
v.（因痛而）叫喊

nestle down
舒服地躺下

fodder
['fɔdə(r)]
n. 饲料，草料

hearth
[hɑ:θ]
n. 炉子

husbandman
['hʌzbəndmən]
n. 农夫

lump
[lʌmp]
n. 块（尤指小块）

plaster
['plɑ:stə(r)]
v. 涂灰泥，涂…

charcoal
['tʃɑ:kəul]
n. 木炭

stride
[straid]
过去式为 strode
v. 大步流星

killed him last night, but they needed thee also. They were looking for thee on the hill."

" I was among the plowed lands. I am ready. See! " Mowgli held up the fire-pot.

"Good! Now, I have seen men thrust a dry branch into that stuff, and presently the Red Flower **blossomed** at the end of it. Art thou not afraid?"

"No. Why should I fear? I remember now—if it is not a dream—how, before I was a Wolf, I lay beside the Red Flower, and it was warm and pleasant."

All that day Mowgli sat in the cave tending his fire pot and dipping dry branches into it to see how they looked. He found a branch that satisfied him, and in the evening when Tabaqui came to the cave and told him rudely enough that he was wanted at the Council Rock, he laughed till Tabaqui ran away. Then Mowgli went to the Council, still laughing.

Akela the Lone Wolf lay by the side of his rock as a sign that the leadership of the Pack was open, and Shere Khan with his following of scrap-fed wolves walked **to and fro** openly being flattered. Bagheera lay close to Mowgli, and the fire pot was between Mowgli's knees. When they were all gathered together, Shere Khan began to speak—a thing he would never have dared to do when Akela was in his prime.

"He has no right," whispered Bagheera. "Say so. He is a dog's son. He will be frightened."

Mowgli sprang to his feet. " Free People, " he cried, "does Shere Khan lead the Pack? What has a tiger to do with our leadership?"

"Seeing that the leadership is yet open, and being asked to speak..." Shere Khan began.

blossom

['blɒsəm]

v. 开花

昨晚就杀死他的，可是他们想连你一块儿杀死。刚才他们还在山上找你呢。"

"我到耕地那里去了。我已经准备好了。瞧！"莫格里举起了装火的罐子。

"好！我见过人们把一根干树枝扔进那玩意儿里去，一会儿，干树枝的一头就会开出红花来。你不怕吗？"

"我不怕，干吗要怕？噢，我记起来了——不知道这是不是一场梦——我记得我变成狼以前，就常常躺在红花旁边，那儿又暖和又舒服。"

那天莫格里一整天都坐在狼穴里照料他的火罐儿，放进一根根干树枝，看它们烧起来是什么样儿。他找到了一根使他满意的树枝，于是到了晚上，当塔巴克来到狼洞，相当无礼地通知他去会议岩开大会的时候，他放声大笑，吓得塔巴克赶紧逃开了。接着，莫格里仍然不住地大笑着来到大会上。

to and fro

来回地，往复地

孤狼阿克拉躺在他那块岩石旁边，表示狼群首领的位置正空着。谢尔汗和那些追随他、吃他的残羹剩饭的狼大摇大摆地走来走去，一副得意的神气。巴希拉紧挨莫格里躺着，那只火罐夹在莫格里的两膝间。狼群到齐以后，谢尔汗开始发言——在阿克拉正当壮年的时候，他是从来不敢这么做的。

"他没有权利，"巴希拉悄声说道，"你来说吧。他是个狗崽子。他会吓坏了的。"

莫格里跳了起来。"自由的兽民们，"他喊道，"难道是谢尔汗在率领狼群吗？我们选头领和一只老虎有什么关系？"

"由于头领的位置空着，同时我又被请来发言……"谢尔汗开口说道。

"By whom?" said Mowgli. "Are we all jackals, to **fawn on** this cattle butcher? The leadership of the Pack is with the Pack alone."

There were yells of "Silence, thou man's cub!" "Let him speak. He has kept our Law"; and at last the seniors of the Pack thundered: "Let the Dead Wolf speak." When a leader of the Pack has missed his kill, he is called the Dead Wolf as long as he lives, which is not long.

Akela raised his old head wearily:

"Free People, and ye too, jackals of Shere Khan, for twelve seasons I have led ye to and from the kill, and in all that time not one has been trapped or **maimed**. Now I have missed my kill. Ye know how that plot was made. Ye know how ye brought me up to an untried buck to make my weakness known. It was cleverly done. Your right is to kill me here on the Council Rock, now. Therefore, I ask, who comes to make an end of the Lone Wolf? For it is my right, by the Law of the Jungle, that ye come one by one."

There was a long hush, for no single wolf cared to fight Akela to the death. Then Shere Khan roared: "Bah! What have we to do with this toothless fool? He **is doomed to** die! It is the man-cub who has lived too long. Free People, he was my meat from the first. Give him to me. I **am weary of** this man-wolf folly. He has troubled the jungle for ten seasons. Give me the man-cub, or I will hunt here always, and not give you one bone. He is a man, a man's child, and from the **marrow** of my bones I hate him!"

Then more than half the Pack yelled: "A man! A man! What has a man to do with us? Let him go to his own

fawn on
奉承,拍马

"是谁请你来的?" 莫格里说, "难道我们都是豺狗,非得讨好你这个宰杀耕牛的屠夫不可吗? 谁当狼群的头领,只有狼群才能决定。"

这时响起了一片叫嚷声。"住嘴,你这人崽儿!""让他发言,他一向是遵守我们的法律的。"最后,几头年长的狼吼道:"让'死狼'说话吧。"当狼群的头领没有能杀死他的猎物时,尽管以后他还活着,也被叫作"死狼",而通常这只狼也是活不久的。

阿克拉疲乏地抬起了他衰老的头:

maim
[meim]
v. 使身体残缺,
残废

"自由的兽民们,还有你们,谢尔汗的豺狗们,我带领你们去打猎,又带领你们回来,已经有许多季节了。在我当头领的时候,从来没有一只狼落进陷阱或者受伤残废。这回我没有逮住猎物,你们明白这是谁设的圈套。你们明白,是你们故意把我引到一头精力旺盛的公鹿那儿,好让我出丑。干得真聪明哇。这会儿你们有权利在会议岩上杀死我。那么,我要问,由谁来结束我这条孤狼的生命呢? '丛林法律'规定我有权利让你们一个一个地上来和我打。"

一片长久的沉默。没有哪一只狼愿意独自去和

be doomed to
注定

阿克拉作决死的战斗。于是谢尔汗咆哮起来:"呸!我们干吗理这个老掉了牙的傻瓜? 他反正是要死的。倒是那个人崽子活得太久了。自由的兽民,他

be weary of
厌倦,厌烦

本来就是我嘴里的肉。把他给我吧,我对这种既是人又是狼的荒唐事儿早就烦透了。他在丛林里惹麻烦已经十个季节了。把人崽子给我,要不我就不走了,我要老是在这里打猎,一根骨头都不给你们留

marrow
['mærəu]
n. 骨髓

下。他是一个人,是个人崽子,我恨他,恨到了骨头缝里!"

接着,狼群里一半以上的狼都嚷了起来:"一个人! 一个人! 人跟我们有什么关系? 让他回他自

place."

" And turn all the people of the villages against us? " clamored Shere Khan. "No, give him to me. He is a man, and none of us can look him between the eyes."

Akela lifted his head again and said, "He has eaten our food. He has slept with us. He has driven game for us. He has broken no word of the Law of the Jungle."

"Also, I paid for him with a bull when he was accepted. The worth of a bull is little, but Bagheera's honor is something that he will perhaps fight for," said Bagheera in his gentlest voice.

"A bull paid ten years ago!" the Pack snarled. "What do we care for bones ten years old?"

"Or for a **pledge**?" said Bagheera, his white teeth bared under his lip. "Well are ye called the Free People!"

"No man's cub can run with the people of the jungle," howled Shere Khan. "Give him to me!"

"He is our brother in all but blood," Akela went on, "and ye would kill him here! In truth, I have lived too long. Some of ye are eaters of cattle, and of others I have heard that, under Shere Khan's teaching, ye go by dark night and snatch children from the villager's doorstep. Therefore I know ye to be **cowards**, and it is to cowards I speak. It is certain that I must die, and my life is of no worth, or I would offer that in the man-cub's place. But for the sake of the Honor of the Pack, —a little matter that by being without a leader ye have forgotten, —I promise that if ye let the man-cub go to his own place, I will not, when my time comes to die, **bare** one tooth against ye. I will die without fighting. That will at least

个儿的地方去。"

"好让他招来所有村里的人反对我们吗?"谢尔汗咆哮道,"不,把他给我。他是个人,我们谁都不敢正眼盯着他瞧。"

阿克拉再次抬起头来说道:"他跟我们一块儿吃食,一块儿睡觉。他替我们把猎物赶过来。他并没有违反'丛林法律'。"

"还有,当初狼群接受他的时候,我为他付出过一头公牛。一头公牛倒值不了什么,但是巴希拉的荣誉可不是件小事,说不定他要为了荣誉斗一场的,"巴希拉用他最温柔的嗓音说道。

"为了十年前付出的一头公牛!"狼群咆哮道,"我们才不管十年前的牛骨头呢!"

pledge
[pledʒ]
n. 誓言,发誓

"那么十年前的誓言呢?"巴希拉说道,他掀起嘴唇,露出了白牙。"怪不得你们叫'自由的兽民'呢!"

"人崽子是不能和丛林的兽民一起生活的,"谢尔汗嗥叫道,"把他给我!"

"他虽说和我们血统不同,却也是我们的兄弟,"阿克拉又说了起来,"你们却想在这儿杀掉他!说实在的,我的确活得太长了。在你们中间,有的成了吃牲口的狼;我听说还有一些狼,在谢尔汗的教

coward
[ˈkauəd]
n. 胆小鬼

唆下,黑夜里到村民家门口去叼走小孩子。所以我知道你们是胆小鬼,我是在对胆小鬼说话。我肯定是要死的。我的命值不了什么,不然的话,我就会代替人崽儿献出生命。可是为了狼群的荣誉——这件小事,你们因为没了首领,好像已经把它忘掉了——我答应你们,如果你们放这个人崽儿回到他

bare
[beə(r)]
v. 露出

自己的地方去,那么,等我的死期到来的时候,我保证连牙都不对你们龇一下。我不和你们斗,让你们把我咬死,那样,狼群里至少有三头狼可以免于

save the Pack three lives. More I cannot do; but if ye will, I can save ye the shame that comes of killing a brother against whom there is no fault—a brother spoken for and bought into the Pack according to the Law of the Jungle."

"He is a man—a man—a man!" snarled the Pack. And most of the wolves began to gather round Shere Khan, whose tail was beginning to **switch**.

"Now the business is in thy hands," said Bagheera to Mowgli. "We can do no more except fight."

Mowgli stood upright—the fire pot in his hands. Then he stretched out his arms, and yawned in the face of the Council; but he was furious with **rage** and sorrow, for, wolflike, the wolves had never told him how they hated him. "Listen you!" he cried. "There is no need for this dog's **jabber**. Ye have told me so often tonight that I am a man (and indeed I would have been a wolf with you to my life's end) that I feel your words are true. So I do not call ye my brothers any more, but sag [dogs], as a man should. What ye will do, and what ye will not do, is not yours to say. That matter is with me; and that we may see the matter more plainly, I, the man, have brought here a little of the Red Flower which ye, dogs, fear."

He flung the fire pot on the ground, and some of the red coals lit a **tuft** of dried moss that **flared up**, as all the Council drew back in terror before the leaping flames.

Mowgli thrust his dead branch into the fire till the twigs lit and crackled, and **whirled** it above his head among the **cowering** wolves.

"Thou art the master," said Bagheera in an undertone.

一死。我只能做到这一点，别的就无能为力了。可是你们如果照我说的办，我就能使你们不至于为杀害一个没有过错的兄弟而丢脸——这个兄弟是按照'丛林法律'，有人替他说话，并且付了代价赎买进狼群来的。"

"他是一个人———一个人———一个人！"狼群咆哮道。大多数的狼开始聚集在谢尔汗周围，他开始晃动起尾巴来。

"现在要看你的了，"巴希拉对莫格里说道，"我们除了打以外，没什么别的办法了。"

莫格里直挺挺地站在那里，双手捧着火罐。接着他伸直了胳臂，面对着大会打了个大哈欠。其实他心里充满了愤怒和忧伤，因为那些狼真狡猾，他们从没对他说过他们是多么仇恨他。"你们听着！"他喊道，"你们不用再咋咋呼呼闹个没完没了。今天晚上你们翻来覆去地说我是一个人（其实，你们不说的话，我倒真愿意和你们在一起，一辈子做一只狼），我觉得你们说得很对。所以从今以后，我再也不把你们叫作我的兄弟了，我要像人应该做的那样，叫你们狗。你们想干什么，你们不想干什么，可就由不得你们了。这事全由我决定。为了让你们把事情看得更清楚些，我，作为人，带来了你们这些狗害怕的一小罐红花。"

他把火罐扔到地上，几块烧红的炭块把一簇干苔藓点着了，一下子烧了起来。全场的狼在跳动的火焰面前，都惊慌地向后退去。

莫格里把他那根枯树枝插进火里，枝条点燃了，劈劈啪啪地烧了起来。他举起树枝在头顶上摇晃，周围的狼全吓得战战兢兢。

"你现在是征服者了，"巴希拉压低了嗓门说道，

switch

[switʃ]

v. 突然或猛然地扯动或挥动

rage

[reidʒ]

n. 愤怒，狂暴

jabber

['dʒæbə(r)]

n. 急促不清的话，喋喋不休

tuft

[tʌft]

n. 一簇，一丛

flare up

突然发出火焰

whirl

[(h)wə:l]

v. 旋转，挥舞

cower

['kauə(r)]

v. 畏缩，退缩

"Save Akela from the death. He was ever thy friend."

Akela, the **grim** old wolf who had never asked for mercy in his life, gave one **piteous** look at Mowgli as the boy stood all naked, his long black hair tossing over his shoulders in the light of the blazing branch that made the shadows jump and quiver.

"Good!" said Mowgli, staring round slowly. "I see that ye are dogs. I go from you to my own people—if they be my own people. The jungle is shut to me, and I must forget your talk and your companionship. But I will be more merciful than ye are. Because I was all but your brother in blood, I promise that when I am a man among men I will not **betray** ye to men as ye have betrayed me." He kicked the fire with his foot, and the sparks flew up. "There shall be no war between any of us in the Pack. But here is a debt to pay before I go." He strode forward to where Shere Khan sat **blinking** stupidly at the flames, and caught him by the tuft on his chin. Bagheera followed in case of accidents. "Up, dog!" Mowgli cried. "Up, when a man speaks, or I will set that coat **ablaze!**"

Shere Khan's ears lay flat back on his head, and he shut his eyes, for the blazing branch was very near.

"This cattle-killer said he would kill me in the Council because he had not killed me when I was a cub. Thus and thus, then, do we beat dogs when we are men. Stir a whisker, Lungri, and I **ram** the Red Flower down thy **gullet!**" He beat Shere Khan over the head with the branch, and the tiger **whimpered** and whined in an **agony** of fear.

"Pah! **Singed** jungle cat—go now! But remember when next I come to the Council Rock, as a man should come, it will be with Shere Khan's hide on my head. For the rest,

grim
[grim]
adj. 坚强的，不屈不挠的

piteous
['pitiəs]
adj. 哀怨的，可怜的

betray
[bi'trei]
v. 出卖，背叛

blink
[bliŋk]
v. 眨眼

ablaze
[ə'bleiz]
adj. 着火的，燃烧的

ram
[ræm]
v. 填塞，灌输

gullet
['gʌlit]
n. 食道，喉咙

whimper
['(h)wimpə(r)]
v. 呜咽，哀诉

agony
['ægəni]
n. 苦恼，极大的痛苦

singe
[sindʒ]
v. 烧焦，烤焦

"救救阿克拉的命吧。他一向是你的朋友。"

一辈子从来没有向谁求过饶的坚强的老狼阿克拉，也乞怜地向莫格里看了一眼。赤身裸体的莫格里站在那里，一头黑黑的长发披在肩后，映照在熊熊燃烧的树枝的火光下。许多黑黑的影子，随着火光跳动、颤抖。

"好！"莫格里不慌不忙地环视着四周说，"我看出你们的确是狗。我要离开你们，到我的自己人那里去——如果他们是我的自己人的话。丛林再也容不下我了，我必须忘记你们的谈话和友谊，但是我比你们更仁慈。既然我除了血统以外，还算得上是你们的兄弟，那么，我答应你们，当我回到人群里，成了一个人以后，我绝不会像你们出卖我那样，把你们出卖给人们。"他用脚踢了一下火，火星迸了出来。"我们人绝不会和狼群交战，可是在我离开以前，还有一笔账要清算。"他大步走到正糊里糊涂地对着火焰眨巴眼睛的谢尔汗身边，抓起他下巴上的一簇虎须。巴希拉紧跟在莫格里后面，以防不测。"站起来，狗！"莫格里喝道，"当人在说话的时候，你必须站起来，不然我就把你这身皮毛烧掉！"

谢尔汗的两只耳朵平平地贴在脑袋上，眼睛也闭上了，因为熊熊燃烧的树枝离他太近了。

"这个专门吃牛的屠夫说，因为我小时候他没有杀死我，他就要在大会上杀我。那么，瞧吧，吃我一记，再吃我一记，我们人打狗就是这样打的。你敢动一根胡子，瘤鬼，我就把红花塞进你喉咙里去。"他抄起树枝抽打谢尔汗的脑袋，老虎被恐怖折磨得呜呜地哀叫。

"呸，燎掉了毛的丛林野猫——滚开！可是要记住，下一次，当我作为人来到会议岩的时候，我的

Akela goes free to live as he pleases. Ye will not kill him, because that is not my will. Nor do I think that ye will sit here any longer, **lolling** out your tongues as though ye were somebodies, instead of dogs whom I drive out—thus! Go!" The fire was burning furiously at the end of the branch, and Mowgli struck right and left round the circle, and the wolves ran howling with the sparks burning their fur. At last there were only Akela, Bagheera, and perhaps ten wolves that had taken Mowgli's part. Then something began to hurt Mowgli inside him, as he had never been hurt in his life before, and he caught his breath and sobbed, and the tears ran down his face.

"What is it? What is it?" he said. "I do not wish to leave the jungle, and I do not know what this is. Am I dying, Bagheera?"

"No, Little Brother. That is only tears such as men use," said Bagheera. "Now I know thou art a man, and a man's cub no longer. The jungle is shut indeed to thee **henceforward**. Let them fall, Mowgli. They are only tears." So Mowgli sat and cried as though his heart would break; and he had never cried in all his life before.

"Now," he said, "I will go to men. But first I must say farewell to my mother." And he went to the cave where she lived with Father Wolf, and he cried on her coat, while the four cubs howled **miserably**.

"Ye will not forget me?" said Mowgli.

" Never while we can follow a **trail**, " said the cubs. "Come to the foot of the hill when thou art a man, and we will talk to thee; and we will come into the croplands to play with thee by night."

头上一定披着谢尔汗的皮。至于其他的事嘛，阿克拉可以随便到哪里去自由地生活。不准你们杀他，因为我不允许。我也不愿看见你们再坐在这儿，伸着舌头，好像你们是什么了不起的家伙，而不是我想撵走的一群狗，瞧，就这样撵！滚吧！"树枝顶端的火焰燃烧得十分旺，莫格里拿着树枝绕着圈儿左右挥舞，火星点燃了狼的毛皮，他们嗥叫着逃跑了。最后，只剩下阿克拉、巴希拉，还有站在莫格里一边的十来只狼。接着，莫格里的心里似乎有什么地方痛了起来，他还从没有这么痛苦过，他哽咽了一下，便抽泣起来，泪珠儿滚下了他的面颊。

"这是什么？这是什么？"他问道，"我不愿意离开丛林，我也不知道这是怎么回事。我要死了吗，巴希拉？"

"不会的，小兄弟。这只不过是人常流的眼泪罢了，"巴希拉说。"现在我看出你的确是个大人，不再是个人娃娃了。从今以后，丛林的确再也容不下你了。让眼泪往下淌吧，莫格里，这只不过是泪水。"于是莫格里坐了下来，放声痛哭起来，好像心都要碎了似的。他打生下来还从来没有哭过呢。

"好吧，"他说，"我要到人那里去了。但是首先我得跟妈妈告别。"于是他来到狼妈妈和狼爸爸住的洞穴，趴在她身上痛哭了一场，四个小狼崽儿也一块儿悲悲切切地哭嚎起来。

"你们不会忘掉我吧？"莫格里问道。

"只要能嗅到你的足迹，我们是绝不会忘掉你的，"狼崽们说。"你做了人以后，可要常常到山脚底下来啊，我们可以在那里和你谈天，我们还会在夜里到庄稼地里去找你一块儿玩。"

"Come soon!" said Father Wolf. "Oh, wise little frog, come again soon; for we be old, thy mother and I."

"Come soon," said Mother Wolf, "little naked son of mine. For, listen, child of man, I loved thee more than ever I loved my cubs."

"I will surely come," said Mowgli. "And when I come it will be to lay out Shere Khan's hide upon the Council Rock. Do not forget me! Tell them in the jungle never to forget me!"

The dawn was beginning to break when Mowgli went down the hillside alone, to meet those **mysterious** things that are called men.

"快点来吧，"狼爸爸说，"噢，聪明的小青蛙，再快点来，我和你妈都已经上了年纪了。"

　　"快点来吧，"狼妈妈说，"我的光着身子的小儿子。听我说吧，人娃娃，我疼爱你比疼我的狼崽儿们还厉害些呢。"

　　"我一定会来的，"莫格里说，"下次我来的时候，一定要把谢尔汗的皮铺在会议岩上。别忘了我！告诉丛林的伙伴们永远别忘了我！"

　　天即将破晓。莫格里独自走下山坡，去会见那些叫作人的神秘动物。

mysterious
[mis'tiəriəs]
adj. 神秘的

Tiger! Tiger!

老虎！老虎！

What of the hunting, hunter bold?
  Brother, the watch was long and cold.
What of the quarry ye went to kill?
  Brother, he crops in the jungle still.
Where is the power that made your pride?
  *Brother, it **ebbs** from my **flank** and **side**.*
Where is the haste that ye hurry by?
  *Brother, I go to my **lair**—to die.*

Now we must go back to the first tale. When Mowgli left the wolf's cave after the fight with the Pack at the Council Rock, he went down to the plowed lands where the villagers lived, but he would not stop there because it was too near to the jungle, and he knew that he had made at least one bad enemy at the Council. So he hurried on, keeping to the rough road that ran down the valley, and followed it at a steady **jog-trot** for nearly twenty miles, till he came to a country that he did not know. The valley opened out into a great plain **dotted** over with rocks and cut up by **ravines**. At one end stood a little village, and at the other the thick jungle came down in a sweep to the **grazing-grounds**, and stopped there as though it had been cut off with a **hoe**. All over the plain, cattle and buffaloes were grazing, and when the little boys in charge of

ebb
[eb]
v. 消失,退去

flank
[flæŋk]
n. 腰窝,侧腹

side
[said]
n. 胁,人类或动物
躯干的左半边或右
半边

lair
[leə(r)]
n. 窝

jog-trot
['ʤɔgtrɒt]
n. 小跑,疾走

dot
[dɔt]
v. 点缀

ravine
[rə'vi:n]
n. 沟壑,峡谷,溪谷

grazing-ground
['greiziŋ-graund]
n. 放牧地

hoe
[həu]
n. 锄头

打猎顺利吗,大胆的猎手?

　　兄弟,我守候猎物,既寒冷又长久。

你捕捉的猎物在哪里?

　　兄弟,他仍然潜伏在丛林里。

你引以为傲的威风又在哪儿?

　　兄弟,它已从我的腰胯和肚腹间消逝。

你这么匆忙要到哪儿去?

　　兄弟,我回我的窝去——去死在那里!

　　我们现在要回头接着上一个故事讲下去。莫格
里和狼群在会议岩斗了一场之后,离开了狼穴,下
山来到村民居住的耕地里。但是他没有在这里停
留,因为这儿离丛林太近了,而他很明白,他在大
会上至少已经结下了一个死敌。于是他匆匆地赶着
路,沿着顺山谷而下的崎岖不平的大路,迈着平稳
的步子赶了将近二十英里地,来到一块不熟悉的地
方。山谷变得开阔了,形成一片广袤的平原,上面
零星散布着块块岩石,还有一条条沟涧穿流其中。
平原尽头有一座小小的村庄。平原的另一头是茂密
的丛林,黑压压一片,一直伸展到牧场旁;牧场边
缘十分清晰,好像有人用一把锄头砍掉了森林。平
原上,到处都是牛群和水牛群在放牧吃草。放牛的

the herds saw Mowgli they shouted and ran away, and the yellow **pariah** dogs that hang about every Indian village barked. Mowgli walked on, for he was feeling hungry, and when he came to the village gate he saw the big thorn-bush that was drawn up before the gate at twilight, pushed to one side.

"Umph!" he said, for he had come across more than one such **barricade** in his night **rambles** after things to eat. "So men are afraid of the People of the Jungle here also." He sat down by the gate, and when a man came out he stood up, opened his mouth, and pointed down it to show that he wanted food. The man stared, and ran back up the one street of the village shouting for the **priest**, who was a big, fat man dressed in white, with a red and yellow mark on his forehead. The priest came to the gate, and with him at least a hundred people, who stared and talked and shouted and pointed at Mowgli.

"They have no manners, these Men Folk," said Mowgli to himself. "Only the gray ape would behave as they do." So he threw back his long hair and frowned at the crowd.

"What is there to be afraid of?" said the priest. "Look at the marks on his arms and legs. They are the bites of wolves. He is but a wolf-child run away from the jungle."

Of course, in playing together, the cubs had often **nipped** Mowgli harder than they intended, and there were white **scars** all over his arms and legs. But he would have been the last person in the world to call these bites, for he knew what real biting meant.

"Arre! Arre!" said two or three women together. "To be bitten by wolves, poor child! He is a handsome boy. He has eyes like red fire. By my honor, Messua, he is not unlike thy

pariah

['pæriə]

n. 贱民（印度的最下阶级）

barricade

[bæri'keid]

n. 路障，障碍物

ramble

['ræmb(ə)l]

v. 漫游，漫步

priest

[pri:st]

n. 祭司，有权执行和指挥宗教仪式的人

小孩们看见了莫格里，顿时喊叫起来，拔脚逃走。那些经常徘徊在每个印度村庄周围的黄毛野狗也汪汪地吠叫起来。莫格里向前走去，因为他觉得饿了。当他来到村庄大门时，看见傍晚用来挡住大门的一棵大荆棘丛这时已挪到一旁。

"哼！"他说，因为他夜间出来寻找食物时，曾经不止一次碰见过这样的障碍物。"看来这儿的人也怕丛林里的兽族。"他在大门边坐下了。等到有个男人走过来的时候，他便站了起来，张大嘴巴，往嘴里指指，表示他想吃东西。那个男人先是盯着他看，然后跑回村里唯一的那条街上，大声叫着祭司。祭司是个高高的胖子，穿着白衣服，额头上涂着红黄色的记号。祭司来到大门前，还有大约一百个人，也跟着他跑来了。他们目不转睛地瞅着，交谈着，喊着，用手指着莫格里。

"这些人类真没有礼貌，"莫格里自言自语地说，"只有灰猿才会像他们这样。"于是他把又黑又长的头发甩到脑后，皱起眉毛看着人群。

"你们害怕什么呀？"祭司说，"瞧瞧他的胳臂上和腿上的疤。都是狼咬的。他只不过是个从丛林里逃出来的狼孩子罢了。"

当然，狼崽们一块儿玩的时候，往往不注意，啃莫格里啃得重了点，所以他的胳臂上和腿上全都是浅色的伤疤。可是他根本不把这叫作咬。他非常清楚真正被咬是什么味道。

nip

[nip]

v. 捏，咬

scar

[skɑ:(r)]

n. 伤痕，疤痕

"哎哟！哎哟！"两三个妇人同声叫了起来，"被狼咬得那个样儿，可怜的孩子！他是个漂亮的男孩子。他的眼睛像红红的火焰。我敢起誓，米苏阿，

boy that was taken by the tiger."

"Let me look," said a woman with heavy **copper** rings on her **wrists** and ankles, and she **peered at** Mowgli under the palm of her hand. "Indeed he is not. He is thinner, but he has the very look of my boy."

The priest was a clever man, and he knew that Messua was wife to the richest villager in the place. So he looked up at the sky for a minute and said **solemnly**: "What the jungle has taken the jungle has restored. Take the boy into thy house, my sister, and forget not to honor the priest who sees so far into the lives of men."

"By the Bull that bought me," said Mowgli to himself, "but all this talking is like another looking-over by the Pack! Well, if I am a man, a man I must become."

The crowd parted as the woman **beckoned** Mowgli to her hut, where there was a red **lacquered bedstead**, a great earthen grain chest with funny raised patterns on it, half a dozen copper cooking pots, an image of a **Hindu** god in a little **alcove**, and on the wall a real looking glass, such as they sell at the country fairs.

She gave him a long drink of milk and some bread, and then she laid her hand on his head and looked into his eyes; for she thought perhaps that he might be her real son come back from the jungle where the tiger had taken him. So she said, "Nathoo, O Nathoo!" Mowgli did not show that he knew the name. "**Dost** thou not remember the day when I gave thee thy new shoes?" She touched his foot, and it was almost as hard as horn. "No," she said sorrowfully, "those feet have never worn shoes, but thou art very like my Nathoo, and thou shalt be my son."

copper
['kɒpə(r)]
n. 铜

wrist
[rist]
n. 手腕,腕关节

peer at
凝视

solemnly
['sɒləmli]
adv. 严肃地,一本正
经地

beckon
['bekən]
v. 招手,召唤

lacquer
['lækə(r)]
v. 用漆涂于…

bedstead
['bedsted]
n. 床架

Hindu
['hindu:]
adj. 印度人的,印度
教的

alcove
['ælkəuv]
n.（室内的）凹室,
壁橱

dost
[dʌst]
v.［古］do 的第二人
称单数现在式

他和你那个被老虎叼走的儿子可真有些相像呢。"

"让我瞧瞧，"一个女人说道。她的手腕和脚踝
上都戴着许多沉甸甸的铜镯子。她手搭凉棚，仔细
望着莫格里。"确实有些相像。他要瘦一点，可是
他的相貌长得和我的孩子一个样。"

祭司是个聪明人。他知道米苏阿是当地最富有
的村民的妻子。于是他仰起头朝天空望了片刻，接
着一本正经地说："被丛林夺去的，丛林又归还了。
把这个男孩带回家去吧，我的姐妹，别忘了向祭司
表示敬意啊，因为他能看透人的命运。"

"我以赎买我的那头公牛起誓，"莫格里自言自
语道，"这一切可真像是又一次被狼群接纳入伙的
仪式啊！好吧，既然我是人，我就必须变成人。"

妇人招手叫莫格里跟她到她的小屋里去，人群
也就散开了。小屋里有一张刷了红漆的床架，一只
陶土制成的收藏粮食的大柜子，上面有许多奇特的
凸出的花纹。六只铜锅。一尊印度神像安放在一个
小小的壁龛里。墙上挂着一面真正的镜子，就是农
村集市上卖的那种镜子。

她给他喝了一大杯牛奶，还给他几块面包，然
后伸手抚摸着他的脑袋，凝视他的眼睛；因为她认
为他也许真是她的儿子，老虎把他拖到森林里，现
在他又回来了。于是她说："纳索，噢，纳索！"但
是莫格里看样子没听过这个名字。"你不记得我给
你穿上新鞋子的那天了吗?"她碰了碰他的脚，这
只脚坚硬得像鹿角。"不，"她悲伤地说，"这双脚
从来没有穿过鞋子。可是你非常像我的纳索，你就
当我的儿子吧。"

Mowgli was uneasy, because he had never been under a roof before. But as he looked at the **thatch**, he saw that he could tear it out any time if he wanted to get away, and that the window had no fastenings. "What is the good of a man," he said to himself at last, "if he does not understand man's talk? Now I am as silly and dumb as a man would be with us in the jungle. I must speak their talk."

It was not for fun that he had learned while he was with the wolves to imitate the **challenge** of bucks in the jungle and the grunt of the little wild pig. So, as soon as Messua pronounced a word Mowgli would imitate it almost perfectly, and before dark he had learned the names of many things in the hut.

There was a difficulty at bedtime, because Mowgli would not sleep under anything that looked so like a panther trap as that hut, and when they shut the door he went through the window. " Give him his will, " said Messua's husband. "Remember he can never till now have slept on a bed. If he is indeed sent in the place of our son he will not run away."

So Mowgli stretched himself in some long, clean grass at the edge of the field, but before he had closed his eyes a soft gray nose **poked** him under the chin.

"Phew!" said Gray Brother (he was the eldest of Mother Wolf's cubs) . "This is a poor reward for following thee twenty miles. Thou smellest of wood smoke and cattle—altogether like a man already. Wake, Little Brother; I bring news."

"Are all well in the jungle?" said Mowgli, hugging him.

" All except the wolves that were burned with the Red Flower. Now, listen. Shere Khan has gone away to hunt far off

thatch
[θætʃ]
n. 茅草屋顶

challenge
['tʃælindʒ]
n. 挑战,对抗

poke
[pəuk]
v. 拱,戳,捅

莫格里心里很不踏实,因为他从来没有在屋顶下面待过。但是他看了看茅草屋顶,发现他如果想逃走,随时可以把茅草屋顶撕开,而且窗上也没有窗栓。"如果听不懂人说的话,"他终于对自己说,"做人又有什么用处呢?现在我什么都不懂,像个哑巴,就跟人来到森林里和我们待在一起一样。我应该学会他们说的话。"

当他在狼群里的时候,他学过森林里大公鹿的挑战声,也学过小野猪的哼哼声,那都不是为了闹着玩儿的。因此,只要米苏阿说出一个字,莫格里就马上学着说,说得一点也不走样。不到天黑,他已经学会了小屋里许多东西的名称。

到了上床睡觉的时候,困难又来了。因为莫格里不肯睡在那么像捕豹的陷阱的小屋里,当他们关上房门的时候,他就从窗子跳了出去。"随他去吧,"米苏阿的丈夫说,"你要记住,直到现在,他还从来没有在床上睡过觉。如果他真是被打发来代替我们的儿子的,他就一定不会逃走。"

于是莫格里伸直了身躯,躺在耕地边上一片长得高高的洁净草地上。但是还没有等他闭上眼睛,一只柔软的灰鼻子就开始拱他的下巴颏了。

"嗬!"灰兄弟说(他是狼妈妈的崽子们中间最年长的一个),"跟踪你跑了二十英里路,得到的是这样的报答,实在太不值得了。你身上尽是篝火气味和牛群的气味,完全像个人了。醒醒吧,小兄弟,我带来了消息。"

"丛林里一切平安吗?"莫格里拥抱了他,说道。

"一切都好,除了那些被红花烫伤的狼。喂,听着。谢尔汗到很远的地方去打猎了,要等到他的皮

till his coat grows again, for he is badly singed. When he returns he **swears** that he will lay thy bones in the Waingunga."

"There are two words to that. I also have made a little promise. But news is always good. I am tired to-night, —very tired with new things, Gray Brother, —but bring me the news always."

"Thou wilt not forget that thou art a wolf? Men will not make thee forget?" said Gray Brother anxiously.

"Never. I will always remember that I love thee and all in our cave. But also I will always remember that I have been cast out of the Pack."

"And that thou mayest be **cast** out of another pack. Men are only men, Little Brother, and their talk is like the talk of frogs in a pond. When I come down here again, I will wait for thee in the bamboos at the edge of the grazing-ground."

For three months after that night Mowgli hardly ever left the village gate, he was so busy learning the ways and customs of men. First he had to wear a cloth round him, which **annoyed** him horribly; and then he had to learn about money, which he did not in the least understand, and about plowing, of which he did not see the use. Then the little children in the village made him very angry. Luckily, the Law of the Jungle had taught him to keep his temper, for in the jungle life and food depend on **keeping your temper**; but when they made fun of him because he would not play games or fly kites, or because he mispronounced some word, only the knowledge that it was **unsportsmanlike** to kill little naked cubs kept him from picking them up and breaking them in two.

He did not know his own strength in the least. In the jungle he knew he was weak compared with the beasts, but

swear
[sweə(r)]
v. 发誓,起誓

cast
[kɑ:st]
v. 以武力赶开,驱逐

annoy
[ə'nɔi]
v. 使苦恼,骚扰

keep one's temper
忍耐

unsportsmanlike
[ʌn'spɔ:tsmənlaik]
adj. 不光明正大的

毛重新长出以后再回来,他的皮毛烧焦得很厉害。他发誓说,他回来以后一定要把你的骨头埋葬在韦根加。"

"那可不一定。我也做了一个小小的保证。不过,有消息总是件好事。我今晚累了,那些新鲜玩意儿弄得我累极了,灰兄弟。可是,你一定要经常给我带来消息啊。"

"你不会忘记你是一头狼吧?那些人不会使你忘记吧?"灰兄弟焦急地说。

"永远不会。我永远记得我爱你,爱我们山洞里的全家。可是我也永远会记得,我是被赶出狼群的。"

"你要记住,另外一群也可能把你赶出去的。人总归是人,小兄弟,他们说起话来,就像池塘里的青蛙说话那样哇哩哇啦的。下次下山,我就在牧场边上的竹林里等你。"

从那个夜晚开始,莫格里有三个月几乎从没走出过村庄大门。他正忙着学习人们的生活习惯和生活方式。首先,他得往身上缠一块布,这使他非常不舒服;其次,他得学会钱的事,可是他一点儿也搞不懂;他还得学耕种,而他看不出耕种有什么用。村里的小娃娃们常惹得他火冒三丈。幸亏"丛林法律"教会了他按捺住火气,因为在丛林里,维持生命和寻找食物全凭着保持冷静。但是他们取笑他不会做游戏或者不会放风筝,或者取笑他某个字发错了音的时候,仅仅是因为他知道杀死赤身裸体的小崽子是不公正的,才使他没有伸手抓起他们,把他们撕成两半。

他一点儿也不知道自己的力气有多大。在丛林里他知道自己比兽类弱,但是在村子里,大家都说

in the village people said that he was as strong as a bull.

And Mowgli had not the faintest idea of the difference that **caste** makes between man and man. When the potter's donkey slipped in the **clay pit**, Mowgli **hauled** it out by the tail, and helped to **stack** the pots for their journey to the market at Khanhiwara. That was very shocking, too, for the potter is a low-caste man, and his donkey is worse. When the priest scolded him, Mowgli threatened to put him on the donkey too, and the priest told Messua's husband that Mowgli had better be set to work as soon as possible; and the village head-man told Mowgli that he would have to go out with the buffaloes next day, and herd them while they grazed. No one was more pleased than Mowgli; and that night, because he had been **appointed** a servant of the village, as it were, he went off to a circle that met every evening on a **masonry** platform under a great fig-tree. It was the village club, and the head-man and the watchman and the barber, who knew all the gossip of the village, and old Buldeo, the village hunter, who had a Tower **musket**, met and smoked. The monkeys sat and talked in the upper branches, and there was a hole under the platform where a cobra lived, and he had his little platter of milk every night because he was **sacred**; and the old men sat around the tree and talked, and pulled at the big huqas (the water-pipes) till far into the night. They told wonderful tales of gods and men and ghosts; and Buldeo told even more wonderful ones of the ways of beasts in the jungle, till the eyes of the children sitting outside the circle **bulged** out of their heads. Most of the tales were about animals, for the jungle was always at their door. The deer and the wild pig **grubbed up** their crops, and now and again the tiger carried off a man at twilight, within sight of the village gates.

caste

[kɑ:st]

n. 印度的世袭阶级,(具有严格等级的)社会地位,种姓

clay pit

黏土矿坑

haul

[hɔ:l]

v. 拖拉

stack

[stæk]

v. 堆叠

appoint

[ə'pɔint]

v. 任命,指派,委派

masonry

['meisnri]

n. 石建筑

musket

['mʌskit]

n. 步枪,火枪

sacred

['seikrid]

adj. 神圣的,宗教的

bulge

[bʌldʒ]

v. 凸出,鼓起

grub up

掘出

他力气大得像头公牛。

　　莫格里也毫不知道种姓在人和人之间造成的差别。有次卖陶器小贩的驴子滑了一跤,摔进了土坑,莫格里攥住驴子的尾巴,把它拉了出来,还帮助小贩码好陶罐,好让他运到卡里瓦拉市场上去卖。这件事使人们大为震惊,因为卖陶器小贩是个贱民,至于驴子,就更加卑贱了。可是祭司责怪莫格里时,莫格里却威胁说要把他也放到驴背上去。于是祭司告诉米苏阿的丈夫,最好打发莫格里去干活,越快越好。村子里的头人告诉莫格里,第二天他就得赶着水牛出去放牧,莫格里高兴极了。当天晚上,由于他已经被指派做村里的雇工,他便去参加村里的晚会。每天晚上,人们都围成一圈,坐在一棵巨大的无花果树底下,围着一块石头砌的台子。这儿是村里的俱乐部,头人、守夜人、剃头师傅(他知道村里所有的小道消息),以及拥有一支陶尔牌老式步枪的村里猎人老布尔迪阿,都来到这儿集会和吸烟。一群猴子坐在枝头高处叽叽喳喳说个没完,石台下面的洞里住着一条眼镜蛇。人们每天晚上向他奉上一小盘牛奶,因为他是神蛇。老人们围坐在树下,谈着话,抽着巨大的水烟袋,直到深夜。他们尽讲一些关于神啦、人啦以及鬼啦的美妙动听的故事,布尔迪阿还常常讲一些更加惊人的丛林兽类的生活方式的故事,听得那些坐在圈子外的小孩儿们的眼睛都差点鼓了出来。大部分故事是关于动物的,因为丛林一直就在他们门外。鹿和野猪常来吃他们的庄稼,有时在薄暮中,老虎公然在村子大门外不远的地方拖走一个男人。

Mowgli, who naturally knew something about what they were talking of, had to cover his face not to show that he was laughing, while Buldeo, the Tower musket across his knees, climbed on from one wonderful story to another, and Mowgli's shoulders shook.

Buldeo was explaining how the tiger that had carried away Messua's son was a ghost-tiger, and his body was **inhabited** by the ghost of a wicked, old money-lender, who had died some years ago. "And I know that this is true," he said, "because Purun Dass always limped from the blow that he got in a riot when his account books were burned, and the tiger that I speak of limps, too, for the tracks of his pads are unequal."

"True, true, that must be the truth," said the gray-beards, nodding together.

"Are all these tales such **cobwebs** and moon talk?" said Mowgli. "That tiger limps because he was born lame, as everyone knows. To talk of the soul of a money-lender in a beast that never had the courage of a jackal is child's talk."

Buldeo was speechless with surprise for a moment, and the head-man stared.

"Oho! It is the jungle **brat**, is it?" said Buldeo. "If thou art so wise, better bring his hide to Khanhiwara, for the Government has set a hundred **rupees** on his life. Better still, talk not when thy elders speak."

Mowgli rose to go. "All the evening I have **lain** here listening," he called back over his shoulder, "and, except once or twice, Buldeo has not said one word of truth concerning the jungle, which is at his very doors. How, then, shall I believe the tales of ghosts and gods and **goblins** which

莫格里对他们谈的东西自然是了解一些的，他只好遮住脸孔，不让他们看见他在笑。于是，当布尔迪阿把陶尔步枪放在膝盖上，兴冲冲地讲着一个又一个神奇的故事时，莫格里的双肩就抖动个不停。

这会儿布尔迪阿正在解释，那只拖走米苏阿儿子的老虎是一只鬼虎。几年前去世的狠毒的老放债人的鬼魂就附在这只老虎身上。"我说的是实话，"他说道，"因为有一回暴动，烧掉了普朗·达斯的账本，他本人也挨了揍，从此他走路总是一瘸一拐的。我刚才说的那只老虎，他也是个瘸子，因为他留下的脚掌痕迹总是一边深一边浅。"

"对，对，这肯定是实话，"那些白胡子老头一齐点头说。

"所有那些故事难道全都是瞎编出来的吗？"莫格里开口说，"那只老虎一瘸一拐的，因为他生下就是瘸腿，这是谁都知道的呀。说什么放债人的魂附到一只从来都比豺还胆小的野兽身上，全是傻话。"

布尔迪阿吃了一惊，有好一会儿说不出话来。头人睁大了眼睛。

"喝！这是那个丛林的小杂种，是吗？"布尔迪阿说道，"你既然这么聪明，为什么不剥下他的皮送到卡里瓦拉去，政府正悬赏一百卢比要他的命呢。要不然，听长辈说话最好别乱插嘴。"

莫格里站起来打算走开。"我躺在这儿听了一晚上，"他回头喊道，"布尔迪阿说了那么多关于丛林的话，除了一两句以外，其余的没有一个字是真的，可是丛林就在他家门口呀。既然是这样，我怎么能相信他讲的那些据说他亲眼见过的鬼呀、神

inhabit
[in'hæbit]
v. 居住,附在…上

cobwebs
['kɔbweb]
n. 杂乱无序
brat
[bræt]
n. 乳臭未干的小子
rupee
['ru:pi:]
n. 卢比(印度、巴基斯坦等国的货币)
lain
[lein]
lie 的过去分词
goblin
['gɔblin]
n. 顽皮的丑小鬼,小妖精

he says he has seen?"

"It is full time that boy went to herding," said the head-man, while Buldeo **puffed** and snorted at Mowgli's **impertinence**.

The custom of most Indian villages is for a few boys to take the cattle and buffaloes out to graze in the early morning, and bring them back at night. The very cattle that would **trample** a white man to death allow themselves to be **banged** and **bullied** and shouted at by children that hardly come up to their noses. So long as the boys keep with the herds they are safe, for not even the tiger will charge a mob of cattle. But if they **straggle** to pick flowers or hunt lizards, they are sometimes carried off. Mowgli went through the village street in the dawn, sitting on the back of Rama, the great herd bull. The **slaty**-blue buffaloes, with their long, backward-sweeping horns and savage eyes, rose out their byres, one by one, and followed him, and Mowgli made it very clear to the children with him that he was the master. He beat the buffaloes with a long, **polished** bamboo, and told Kamya, one of the boys, to graze the cattle by themselves, while he went on with the buffaloes, and to be very careful not to **stray** away from the herd.

An Indian grazing ground is all rocks and scrub and **tussocks** and little ravines, among which the herds scatter and disappear. The buffaloes generally keep to the pools and muddy places, where they lie wallowing or basking in the warm mud for hours. Mowgli drove them on to the edge of the plain where the Waingunga came out of the jungle; then he dropped from Rama's neck, trotted off to a bamboo clump, and found Gray Brother. "Ah," said Gray Brother, "I have

puff

[pʌf]

v. 喘气

impertinence

[im'pə:tinəns]

n. 鲁莽,无礼

trample

['træmp(ə)l]

v. 践踏,踩坏

bang

[bæŋ]

v. 猛撞

bully

['buli]

v. 威吓,欺侮,以强
凌弱

straggle

['stræg(ə)l]

v. 散乱地伸展,四
处跑

slaty

['sleiti]

adj. 石板色的

polish

['pɔliʃ]

v. 磨光,擦亮

stray

[strei]

v. 走离,迷路

tussock

['tʌsək]

n. 草丛

呀、妖怪呀等等的故事呢?"

"这孩子确实应该去放牛了,"头人说。布尔迪阿被莫格里的大胆无礼气得呼哧呼哧地喘着粗气。

大多数印度村子的习惯是在大清早派几个孩子赶着牛群和水牛群出去放牧,晚上再把它们赶回来。那些牛群能把一个白人踩成肉泥,却老老实实地让一些还够不着他们鼻子的孩子们打骂和欺负。这些孩子只要和牛群待在一块儿,就非常安全,连老虎也不敢袭击一大群牛。可孩子们如果跑开去采摘花儿,或者捕捉蜥蜴,他们有时就会被老虎叼走。莫格里骑在牛群头领大公牛拉玛的背上,穿过村庄的大街。那些蓝灰色的水牛,长着向后弯曲的长角和凶猛的眼睛,一头头地从他们的牛棚里走出来,跟在他后面。莫格里非常明确地向一同放牧的孩子表示:他是头领。他用一根磨得光溜溜的长竹竿敲打着水牛,又告诉一个叫卡米阿的小男孩,叫他们自己去放牧牛群,他要赶着水牛往前走,并且叫他们要多加小心,别离开牛群乱跑。

印度人的牧场到处是岩石、矮树丛、杂草和一条条小溪流,牛群一到这儿就分散开去,消失不见了。水牛一般总待在池塘和泥沼里,他们常常一连几个小时躺在温暖的烂泥里打滚、晒太阳。莫格里把水牛赶到平原边上,韦根加河流出丛林的地方。接着他从拉玛的脖子上跳下来,一溜烟儿跑到一丛竹子那儿,找到了灰兄弟。"喂!"灰兄弟说,"我

waited here very many days. What is the meaning of this cattle-herding work?"

"It is an order," said Mowgli. "I am a village herd for a while. What news of Shere Khan?"

"He has come back to this country, and has waited here a long time for thee. Now he has gone off again, for the game is **scarce**. But he means to kill thee."

"Very good," said Mowgli. "So long as he is away do thou or one of the four brothers sit on that rock, so that I can see thee as I come out of the village. When he comes back wait for me in the ravine by the dhaka tree in the center of the plain. We need not walk into Shere Khan's mouth."

Then Mowgli picked out a shady place, and lay down and slept while the buffaloes grazed round him. Herding in India is one of the laziest things in the world. The cattle move and **crunch**, and lie down, and move on again, and they do not even **low**. They only grunt, and the buffaloes very seldom say anything, but get down into the muddy pools one after another, and work their way into the mud till only their noses and staring **china-blue** eyes show above the surface, and then they lie like logs. The sun makes the rocks dance in the heat, and the herd children hear one kite (never any more) whistling almost out of sight overhead, and they know that if they died, or a cow died, that kite would sweep down, and the next kite miles away would see him drop and follow, and the next, and the next, and almost before they were dead there would be a score of hungry kites come out of nowhere. Then they sleep and wake and sleep again, and weave little baskets of dried grass and put grasshoppers in them; or catch two praying **mantises** and make them fight; or **string** a

在这里等你好多天了。你怎么干起了放牛的活儿?"

"这是命令," 莫格里说, "我暂时是村里的放牛娃。谢尔汗有什么消息吗?"

"他已经回到这个地区来了,他在这里等了你很久。眼下他走了,因为猎物太少。但是他一心要杀死你。"

"很好," 莫格里说, "他不在的时候,你或者四个兄弟里的一个就坐在岩石上,好让我一出村就能够看见你。他回来以后,你就在平原正中间那棵达克树下的小溪边等我。我们不用自己走进谢尔汗的嘴里去。"

然后莫格里挑选了一块阴凉的地方,躺下睡着了,水牛在他四周吃着草。在印度,放牛是天下最逍遥自在的活儿之一。牛群走动着,嚼着草,躺下,然后又爬起来向前走动,他们甚至不哞哞地叫,他们只哼哼。水牛们更是很少说什么,只是一头挨一头地走进烂泥塘去,他们一点点钻进污泥里,最后只剩下他们的鼻孔和呆呆瞪着的青瓷色眼睛露在水面上,他们就像一根根圆木头那样躺在那里。酷热的太阳晒得石头跳起了舞,放牛的孩子听见一只鸢(永远只是一只)在头顶上高得几乎望不见的地方发出呼啸声,他们知道,如果他们死了,或者是一头母牛死了,那只鸢就会扑下来。而在遥远的地方,另一只鸢会看见他下降,于是就跟着飞下来,接着又是一只,又是一只,几乎在他们断气以前,不知从哪里就会出现二十只饿鸢。接着,孩子们睡了,醒来,又睡了。他们用干枯的草叶编了些小篮子,把蚂蚱放进去;或是捉两只螳螂,让他们打架;

scarce
[skɛəs]
adj. 缺乏的,稀有的

crunch
[krʌntʃ]
v. 嘎吱嘎吱地咀嚼

low
[ləu]
v. (牛)哞哞叫

china-blue
n. 青瓷色

mantis
['mæntis]
n. 螳螂

string
[striŋ]
v. 穿成一串,排起

necklace of red and black jungle nuts; or watch a lizard basking on a rock, or a snake hunting a frog near the wallows. Then they sing long, long songs with odd native quavers at the end of them, and the day seems longer than most people's whole lives, and perhaps they make a mud castle with mud figures of men and horses and buffaloes, and put **reeds** into the men's hands, and pretend that they are kings and the figures are their armies, or that they are gods to be worshiped. Then evening comes and the children call, and the buffaloes **lumber** up out of the sticky mud with noises like gunshots going off one after the other, and they all string across the gray plain back to the **twinkling** village lights.

Day after day Mowgli would lead the buffaloes out to their wallows, and day after day he would see Gray Brother's back a mile and a half away across the plain (so he knew that Shere Khan had not come back), and day after day he would lie on the grass listening to the noises round him, and dreaming of old days in the jungle. If Shere Khan had made a false step with his lame paw up in the jungles by the Waingunga, Mowgli would have heard him in those long, still mornings.

At last a day came when he did not see Gray Brother at the signal place, and he laughed and headed the buffaloes for the ravine by the dhaka tree, which was all covered with golden-red flowers. There sat Gray Brother, every bristle on his back lifted.

"He has hidden for a month to throw thee off thy guard. He crossed the ranges last night with Tabaqui, hot-foot on thy trail," said the Wolf, panting.

Mowgli frowned. "I am not afraid of Shere Khan, but

reed
[ri:d]
n. 芦苇
lumber
['lʌmbə]
v. 笨重、缓慢地
移动
twinkling
['twiŋk(ə)liŋ]
adj. 闪烁的

要不他们就用丛林的红色坚果和黑色坚果编成一串项链；或是观察一只趴在岩石上晒太阳的蜥蜴或是一条在水坑旁边抓青蛙的蛇。然后他们唱起了漫长的歌曲，结尾的地方都带着当地人奇特的颤音，这样的白天仿佛比大多数人的整个一生还要长。他们或许用泥捏一座城堡，还捏些泥人和泥马、泥水牛，在泥人手里插上芦苇，他们自己装作国王，泥人是他们的军队，或者他们假装是受人礼拜的神。傍晚到来了，孩子们呼唤着，水牛迟钝地爬出黏糊糊的污泥，发出一声又一声像枪声一样响亮的声音，然后一个挨着一个穿过灰暗的平原，回到村子里闪亮的灯火那里。

莫格里每天都领着水牛到他们的泥塘里去，每天他都能看见一英里半以外平原上灰兄弟的脊背（于是他知道谢尔汗还没有回来），每天他都躺在草地上倾听四周的声音，梦想着过去在丛林里度过的时光。在那些漫长而寂静的早晨，哪怕谢尔汗在韦根加河边的丛林里伸出瘸腿迈错了一步，莫格里也会听见的。

终于有一天，在约好的地方他没有看见灰兄弟，他笑了，领着水牛来到了达克树旁的小溪边。达克树上开满了金红色的花朵。灰兄弟就坐在那里，背上的毛全竖了起来。

"他躲了一个月，好叫你放松警惕。昨天夜里他和塔巴克一块儿翻过了山，正紧紧追踪着你呢。"灰狼喘着气说道。

莫格里皱起了眉头。"我倒不怕谢尔汗，但塔

Tabaqui is very cunning."

"Have no fear," said Gray Brother, licking his lips a little. "I met Tabaqui in the dawn. Now he is telling all his wisdom to the kites, but he told me everything before I broke his back. Shere Khan's plan is to wait for thee at the village gate this evening—for thee and for no one else. He is lying up now, in the big dry ravine of the Waingunga."

" Has he eaten today, or does he hunt empty? " said Mowgli, for the answer meant life and death to him.

" He killed at dawn, —a pig, —and he has drunk too. Remember, Shere Khan could never fast, even for the sake of **revenge**."

" Oh! Fool, fool! What a cub's cub it is! Eaten and drunk too, and he thinks that I shall wait till he has slept! Now, where does he lie up? If there were but ten of us we might pull him down as he lies. These buffaloes will not charge unless they wind him, and I cannot speak their language. Can we get behind his track so that they may smell it?"

"He swam far down the Waingunga to cut that off," said Gray Brother.

" Tabaqui told him that, I know. He would never have thought of it alone." Mowgli stood with his finger in his mouth, thinking. "The big ravine of the Waingunga. That opens out on the plain not half a mile from here. I can take the herd round through the jungle to the head of the ravine and then sweep down —but he would **slink** out at the foot. We must block that end. Gray Brother, canst thou cut the herd in two for me?"

"Not I, perhaps—but I have brought a wise helper." Gray Brother trotted off and dropped into a hole. Then there lifted up a huge gray head that Mowgli knew well, and the hot air

巴克是很狡猾的。"

"不用怕，"灰兄弟稍稍舔了舔嘴唇说道，"黎明时我遇见了塔巴克，现在他正在对鸢鹰们卖弄他的聪明呢。但是，在我折断他的脊梁骨以前，他把一切都告诉了我。谢尔汗的打算是今天傍晚在村庄大门口等着你——专门等着你，不是等别人。他现在正躺在韦根加的那条干涸的大河谷里。"

"他吃过食了吗？他是不是空着肚子出来打猎的？"莫格里说。这问题的回答对他是生死攸关的。

"他在天刚亮时杀了猎物———头猪，他也饮过水了。记住，谢尔汗是从来不肯节食的，哪怕是为了报仇。"

revenge
[ri'vendʒ]
n. 报仇,复仇

"噢，蠢货，蠢货！简直像个不懂事的崽子！他又吃又喝，还以为我会等到他睡过觉再动手呢！喂，他躺在哪儿？假如我们有十个，就可以在他躺的地方干掉他。这些水牛不嗅到他的气味是不会冲上去的，而我又不会说他们的话。我们是不是能转到他的脚印的背后，好让他们嗅出他来？"

"他跳进韦根加河，游下去好长一段路，来消灭自己的踪迹。"灰兄弟说。

"这一定是塔巴克教他的，我知道。他自己是绝不会想出这个办法的。"莫格里把手指放进嘴里思索着。"韦根加河的大河谷。它通向离这儿不到半英里的平原。我可以带着牛群，绕道丛林，一直把他们带到河谷的出口，然后横扫过去——不过他会从另一头溜掉的。我们必须堵住那边的出口。灰兄弟，你能帮我把牛分成两群吗？"

slink
[sliŋk]
v. 潜逃

"我可能不行，——不过我带来了一个聪明的帮手。"灰兄弟走开了，跳进一个洞里。接着洞里伸出一个灰色的大脑袋，那是莫格里十分熟悉的，炎

was filled with the most **desolate** cry of all the jungle—the hunting howl of a wolf at midday.

"Akela! Akela!" said Mowgli, clapping his hands. "I might have known that thou wouldst not forget me. We have a big work in hand. Cut the herd in two, Akela. Keep the cows and calves together, and the bulls and the plow buffaloes by themselves."

The two wolves ran, ladies'-chain fashion, in and out of the herd, which snorted and threw up its head, and separated into two clumps. In one, the cow-buffaloes stood with their calves in the center, and glared and pawed, ready, if a wolf would only stay still, to charge down and trample the life out of him. In the other, the bulls and the young bulls snorted and stamped, but though they looked more **imposing** they were much less dangerous, for they had no calves to protect. No six men could have divided the herd so neatly.

"What orders!" panted Akela. "They are trying to join again."

Mowgli **slipped** on to Rama's back. "Drive the bulls away to the left, Akela. Gray Brother, when we are gone, hold the cows together, and drive them into the foot of the ravine."

"How far?" said Gray Brother, panting and snapping.

"Till the sides are higher than Shere Khan can jump," shouted Mowgli. "Keep them there till we come down." The bulls swept off as Akela bayed, and Gray Brother stopped in front of the cows. They **charged** down on him, and he ran just before them to the foot of the ravine, as Akela drove the bulls far to the left.

"Well done! Another charge and they are fairly started.

desolate
['desəlit]
adj. 凄凉的

热的空气里响起了丛林里最凄凉的叫声——一头在正午时分猎食的狼的吼叫。

"阿克拉！阿克拉！"莫格里拍起巴掌叫道，"我早该知道，你是不会忘记我的。我们手头有要紧的工作呢。把牛群分成两半，阿克拉。让母牛和小牛待在一起，公牛和耕地的水牛在一起。"

两只狼跳开了四对舞的花样，在牛群里穿进穿出，牛群呼哧呼哧地喷着鼻息，昂起脑袋，分成了两堆。母水牛站在一堆，把她们的小牛围在中间。她们瞪起眼睛，前蹄敲着地面，只要哪只狼稍稍停下，她们就会冲上前去把他踩死。在另一群里，成年公牛和年轻公牛喷着鼻息，跺着蹄子。不过，他

imposing
[im'pəuziŋ]
adj. 有气势的，吓人的

们虽说看起来更吓人，实际上却并不那么凶恶，因为他们不需要保护小牛。就连六个男人也没法这样利索地把牛群分开。

"还有什么指示？"阿克拉喘着气说，"他们又要跑到一块儿去了。"

slip
[slip]
v. 顺利地滑动，麻利地爬

莫格里跨到拉玛背上。"把公牛赶到左边去，阿克拉。灰兄弟，等我们走了以后，你把母牛集中到一堆，把她们赶进河谷里面去。"

"赶多远？"灰兄弟问道，他一面喘着气，一面又咬又扑。

charge
[tʃɑːʤ]
v. 冲锋，冲向

"赶到河岸高得谢尔汗跳不上去的地方，"莫格里喊道，"让她们留在那里，直到我们下来。"阿克拉吼着，公牛一阵风似的奔了开去，灰兄弟拦住了母牛。母牛向灰兄弟冲去，灰兄弟稍稍跑在她们的前面，带着她们向河谷底跑去。而阿克拉这时已把公牛赶到左边很远的地方了。

"干得好！再冲一下他们就开始跑了。小心，现

Careful, now—careful, Akela. A snap too much and the bulls will charge. Hujah! This is wilder work than driving black-buck. Didst thou think these creatures could move so swiftly? " Mowgli called.

" I have—have hunted these too in my time, " gasped Akela in the dust. "Shall I turn them into the jungle?"

" Ay! Turn. Swiftly turn them! Rama is mad with rage. Oh, if I could only tell him what I need of him to-day."

The bulls were turned, to the right this time, and **crashed** into the standing thicket. The other herd children, watching with the cattle half a mile away, hurried to the village as fast as their legs could carry them, crying that the buffaloes had gone mad and run away.

But Mowgli's plan was simple enough. All he wanted to do was to make a big circle uphill and get at the head of the ravine, and then take the bulls down it and catch Shere Khan between the bulls and the cows; for he knew that after a meal and a full drink Shere Khan would not be in any condition to fight or to **clamber** up the sides of the ravine. He was **soothing** the buffaloes now by voice, and Akela had dropped far to the **rear**, only whimpering once or twice to hurry the rear-guard. It was a long, long circle, for they did not wish to get too near the ravine and give Shere Khan warning. At last Mowgli rounded up the bewildered herd at the head of the ravine on a grassy **patch** that **sloped steeply** down to the ravine itself. From that height you could see across the tops of the trees down to the plain below; but what Mowgli looked at was the sides of the ravine, and he saw with a great deal of satisfaction that they ran nearly straight up and down, while the vines and **creepers** that hung over them would give no **foothold** to a tiger

在要小心了，阿克拉。你再扑一下，他们就会向前冲过去了。喔嗨！这可比驱赶黑公鹿要来劲得多。你没想到这些家伙会跑得这么快吧?"，莫格里叫道。

"我年轻的时候也……也捕猎过这些家伙，"阿克拉在尘埃中气喘吁吁地说道，"要我把他们赶进丛林里去吗?"

"哎，赶吧! 快点赶他们吧! 拉玛已经狂怒起来了。唉，要是我能告诉他，今天我需要他帮什么忙，那该有多好!"

这回公牛被赶向右边，他们横冲直撞，闯进了高高的灌木丛。在半英里外带着牛群观望着的其他放牛孩子拼命跑回村里，喊叫着说水牛全都发了狂，说他们都跑掉了。

其实莫格里的计划是相当简单的。他只不过想在山上绕一个大圆圈，绕到河谷出口的地方，然后带着公牛下山，把谢尔汗夹在公牛和母牛群中间，然后捉住他。因为他知道，谢尔汗在吃过食，饮过大量水以后，是没有力气战斗的，并且也爬不上河谷的两岸。他现在用自己的声音安慰着水牛。阿克拉已经退到牛群的后面，只是有时哼哼一两声，催着殿后的水牛快点走。他们绕了个很大很大的圆圈，因为他们不愿离河谷太近，引起谢尔汗的警觉。最后，莫格里终于把弄糊涂了的牛群带到了河谷出口，来到一块急转直下、斜插入河谷的草地上。站在那块高坡上，可以越过树梢俯瞰下面的平原，但是莫格里却只注视河谷的两岸。他非常满意地看见，两岸非常陡峭，几乎是直上直下，岸边长满了藤蔓和爬山虎，一只想逃出去的老虎，在这里

crash
[kræʃ]
v. 横冲直撞,碰撞

clamber
['klæmbə(r)]
v. 爬上,攀登

soothe
[su:ð]
v. 抚慰,安慰

rear
[riə(r)]
n. 后面,背后,后方

patch
[pætʃ]
n. 一小块土地

slope
[sləup]
v. (使)倾斜

steeply
['sti:pli]
adv. 险峻地

creeper
['kri:pə(r)]
n. 蔓草,攀缘植物

foothold
['futhəuld]
n. 立足处

who wanted to get out.

" Let them breathe, Akela, " he said, holding up his hand. " They have not winded him yet. Let them breathe. I must tell Shere Khan who comes. We have him in the trap."

He put his hands to his mouth and shouted down the ravine—it was almost like shouting down a tunnel—and the **echoes** jumped from rock to rock.

After a long time there came back the drawling, sleepy snarl of a full-fed tiger just wakened.

"Who calls?" said Shere Khan, and a splendid peacock **fluttered** up out of the ravine **screeching**.

"I, Mowgli. Cattle thief, it is time to come to the Council Rock! Down—hurry them down, Akela! Down, Rama, down!"

The herd paused for an instant at the edge of the slope, but Akela gave tongue in the full hunting-yell, and they **pitched** over one after the other, just as steamers shoot rapids, the sand and stones **spurting** up round them. Once started, there was no chance of stopping, and before they were fairly in the bed of the ravine Rama winded Shere Khan and bellowed.

" Ha! Ha! " said Mowgli, on his back. " Now thou knowest!" and the **torrent** of black horns, **foaming muzzles**, and staring eyes whirled down the ravine just as boulders go down in floodtime; the weaker buffaloes being shouldered out to the sides of the ravine where they tore through the creepers. They knew what the business was before them—the terrible charge of the buffalo herd against which no tiger can hope to stand. Shere Khan heard the thunder of their hoofs, picked himself up, and lumbered down the ravine, looking

是找不到立足点的。

"让他们歇口气，阿克拉，"他抬起一只手说，"他们还没有嗅到他的气味呢，让他们歇口气。我得告诉谢尔汗是谁来了，我们已经使他落进了陷阱。"

他把双手围在嘴边，冲着下面的河谷高喊——这简直像冲着一条隧洞叫喊一样——回声从一块岩石弹到另一块岩石上。

过了很久，传来了一头刚刚醒来的、吃得饱饱的老虎慢吞吞的带着倦意的咆哮声。

"是谁在叫？"谢尔汗说。这时，一只华丽的孔雀惊叫着从河谷里振翅飞了出来。

"是我，莫格里。偷牛贼，现在是你到会议岩去的时候了！下去！快赶他们下去，阿克拉！下去，拉玛，下去！"

牛群在斜坡边上停顿了片刻，但是阿克拉放开喉咙发出了狩猎的吼叫，牛便一个接一个地像轮船穿过激流似的飞奔下去，沙子和石头在他们周围高高地溅起。一旦奔跑起来，就不可能停住了。他们还没有进入峡谷的河床，拉玛就嗅出了谢尔汗的气味，吼叫起来。

"哈！哈！"莫格里骑在他背上说，"这下你可明白了！"只见乌黑的牛角、喷着白沫的牛鼻子、鼓起的眼睛，像洪流一般冲下河谷，如同山洪暴发时大圆石头滚下山去一样。体弱的水牛都被挤到河谷两边，他们冲进了爬山虎藤里。他们知道眼下要干什么——水牛群要疯狂地冲锋了，任何老虎都挡不住他们。谢尔汗听见了他们雷鸣般的蹄声，便爬起身来，笨重地走下河谷，左瞧右瞧，想找一条路逃

echo
['ekəu]
n. 回声,回音

flutter
['flʌtə(r)]
v. 振翅,鼓翼

screech
[skri:tʃ]
v. 尖叫

pitch
[pitʃ]
v. 向前跌或冲,头向前摔出

spurt
[spə:t]
v. 喷出,迸发

torrent
['tɔrənt]
n. 急流,洪流

foam
[fəum]
v. 起泡沫,吐白沫

muzzle
['mʌz(ə)l]
n. 动物之鼻口

from side to side for some way of escape, but the walls of the ravine were straight and he had to hold on, heavy with his dinner and his drink, willing to do anything rather than fight. The herd splashed through the pool he had just left, bellowing till the narrow cut rang. Mowgli heard an answering bellow from the foot of the ravine, saw Shere Khan turn (the tiger knew if the worst came to the worst it was better to meet the bulls than the cows with their calves), and then Rama tripped, stumbled, and went on again over something soft, and, with the bulls at his heels, crashed full into the other herd, while the weaker buffaloes were lifted clean off their feet by the shock of the meeting. That charge carried both herds out into the plain, **goring** and stamping and snorting. Mowgli watched his time, and slipped off Rama's neck, laying about him right and left with his stick.

"Quick, Akela! Break them up. **Scatter** them, or they will be fighting one another. Drive them away, Akela. Hai, Rama! Hai, hai, hai! my children. Softly now, softly! It is all over."

Akela and Gray Brother ran to and fro nipping the buffaloes' legs, and though the herd wheeled once to charge up the ravine again, Mowgli managed to turn Rama, and the others followed him to the wallows.

Shere Khan needed no more trampling. He was dead, and the kites were coming for him already.

"Brothers, that was a dog's death," said Mowgli, feeling for the knife he always carried in a **sheath** round his neck now that he lived with men. "But he would never have shown fight. His hide will look well on the Council Rock. We must get to work swiftly."

A boy trained among men would never have dreamed of

出去；可是河谷两边的高坡是笔直的，他只好向前走去，肚里沉甸甸地装满了食物和饮水，这会儿叫他干什么别的都可以，他就是不想战斗。牛群践踏着他刚才离开的泥沼，不停地吼叫着，直到狭窄的河沟里充满了回响。莫格里听见河谷底下传来了回应的吼声，看见谢尔汗转过身来（老虎知道，到了紧急关头，面向着公牛比向着带了小牛的母牛总要好一点儿），接着拉玛被绊了一下，打了个趔趄，踩着什么软软的东西过去了。那些公牛都跟在他身后，他们迎头冲进了另一群牛当中，那些不那么强壮的水牛挨了这一下冲撞，都被掀得四蹄离了地。这次冲刺使两群牛都涌进了平原，他们用角抵，用蹄子践踏，喷着鼻息。莫格里看准了时机，从拉玛脖子上出溜下来，拿起他的棍子左右挥舞。

"快些，阿克拉！把他们分开。叫他们散开，不然他们彼此会斗起来的。把他们赶开，阿克拉。嗨，拉玛！嗨！嗨！嗨！我的孩子们，现在慢些，慢些！一切都结束了。"

阿克拉和灰兄弟跑来跑去，咬着水牛腿。牛群虽说又一次想回过头冲进河谷，莫格里却设法叫拉玛掉转了头，其余的牛便跟着他到了牛群打滚的池沼。

谢尔汗不需要牛群再去践踏他了。他死了，鸢鹰们已经飞下来啄食他了。

"弟兄们，他死得像条狗，"莫格里说，一面摸着他的刀。他和人生活在一起以后，这把刀老是挂在他脖子上的一个刀鞘里。"不过，反正他是根本不想战斗的，他的毛皮放在会议岩上一定很漂亮，我们得赶快动手干起来。"

一个在人们中间教养大的孩子，做梦也不会想

gore

[gɔː]

v. 用角顶伤

scatter

['skætə(r)]

v. 分散, 驱开

sheath

[ʃiːθ]

n. 刀鞘

skinning a ten-foot tiger alone, but Mowgli knew better than anyone else how an animal's skin is fitted on, and how it can be taken off. But it was hard work, and Mowgli **slashed** and tore and grunted for an hour, while the wolves lolled out their tongues, or came forward and **tugged** as he ordered them.

Presently a hand fell on his shoulder, and looking up he saw Buldeo with the Tower musket. The children had told the village about the buffalo **stampede**, and Buldeo went out angrily, only too anxious to correct Mowgli for not taking better care of the herd. The wolves dropped out of sight as soon as they saw the man coming.

"What is this folly?" said Buldeo angrily. "To think that thou canst skin a tiger! Where did the buffaloes kill him? It is the Lame Tiger too, and there is a hundred rupees on his head. Well, well, we will overlook thy letting the herd run off, and perhaps I will give thee one of the rupees of the reward when I have taken the skin to Khanhiwara." He **fumbled** in his waist cloth for **flint** and steel, and **stooped down** to singe Shere Khan's whiskers. Most native hunters always singe a tiger's whiskers to prevent his ghost from **haunting** them.

"Hum!" said Mowgli, half to himself as he **ripped** back the skin of a forepaw. "So thou wilt take the hide to Khanhiwara for the reward, and perhaps give me one rupee? Now it is in my mind that I need the skin for my own use. Heh! Old man, take away that fire!"

"What talk is this to the chief hunter of the village? Thy luck and the stupidity of thy buffaloes have helped thee to this kill. The tiger has just fed, or he would have gone twenty miles by this time. Thou canst not even skin him properly, little beggar brat, and **forsooth** I, Buldeo, must be told not to

独自去剥掉一只十英尺长的老虎皮，但是莫格里比谁都了解一头动物的皮是怎样长上的，也知道怎样把它剥下来。然而这件活儿确实很费力气，莫格里用刀又砍又撕，累得嘴里直哼哼，干了一个钟头；两只狼在一边懒洋洋地伸出舌头，当他命令他们的时候，他们就上前帮忙拽。

一会儿，一只手搭上了他的肩头。他抬头一看，是那个有根陶尔步枪的布尔迪阿。孩子们告诉村里人，水牛全惊跑了，布尔迪阿怒冲冲地跑出来，一心要教训莫格里一番，因为他没有照顾好牛群。狼一看有人来了，便立刻溜开了。

"这是什么蠢主意？"布尔迪阿生气地说，"你以为你能剥下老虎的皮！水牛是在哪里踩死他的？哦，这还是那只跛脚虎哩，他的头上还悬了一百卢比的赏金。好啦，好啦，把牛群吓跑的事，我们就不跟你计较了，等我把虎皮拿到卡里瓦拉去，也许还会把赏金分给你一卢比。"他在围腰布里摸出打火石和火镰，蹲下身子去烧掉谢尔汗的胡须。当地许多猎人总是烧掉老虎的胡须，免得老虎的鬼魂缠上自己。

"哼！"莫格里仿佛是对自己说，同时撕下了老虎前爪的皮。"原来你想把虎皮拿到卡里瓦拉去领赏钱，也许还会给我一个卢比？可是我有我的打算，我要留下虎皮自己用。喂，老头子，把火拿开！"

"你就这样对村里的猎人头领说话吗？你杀死这头老虎，全凭了你的运气和你那群水牛的蠢劲。这只老虎刚刚吃过食，不然，到这时他早已跑到二十英里之外去了。你连怎么好好剥他的皮都不会，小讨饭娃。好哇，你确实应该教训我不要烧他的胡

---

slash

[slæʃ]

v. 猛砍,乱砍

tug

[tʌg]

v. 用力或使劲拉动

stampede

[stæm'pi:d]

n. 惊跑

fumble

['fʌmb(ə)l]

v. 乱摸,摸索

flint

[flint]

n. 打火石

stoop down

弯腰

haunt

[hɔ:nt]

v. 指鬼魂重回或常去,萦绕

rip

[rip]

v. 撕,剥

forsooth

[fə'su:θ]

adv. 确实,的确

singe his whiskers. Mowgli, I will not give thee one **anna** of the reward, but only a very big beating. Leave the **carcass**!"

"By the Bull that bought me," said Mowgli, who was trying to get at the shoulder, "must I stay **babbling** to an old ape all noon? Here, Akela, this man **plagues** me."

Buldeo, who was still stooping over Shere Khan's head, found himself **sprawling** on the grass, with a gray wolf standing over him, while Mowgli went on skinning as though he were alone in all India.

"Ye-es," he said, between his teeth. "Thou art altogether right, Buldeo. Thou wilt never give me one anna of the reward. There is an old war between this lame tiger and myself—a very old war, and—I have won."

To do Buldeo justice, if he had been ten years younger he would have taken his chance with Akela had he met the wolf in the woods, but a wolf who obeyed the orders of this boy who had private wars with man-eating tigers was not a common animal. It was **sorcery**, magic of the worst kind, thought Buldeo, and he wondered whether the **amulet** round his neck would protect him. He lay as still, expecting every minute to see Mowgli turn into a tiger too.

"Maharaj! Great King," he said at last in a husky whisper.

"Yes," said Mowgli, without turning his head, **chuckling** a little.

"I am an old man. I did not know that thou wast anything more than a herdsboy. May I rise up and go away, or will thy servant tear me to pieces?"

"Go, and peace go with thee. Only, another time do not **meddle with** my game. Let him go, Akela."

须，莫格里，这下子我一个安那赏钱也不给你了，还要给你一顿好揍。离开这具尸体！"

"凭赎买我的公牛起誓，"莫格里说，他正在设法剥下老虎的肩胛皮。"难道整个中午我就这么听一只老人猿唠叨个没完吗？喂，阿克拉，这个人老缠着我。"

布尔迪阿正弯腰朝着老虎脑袋，突然发现自己被仰面掀翻在草地上，一头灰狼站他身边，而莫格里继续剥着皮，仿佛整个印度只有他一个人。

"好——吧，"他低声说道，"你说得完全对，布尔迪阿。你永远也不会给我一安那赏钱。这头跛老虎过去和我有过冲突——很久以前的冲突，而我赢了。"

说句公道话，如果布尔迪阿年轻十岁的话，他在森林里遇见了阿克拉，是会和他较量一下的，但是一头听这孩子命令的狼——而这个孩子又和吃人的老虎在很久以前有过私人冲突，这头狼就不是一头普通的野兽了。布尔迪阿认为这是巫术，是最厉害的妖法，他很想知道，他脖子上戴的护身符是不是能够保护他。他躺在那里，一动也不敢动，随时准备看见莫格里也变成一只老虎。

"王爷！伟大的国王！"他终于嘶哑着嗓子低声说道。

"嗯，"莫格里没有扭过头来，抿着嘴轻声笑了。

"我是个老头子。我不知道你是个非同一般的放牛孩子。你能让我站起来离开这儿吗？你的仆人会把我撕成碎片吗？"

"去吧，祝你一路平安。只不过下一次再也不要乱插手我的猎物了。放他走吧，阿克拉。"

Buldeo **hobbled** away to the village as fast as he could, looking back over his shoulder in case Mowgli should change into something terrible. When he got to the village he told a tale of magic and **enchantment** and sorcery that made the priest look very grave.

Mowgli went on with his work, but it was nearly twilight before he and the wolves had drawn the great gay skin clear of the body.

"Now we must hide this and take the buffaloes home! Help me to herd them, Akela."

The herd rounded up in the misty twilight, and when they got near the village Mowgli saw lights, and heard the **conches** and bells in the temple blowing and banging. Half the village seemed to be waiting for him by the gate. "That is because I have killed Shere Khan," he said to himself. But a shower of stones whistled about his ears, and the villagers shouted: "Sorcerer! Wolf's brat! Jungle demon! Go away! Get hence quickly or the priest will turn thee into a wolf again. Shoot, Buldeo, shoot!"

The old Tower musket went off with a bang, and a young buffalo bellowed in pain.

"More sorcery!" shouted the villagers. "He can turn bullets. Buldeo, that was thy buffalo."

"Now what is this?" said Mowgli, bewildered, as the stones flew thicker.

"They are not unlike the Pack, these brothers of thine," said Akela, sitting down **composedly**. "It is in my head that, if bullets mean anything, they would cast thee out."

"Wolf! Wolf's cub! Go away!" shouted the priest, waving a **sprig** of the sacred tulsi plant.

hobble
['hɔb(ə)l]
v. 蹒跚

enchantment
[in'tʃɑːntmənt]
n. 魔法，妖术

conch
[kɒntʃ]
n. 海螺

composedly
[kəm'pəuzdli]
adv. 镇定地，沉着
地，从容地

sprig
[sprig]
n. 小枝

布尔迪阿一瘸一拐地拼命朝村里跑去，他不住地回头瞧，害怕莫格里会变成什么可怕的东西。他一到村里，就讲出了一个尽是魔法、妖术和巫术的故事，使得祭司听了脸色变得十分阴沉。

莫格里继续干他的活儿，但直到将近傍晚，他和狼才把那张巨大的花斑皮从老虎身上剥下来。

"我们现在先把它藏起来，把水牛赶回家。来帮我把他们赶到一块儿吧，阿克拉。"

牛群在雾蒙蒙的暮色中聚到一块儿了。当他们走近村子时，莫格里看见了火光，听见海螺呜呜地响，铃儿叮当地摇。村里一半的人似乎都在大门那里等着他。"这是因为我杀死了谢尔汗，"他对自己说；但是一阵雨点似的石子在他耳边呼啸而过，村民们喊道："巫师！狼崽子！丛林魔鬼！滚开！快些滚开，不然祭司会把你再变成一头狼。开枪，布尔迪阿，开枪呀！"

那支旧陶尔步枪砰的一声开火了，一头年轻的水牛痛得吼叫起来。

"这也是巫术！"村民叫喊道，"他会叫子弹拐弯。布尔迪阿，那是你的水牛。"

"这是怎么回事呀？"石头越扔越密，莫格里摸不着头脑地说。

"你这些兄弟跟狼群没什么两样，"阿克拉镇定自若地坐下说。"我看，假如子弹能说明什么的话，那他们是想把你驱逐出去。"

"狼！狼崽子！滚开！"祭司摇晃着一根神圣的罗勒树枝叫喊道。

"Again? Last time it was because I was a man. This time it is because I am a wolf. Let us go, Akela."

A woman—it was Messua—ran across to the herd, and cried: "Oh, my son, my son! They say thou art a sorcerer who can turn himself into a beast at will. I do not believe, but go away or they will kill thee. Buldeo says thou art a **wizard**, but I know thou hast **avenged** Nathoo's death."

"Come back, Messua!" shouted the crowd. "Come back, or we will stone thee."

Mowgli laughed a little short ugly laugh, for a stone had hit him in the mouth. "Run back, Messua. This is one of the foolish tales they tell under the big tree at dusk. I have at least paid for thy son's life. Farewell; and run quickly, for I shall send the herd in more swiftly than their **brickbats**. I am no wizard, Messua. Farewell!"

"Now, once more, Akela," he cried. "Bring the herd in."

The buffaloes were anxious enough to get to the village. They hardly needed Akela's yell, but charged through the gate like a **whirlwind**, scattering the crowd right and left.

"Keep count!" shouted Mowgli **scornfully**. "It may be that I have stolen one of them. Keep count, for I will do your herding no more. Fare you well, children of men, and thank Messua that I do not come in with my wolves and hunt you up and down your street."

He turned on his heel and walked away with the Lone Wolf, and as he looked up at the stars he felt happy. "No more sleeping in traps for me, Akela. Let us get Shere Khan's skin and go away. No, we will not hurt the village, for Messua was kind to me."

wizard
['wizəd]
n. 男巫,术士

avenge
[ə'vendʒ]
v. 为…报复,报仇

brickbat
['brikbæt]
n. 用作武器或投射物的碎块,尤指砖块

whirlwind
['wə:lwind]
n. 旋风

scornfully
['skɔ:nfuli]
adv. 轻蔑地,藐视地

"又叫我滚吗?上次叫我滚,因为我是一个人。这次却因为我是只狼。我们走吧,阿克拉。"

一个妇人——她是米苏阿——跑到牛群这边来了,她喊道:"啊,我儿,我儿!他们说你是个巫师,能随便把自己变成一头野兽。我不相信,但是你快走吧,不然他们会杀死你的。布尔迪阿说你是个巫师,可是我知道,你替纳索的死报了仇。"

"回来,米苏阿!"人们喊道,"回来,不然我们就要向你扔石头了。"

莫格里恶狠狠地、短促地笑了一声,因为一块石头正好打在他的嘴巴上。"跑回去吧,米苏阿。这是他们黄昏时在大树下面编的一个荒唐的故事。我至少为你儿子的生命报了仇。再会了,快点儿跑吧,因为我要把牛群赶过去了,他们跑得会比碎砖头块还快呢。我不是巫师,米苏阿。再会!"

"好啦,再赶一次,阿克拉,"他叫道,"把牛群赶进去。"水牛也急于回到村里。他们几乎不需要阿克拉的咆哮,就像一阵旋风似的冲进了大门,把人群冲得七零八散。

"好好数数吧!"莫格里轻蔑地喊道,"没准儿我偷走了一头牛呢。好好数数吧,因为我再也不会给你们放牛了。再见吧,人的孩子们,你们得感谢米苏阿,因为她,我才没有带着我的狼沿着你们的街道追捕你们。"

他转过身,带着孤狼走开了。当他仰望着星星时,他觉得很幸福。"我不必再在陷阱里睡觉了,阿克拉。我们去取出谢尔汗的皮,离开这里吧。不,我们绝不伤害这个村庄,因为米苏阿待我是那么好。"

When the moon rose over the plain, making it look all milky, the horrified villagers saw Mowgli, with two wolves at his heels and a **bundle** on his head, trotting across at the steady wolf's trot that eats up the long miles like fire. Then they banged the temple bells and blew the conches louder than ever. And Messua cried, and Buldeo **embroidered** the story of his adventures in the jungle, till he ended by saying that Akela stood up on his hind legs and talked like a man.

The moon was just going down when Mowgli and the two wolves came to the hill of the Council Rock, and they stopped at Mother Wolf's cave.

"They have cast me out from the Man-Pack, Mother," shouted Mowgli, "but I come with the hide of Shere Khan to keep my word." Mother Wolf walked stiffly from the cave with the cubs behind her, and her eyes **glowed** as she saw the skin.

"I told him on that day, when he **crammed** his head and shoulders into this cave, hunting for thy life, Little Frog—I told him that the hunter would be the hunted. It is well done."

"Little Brother, it is well done," said a deep voice in the thicket. "We were lonely in the jungle without thee, and Bagheera came running to Mowgli's bare feet. They clambered up the Council Rock together, and Mowgli spread the skin out on the flat stone where Akela used to sit, and **pegged it down** with four slivers of bamboo, and Akela lay down upon it, and called the old call to the Council, "Look—look well, O Wolves," exactly as he had called when Mowgli was first brought there.

Ever since Akela had been **deposed**, the Pack had been without a leader, hunting and fighting at their own pleasure. But they answered the call from habit; and some of them were

当月亮升起在平原上空,使一切变成了乳白色的时候,吓坏了的村民看见了身后跟着两只狼的莫格里,他的头上顶着一包东西,正用狼的平稳小跑姿势赶着路,狼的小跑就像大火一样,把漫长的距离一下子就消灭掉了。于是他们更加使劲地敲起了庙宇的钟,更响地吹起了海螺;米苏阿痛哭着,布尔迪阿把他在丛林里历险的故事添枝加叶,讲了又讲,最后竟说,阿克拉用后脚直立起来,像人一样说话。

莫格里和两只狼来到会议岩的山上,月亮正在下沉,他们先在狼妈妈的山洞停下了。

"他们把我从人群里赶了出来,妈妈,"莫格里喊道,"可是我实现了诺言,带来了谢尔汗的皮。"狼妈妈从洞里费力地走了出来,后面跟着狼崽们;她一见虎皮,眼睛便发亮了。

"那天他把脑袋和肩膀塞进这个洞口,想要你的命,小青蛙。我就对他说:'捕猎别人的,总归要被人捕猎的。'干得好。"

"小兄弟,干得好,"一个低沉的声音从灌木丛里传来。"你离开了丛林,我们都觉得寂寞。"巴希拉跑到莫格里赤裸的双脚下。他们一块儿爬上会议岩,莫格里把虎皮铺在阿克拉常坐的那块扁平石头上,用四根竹钉钉把它固定住。阿克拉在上面躺了下来,发出了以前召集大会时的召唤声:"瞧啊——仔细瞧瞧,狼群诸君!"那声音正和莫格里初次被带到这里时他的呼叫一模一样。

自从阿克拉被赶下台以后,狼群就没有了首领,他们可以随心所欲地行猎和殴斗。但是他们出于习惯,回答了召唤。他们中间,有些跌进了陷阱,

lame from the traps they had fallen into, and some limped from shot wounds, and some were mangy from eating bad food, and many were missing. But they came to the Council Rock, all that were left of them, and saw Shere Khan's striped hide on the rock, and the huge claws **dangling** at the end of the empty dangling feet. It was then that Mowgli made up a song that came up into his throat all by itself, and he shouted it aloud, leaping up and down on the rattling skin, and beating time with his heels till he had no more breath left, while Gray Brother and Akela howled between the verses.

"Look well, O Wolves. Have I kept my word?" said Mowgli. And the wolves bayed "Yes," and one **tattered** wolf howled:

"Lead us again, O Akela. Lead us again, O Man-cub, for we be sick of this **lawlessness**, and we would be the Free People once more."

"Nay," purred Bagheera, "that may not be. When ye are full-fed, the madness may come upon you again. Not for nothing are ye called the Free People. Ye fought for freedom, and it is yours. Eat it, O Wolves."

"Man-Pack and Wolf-Pack have cast me out," said Mowgli. "Now I will hunt alone in the jungle."

"And we will hunt with thee," said the four cubs.

So Mowgli went away and hunted with the four cubs in the jungle from that day on. But he was not always alone, because, years afterward, he became a man and married.

But that is a story for grown-ups.

变成了瘸子；有些中了枪弹，走起来一拐一拐的；另一些吃了不洁的食物，全身的毛变得癞巴巴的。还有许多头狼下落不明，但是剩下的狼全都来了。他们来到会议岩，看见了谢尔汗的花斑毛皮摊在岩石上，巨大的虎爪连在空荡荡的虎脚上，在空中晃来晃去。就是在这时，莫格里编了一首不押韵的歌，这首歌自然而然地涌上了他的喉头，他便高声把它喊了出来。他一面喊，一面在那张嘎嘎响的毛皮上蹦跳，用脚后跟打着拍子，直到他喘不过气来为止。灰兄弟和阿克拉也夹在他的诗节中间吼叫着。

"仔细瞧吧，噢，狼群诸君！我是否遵守了诺言？"莫格里喊完以后说；狼群齐声叫道："是的。"一头毛皮凌乱的狼嚎叫道：

"还是你来领导我们吧，啊，阿克拉。再来领导我们吧，啊，人娃娃，我们厌烦了这种没有法律的生活，我们希望重新成为自由的兽民。"

"不，"巴希拉柔声说道，"不行。等你们吃饱了，那种疯狂劲又会上来的。把你们叫作自由的兽民，不是没有缘故的。你们不是为了自由而战斗过了吗，现在你们得到了自由。好好享受它吧，狼群诸君。"

"人群和狼群都驱逐了我，"莫格里说，"现在我要独自在丛林里打猎了。"

"我们和你一起打猎，"四只小狼说。

于是从那天起，莫格里便离开了那里，和四只小狼在丛林中打猎。但是他并没有孤独一辈子，因为许多年以后，他长大成人，结了婚。

不过，那是一个讲给成年人听的故事了。

dangle
['dæŋg(ə)l]
v. 摇摆

tatter
['tætə(r)]
v. 使变得破破烂烂

lawlessness
['lɔ:lisnis]
n. 无法律的状态

The White Seal

白海豹

Oh! hush thee, my baby, the night is behind us,
*And black are the waters that **sparkled** so green.*
The moon, o'er the combers, looks downward to find us
*At rest in the **hollows** that rustle between.*
*Where **billow** meets billow, then soft be thy pillow,*
*Ah, weary wee **flipperling**, curl at thy ease!*
The storm shall not wake thee, nor shark overtake thee,
Asleep in the arms of the slow-swinging seas!

—Seal Lullaby

All these things happened several years ago at a place called Novastoshnah, or North East Point, on the Island of St. Paul, away and away in the Bering Sea. Limmershin, the Winter Wren, told me the tale when he was blown on to the **rigging** of a steamer going to Japan, and I took him down into my cabin and warmed and fed him for a couple of days till he was fit to fly back to St. Paul's again. Limmershin is a very **quaint** little bird, but he knows how to tell the truth.

Nobody comes to Novastoshnah except on business, and the only people who have regular business there are the seals. They come in the summer months by hundreds and hundreds of thousands out of the cold gray sea. For Novastoshnah Beach has the finest **accommodation** for seals of any place in

啊，不要闹，我的宝宝，我们背后就是黑夜，
　　漆黑的海水泛着墨绿的光芒。
滚滚的波涛上面，月亮正低头看着我们
　　在絮絮低语般起伏的浪窝里歇息。
一个接一个拍打的浪花，就是你柔软的枕头；
　　啊，带鳍的小人儿疲倦了，舒舒服服地
　　蜷着身子睡觉吧！
风暴不会闹醒你，鲨鱼不会追赶你，
　　在轻柔起伏的大海怀抱里酣睡吧。

——《海豹摇篮曲》

　　所有这一切都是几年以前发生在一个叫诺瓦斯托西纳的地方的事情。诺瓦斯托西纳又叫东北岬，在白令海那边遥远的圣保罗岛上。这个故事是一只名叫利默欣的冬鹟鹩告诉我们的。有一次他被风刮到了一只驶往日本的轮船的帆缆上，我把他救了下来，带回我的船舱，让他暖和过来，又喂养了他两天，直到他有气力飞回圣保罗岛为止。利默欣是一只非常古怪的小鸟，但是他知道怎样讲真话。

　　除非有事情要办，否则人们是不会到诺瓦斯托西纳来的，而在那里经常有事情要办的是海豹。夏天里，他们从寒冷的灰蒙蒙的大海来到这里，一下子就是几十万只；因为诺瓦斯托西纳海滩是世界上

all the world.

Sea Catch knew that, and every spring would swim from whatever place he happened to be in—would swim like a torpedo-boat straight for Novastoshnah and spend a month fighting with his companions for a good place on the rocks, as close to the sea as possible. Sea Catch was fifteen years old, a huge gray fur seal with almost a mane on his shoulders, and long, wicked dog teeth. When he heaved himself up on his front flippers he stood more than four feet clear of the ground, and his weight, if anyone had been bold enough to weigh him, was nearly seven hundred pounds. He was scarred all over with the marks of savage fights, but he was always ready for just one fight more. He would put his head on one side, as though he were afraid to look his enemy in the face; then he would shoot it out like lightning, and when the big teeth were firmly fixed on the other seal's neck, the other seal might get away if he could, but Sea Catch would not help him.

Yet Sea Catch never chased a beaten seal, for that was against the Rules of the Beach. He only wanted room by the sea for his nursery. But as there were forty or fifty thousand other seals hunting for the same thing each spring, the whistling, bellowing, roaring, and blowing on the beach was something frightful.

From a little hill called Hutchinson's Hill, you could look over three and a half miles of ground covered with fighting seals; and the surf was dotted all over with the heads of seals hurrying to land and begin their share of the fighting. They fought in the breakers, they fought in the sand, and they fought on the smooth-worn basalt rocks of the nurseries, for they were just as stupid and unaccommodating as men. Their

Sea Catch
此处是一只海豹的
名字,西卡奇
torpedo-boat
n. 鱼雷艇
mane
[mein]
n. 鬃毛
heave
[hi:v]
v. 举起

最适合海豹居住的地方。

西卡奇知道这一点。因此每年一到春天,不管他当时正在什么地方,他总是要像一艘鱼雷艇那样笔直游向诺瓦斯托西纳,并且花费一个月的时间和他的同伴们打架,好夺取一块离海最近的岩石上面的好地盘。西卡奇已经十五岁了,他是一头巨大的灰色海豹,肩胛上的鬃毛又长又密,还有长长的恶狠狠的犬牙。当他用前肢的阔鳍支撑着站直了的时候,离地足有四英尺高。他的体重——假如有人胆敢去称他的体重的话——大约是七百磅。他遍体是伤疤,全是多次恶战留下的痕迹,可是他还是跃跃欲试,随时准备再进行一次新的战斗。他常常故意歪着头,仿佛不敢正眼瞧他的敌手,接着他就会闪电般地发起袭击,他的长牙就会狠狠咬住另一头海豹的脖子,那头海豹也许拼命想逃,但西卡奇是绝不会轻易放开他的。

nursery
['nə:səri]
n. 养育后代的地方
surf
[sə:f]
n. 海浪
breaker
['breikə(r)]
n. 碎浪,浪花
unaccommodat-
ing
[,ʌnə'kɔmədeitiŋ]
adj. 不与人方便的,
不随和的

然而西卡奇从来没有追过一头打败了的海豹,因为那是违犯海滩上的规则的。他只想在海边找块地方做喂养小海豹的窝。但是,每年春天总有四万到五万头海豹也到这儿找地方做窝,所以,海滩上便响起一片惊人的尖叫声、咆哮声、怒吼声和撞击声。

你要是站在一个名叫哈钦森山的小山头上,就可以眺望到周围三英里半的地方。这块地方密密麻麻全是正在打架的海豹。而在浅海滩边,只见到处是海豹的头在海水中攒动,他们急着要登上陆地,好参加打架的行列。他们在浪花里打架,在沙滩上打架,也在被磨得光溜溜的做海豹窝的玄武岩上打架,因为他们跟男人们一样愚蠢和倔强。他们的妻

wives never came to the island until late in May or early in June, for they did not care to be torn to pieces; and the young two-, three-, and four-year-old seals who had not begun **housekeeping** went inland about half a mile through the ranks of the fighters and played about on the sand **dunes** in **droves** and **legions**, and **rubbed off** every single green thing that grew. They were called the holluschickie—the bachelors— and there were perhaps two or three hundred thousand of them at Novastoshnah alone.

Sea Catch had just finished his forty-fifth fight one spring when Matkah, his soft, sleek, gentle-eyed wife, came up out of the sea, and he caught her by the **scruff** of the neck and **dumped** her down on his reservation, saying **gruffly**: "Late as usual. Where have you been?"

It was not the fashion for Sea Catch to eat anything during the four months he stayed on the beaches, and so his temper was generally bad. Matkah knew better than to answer back. She looked round and **cooed**: "How thoughtful of you. You've taken the old place again."

"I should think I had," said Sea Catch. "Look at me!" He was scratched and bleeding in twenty places; one eye was almost out, and his sides were torn to **ribbons**.

"Oh, you men, you men!" Matkah said, fanning herself with her hind flipper. "Why can't you be sensible and settle your places quietly? You look as though you had been fighting with the Killer Whale."

"I haven't been doing anything but fight since the middle of May. The beach is disgracefully crowded this season. I've met at least a hundred seals from Lukannon Beach, house hunting. Why can't people stay where they belong?"

子一直要等到五月底或者六月初才到岛上来，因为她们才不愿意被撕成碎片呢。那些还没有成家的两岁、三岁和四岁的年轻海豹，则穿过打架的斗士们的行列，进入离大海一英里半的内陆，他们结伙成帮，在沙丘上嬉戏，把地上长出来的带点绿颜色的草呀、小树呀，全都蹭个精光。人家把他们叫作"霍卢斯契基"，也就是单身汉的意思。仅仅在诺瓦斯托西纳，就有二三十万头这样的海豹。

一个春天，西卡奇刚刚打完第四十五场架，这时，他那毛皮柔软光滑、眼神温柔的妻子玛特卡正好爬出海来，他一口咬住她颈背上的皮，把她提起来放在他占据的地盘里，没好气地说："又来晚了。你究竟到哪儿去了？"

通常西卡奇要在海滩上停留四个月，在这段时间里他是不作兴吃任何东西的，所以他的脾气总是很坏。玛特卡知道自己最好别还嘴。她看看四周，温柔地说："你考虑得多周到呀！找的还是老地方。"

"当然找老地方喽，"西卡奇说，"瞧瞧我！"他身上到处是破口子，有二十块伤口在流着血，一只眼睛几乎都瞎了，两边腰上满是一条条的伤痕。

"唉，你们这些男人哪，你们这些男人哪！"玛特卡用前鳍给自己扇着风，说道，"你们干吗不能通情达理，安安静静地商量一下分配地盘的事呢？瞧你那样儿，好像和逆戟鲸打过仗似的。"

"我从五月中旬开始，除了打架就没有干别的事。今年这块儿海滩挤得太不像话了。我至少遇见了上百头从卢坎龙海滩来这儿找住处的海豹。那些家伙为什么不待在他们自己的地方呢？"

"I've often thought we should be much happier if we hauled out at Otter Island instead of this crowded place," said Matkah.

"Bah! Only the holluschickie go to Otter Island. If we went there they would say we were afraid. We must preserve appearances, my dear."

Sea Catch sunk his head proudly between his fat shoulders and pretended to go to sleep for a few minutes, but all the time he was keeping a sharp lookout for a fight. Now that all the seals and their wives were on the land, you could hear their clamor miles out to sea above the loudest **gales**. At the lowest counting there were over a million seals on the beach—old seals, mother seals, tiny babies, and holluschickie, fighting, **scuffling**, **bleating**, crawling, and playing together— going down to the sea and coming up from it in gangs and **regiments**, lying over every foot of ground as far as the eye could reach, and **skirmishing** about in **brigades** through the fog. It is nearly always foggy at Novastoshnah, except when the sun comes out and makes everything look all pearly and rainbow-colored for a little while.

Kotick, Matkah's baby, was born in the middle of that confusion, and he was all head and shoulders, with pale, watery blue eyes, as tiny seals must be, but there was something about his coat that made his mother look at him very closely.

"Sea Catch," she said, at last, "our baby's going to be white!"

"Empty clam-shells and dry seaweed!" snorted Sea Catch. "There never has been such a thing in the world as a white seal."

gale
[geil]
n. 大风,强风

scuffle
['skʌf(ə)l]
v. 混战

bleat
[bli:t]
v. (牛)哞哞叫,(羊)
咩咩叫

regiment
['redʒimənt]
n. 团,大群

skirmish
['skə:miʃ]
v. 进行遭遇战

brigade
[bri'geid]
n. 旅,队

"我常常想,我们要是换个地方,不到这块儿拥挤得要命的地方来,而到水獭岛去,我们会快活得多的。"玛特卡说。

"呸!只有霍卢斯契基才到水獭岛去。我们要是去的话,他们会说我们胆怯了。我们得顾点儿体面呀,亲爱的。"

西卡奇骄傲地把脑袋埋进他肥胖的双肩里,待了几分钟,假装已经睡着了。其实他一直在警惕地注意着,随时准备打架。现在,所有的海豹和他们的伴侣都已经登上了陆地,在好多英里外的海面上就可以听见他们的喧闹声,这闹声压倒了最猛烈的风暴的呼啸。在这个海滩上,少说也有一百多万头海豹——老海豹、海豹妈妈、小不点儿海豹娃娃,还有霍卢斯契基。他们打架斗殴,混战一场,咩咩地叫着爬来爬去,在一块儿做游戏,成群结队地爬进海里,又爬出海面。海滩上一眼望去,密密麻麻全是海豹躺在那里,他们透过雾气,一小队一小队出发去进行战斗。在诺瓦斯托西纳几乎整天下着雾,但是一旦太阳出来,霎时间一切就显得银光闪闪,五彩缤纷。

玛特卡的婴儿柯蒂克就诞生在这片混乱之中。像所有的小海豹一样,他的头部和肩部显得特别大,他的眼睛也是水汪汪的浅蓝色,但是他的皮毛却有点儿特别,使得他的母亲不禁要非常仔细地瞧着他。

"西卡奇,"她终于说道,"我们的宝宝将来会长成白色的。"

"胡说八道!"西卡奇喷着鼻息说,"世界上根本没有白色的海豹。"

107

"I can't help that," said Matkah; "there's going to be now." And she sang the low, **crooning** seal song that all the mother seals sing to their babies:

You mustn't swim till you're six weeks old,
Or your head will be sunk by your heels;
And summer gales and Killer Whales
Are bad for baby seals.

Are bad for baby seals, dear rat,
As bad as bad can be;
But splash and grow strong,
And you can't be wrong.
Child of the Open Sea!

Of course the little fellow did not understand the words at first. He **paddled** and **scrambled** about by his mother's side, and learned to scuffle out of the way when his father was fighting with another seal, and the two rolled and roared up and down the slippery rocks. Matkah used to go to sea to get things to eat, and the baby was fed only once in two days, but then he ate all he could and throve upon it.

The first thing he did was to crawl inland, and there he met tens of thousands of babies of his own age, and they played together like **puppies**, went to sleep on the clean sand, and played again. The old people in the nurseries took no notice of them, and the holluschickie kept to their own grounds, and the babies had a beautiful playtime.

When Matkah came back from her deep-sea fishing she would go straight to their playground and call as a sheep calls

croon
[kru:n]
v. 低声歌唱,低声
哼,低吟

"那我可没有办法,"玛特卡说, "反正从今以后就会有了。"于是她低声唱起了温柔的海豹歌谣,所有的海豹妈妈都是这样对她们的宝宝唱的:

没长够六个星期,你可不要去游泳呀,
　　不然你就会头朝下脚朝上沉到水底;
夏天的风暴和那逆戟鲸
　　都是海豹娃娃的死对头啊。

都是海豹娃娃的死对头,亲爱的小耗子,
　　最凶最凶的死对头;
但是玩水吧,长得壮壮的吧,
那样你就会万事如意,
　　大海的孩子啊!

paddle
['pæd(ə)l]
v. 拍打,戏水
scramble
['skræmb(ə)l]
v. 攀爬,爬行

那个小家伙一开始当然听不懂这些话。他挨在母亲身边,划动前鳍,爬来爬去。他懂得每当父亲和别的海豹打起架来,吼叫着在滑溜溜的岩石上边滚上滚下的时候,他就爬到旁边去。玛特卡常常到海里去找食物吃,两天才喂一次孩子,但是喂他的时候他总是放开肚皮饱餐一顿,倒也长得很壮实。

puppy
['pʌpi]
n. (常指未满一岁的)小狗,小动物

他自个儿做的第一件事是朝着内陆爬去,他在那里看见了几万只和自己一样大的小海豹,他们像小狗一样在一块儿玩耍,在干净的沙子上睡觉,睡醒了再玩。待在海豹窝那边的老海豹们不理睬他们,霍卢斯契基们只在自己那块儿地盘上玩,于是海豹娃娃们自个儿玩得可痛快啦。

玛特卡从深海捕鱼回来就立刻来到他们的游戏场。她像母羊呼唤小羊羔那样叫唤起来,直到听见

109

for a lamb, and wait until she heard Kotick bleat. Then she would take the straightest of straight lines in his direction, striking out with her fore flippers and knocking the youngsters head over heels right and left. There were always a few hundred mothers hunting for their children through the playgrounds, and the babies were kept lively. But, as Matkah told Kotick, "So long as you don't lie in muddy water and get mange, or rub the hard sand into a cut or scratch, and so long as you never go swimming when there is a heavy sea, nothing will hurt you here."

Little seals can no more swim than little children, but they are unhappy till they learn. The first time that Kotick went down to the sea a wave carried him out beyond his depth, and his big head sank and his little hind flippers flew up exactly as his mother had told him in the song, and if the next wave had not thrown him back again he would have drowned.

After that, he learned to lie in a beach pool and let the wash of the waves just cover him and lift him up while he paddled, but he always kept his eye open for big waves that might hurt. He was two weeks learning to use his flippers; and all that while he **floundered** in and out of the water, and coughed and grunted and crawled up the beach and took **catnaps** on the sand, and went back again, until at last he found that he truly belonged to the water.

Then you can imagine the times that he had with his companions, ducking under the rollers; or coming in on top of a **comber** and landing with a **swash** and a splutter as the big wave went whirling far up the beach; or standing up on his tail and scratching his head as the old people did; or

柯蒂克的咩咩叫声为止。然后她就笔直地向他走过去，用前鳍打开一条路，把小海豹们掀翻在地，左右推开。在游戏场上，老是有几百个海豹妈妈在找自己的孩子，于是娃娃们也老是不得安宁，但是玛特卡是这样告诉柯蒂克的："只要你不躺在泥水里头，把皮毛弄得癞巴巴的，也不把硬砂子揉进划破的伤口里去，只要你不在大风大浪里游泳，这儿就没有什么能够伤害你。"

小海豹就跟小娃娃一个样，他们本来是不会游泳的，但是他们只要还没有学会游泳，心里就老痒痒。柯蒂克头一次下海，就被一个浪头把他卷进了没顶的深水里，他的大脑袋沉了下去，他的小小的后鳍翘了起来，正像他妈妈在那首歌谣里对他讲的那样。如果不是第二个浪头又把他打了回来，他一定会淹死了。

从那以后，他学会了躺在海滩边的水洼里，让波浪刚好盖住他的身体，他一划动双鳍就漂浮起来。但是他总是小心翼翼地躲开那些会伤害他的大浪头。他花了两个星期才学会用鳍划水。在这两星期里，他不停地在水里跟跟跄跄地沉下去又浮起来，一边呛水，一边哼哼。有时他爬上海滩，在沙堆里打会儿瞌睡，然后又下到海里，直到他终于觉得，他在水里就像到了家啦。

接着，你可以想象得出他和他的伙伴们是多么兴高采烈，他们迎着大浪头扎猛子，或是跨上一个高高的卷浪，跟着这个大浪头涌向海岸很远的沙滩上，然后扑通一声，水花四溅地落到地上；要不就学老海豹那样，用尾巴直立起来，搔着自己的脑袋；或是爬到伸出浅海湾的、上头长满杂草的滑溜

flounder
['flaundə(r)]
v.（在水中）挣扎，困难地往前走

catnap
['kætnæp]
n. 小睡，小憩

comber
['kəumə]
n. 卷浪，拍岸浪

swash
[swɔʃ]
n. 冲击，拍打

playing " I'm the King of the Castle" on slippery, weedy rocks that just stuck out of the wash. Now and then he would see a thin **fin**, like a big shark's fin, drifting along close to shore, and he knew that that was the Killer Whale, the Grampus, who eats young seals when he can get them; and Kotick would head for the beach like an arrow, and the fin would **jig** off slowly, as if it were looking for nothing at all.

Late in October the seals began to leave St. Paul's for the deep sea, by families and tribes, and there was no more fighting over the nurseries, and the holluschickie played anywhere they liked. "Next year," said Matkah to Kotick, "you will be a holluschickie; but this year you must learn how to catch fish."

They set out together across the Pacific, and Matkah showed Kotick how to sleep on his back with his flippers **tucked** down by his side and his little nose just out of the water. No **cradle** is so comfortable as the long, rocking swell of the Pacific. When Kotick felt his skin **tingle** all over, Matkah told him he was learning the "feel of the water," and that tingly, **prickly** feelings meant bad weather coming, and he must swim hard and get away.

"In a little time," she said, "you'll know where to swim to, but just now we'll follow Sea Pig, the **Porpoise**, for he is very wise." A **school** of porpoises were ducking and tearing through the water, and little Kotick followed them as fast as he could. "How do you know where to go to?" he panted. The leader of the school rolled his white eye and ducked under. "My tail tingles, youngster," he said. "That means there's a gale behind me. Come along! When you're south of the Sticky Water [he meant the **Equator**] and your tail tingles,

fin
[fin]
n. 鳍,鱼翅

jig
[dʒig]
v. 急促地上下跳动

tuck
[tʌk]
v. 卷起,折起,收拢

cradle
['kreid(ə)l]
n. 摇篮,发源地

tingle
['tiŋ(ə)l]
v. 使感刺痛

prickly
['prikli]
adj. 刺痛的

porpoise
['pɔ:pəs]
n. 海豚,小鲸

school
[sku:l]
n. 鱼群

equator
[i'kweitə(r)]
n. 赤道

溜岩石顶上做"我是城堡国王"的游戏。有时他看见水里有一条薄薄的鱼翅,非常像大鲨鱼的鱼翅,正紧贴着海岸漂过来,于是他知道,这是逆戟鲸格兰普斯,他要是抓得着年轻的海豹,就会毫不客气地吃掉他们。于是柯蒂克就会像支箭似的吱溜一下朝海滩逃去,那只鱼翅便会慢吞吞地扭摆开去,仿佛它根本就没打算寻找什么似的。

到了十月,一家一户的和整个部族的海豹开始离开圣保罗岛,迁移到深海区去。这时,再也没有人为了争夺喂养小海豹的窝而打架,那些霍卢斯契基也可以任意地到处自由玩耍了。玛特卡对柯蒂克说:"打明年起你就是霍卢斯契基了,但是今年你首先得学会捕鱼。"

他们一块儿出发横渡太平洋。玛特卡教柯蒂克怎样仰天躺着睡觉,把他的鳍贴着身子收拢起来,让他的小鼻子露出一点儿在水面上。什么样儿的摇篮也没有太平洋摇荡起伏的漫长的波浪那么舒服。柯蒂克觉得他全身的皮肤都痒酥酥的。玛特卡告诉他,他现在正体会着"海水的味道",那带点刺痛的酸麻感觉说明坏天气要到来了,他应该快点游,好离开这儿。

"用不了多少时间,"她说,"你就会知道该往哪儿游了。不过我们现在就跟在海豚波帕斯后面吧,他是非常聪明的。"一大群海豚扎进海底,正在飞快地赶着路,小柯蒂克使劲儿跟在他们后面。"你们怎么知道该朝哪儿游呢?"他喘着气问道。这群海豚的头领翻动着白眼,一头扎了下去。"我的尾巴觉得有点刺痛,小伙子,"他说道,"那就是说,一场风暴正跟在我背后。来吧!假如你在'黏糊糊的海水'(他的意思是指赤道)的南边的时候,你的尾巴开始觉得刺痛,那就是说,你的前头有一

that means there's a gale in front of you and you must head north. Come along! The water feels bad here."

This was one of very many things that Kotick learned, and he was always learning. Matkah taught him to follow the **cod** and the **halibut** along the under-sea banks and **wrench** the rockling out of his hole among the weeds; how to **skirt** the wrecks lying a hundred **fathoms** below water and dart like a rifle bullet in at one porthole and out at another as the fishes ran; how to dance on the top of the waves when the lightning was racing all over the sky, and wave his flipper politely to the **stumpy-tailed** Albatross and the Man-of-war Hawk as they went down the wind; how to jump three or four feet clear of the water like a dolphin, flippers close to the side and tail curved; to leave the flying fish alone because they are all bony; to take the shoulder-piece out of a cod at full speed ten fathoms deep, and never to stop and look at a boat or a ship, but particularly a row-boat. At the end of six months what Kotick did not know about deep-sea fishing was not worth the knowing. And all that time he never set flipper on dry ground.

One day, however, as he was lying half asleep in the warm water somewhere off the Island of Juan Fernandez, he felt faint and lazy all over, just as human people do when the spring is in their legs, and he remembered the good firm beaches of Novastoshnah seven thousand miles away, the games his companions played, the smell of the seaweed, the seal roar, and the fighting. That very minute he turned north, swimming steadily, and as he went on he met scores of his mates, all **bound for** the same place, and they said: "Greeting, Kotick! This year we are all holluschickie, and we

cod

[kɔd]

n. 鳕

halibut

[ˈhælibət]

n. 大比目鱼

wrench

[rentʃ]

v. 扭拉

skirt

[skə:t]

v. 绕行,环绕

fathom

[ˈfæð(ə)m]

n. 英寻(长度单位,
1 英寻＝6 英尺)

stumpy-tailed

短尾巴的

场风暴,你就必须朝北边去。来吧,这儿的海水我
觉得不太对头。"

　　这就是柯蒂克学会的许多许多件事情中的一
件,他时刻都在学。玛特卡教他沿着海底的沙洲追
逐鳕鱼和大比目鱼,从海草丛中的洞穴里抠出黑鲅
来;还教他怎样绕过海底一百英寻深的地方的沉船
残骸,在鱼群中间像一颗步枪子弹一样掠进这边的
舷窗,又从另一边的舷窗里游出来。当整个天空到
处是闪电的时候,玛特卡教他怎样在浪尖上跳舞,
并且有礼貌地向顺风而下的短尾巴信天翁和战舰鹰
晃动自己的鳍;还教他怎么样让他的鳍紧贴住身
子,把尾巴弯起来,像一只海豚一样跃出水面三四
英尺高;她告诉他不要理睬飞鱼,因为他们身上尽
是骨头;她教他在海底十英寻深的地方全速前进
时,怎样一口咬下一只鳕鱼的肩胛肉;还教他绝不
要停下来看一只小船或是一艘海船,尤其是一只划
艇。六个月以后,柯蒂克可以算是完全精通深海捕
鱼的本领了。在这段时间里,他的鳍从来没有挨过
干燥的陆地。

　　然而有一天,他正半睡半醒地躺在胡安·费尔
南德斯岛附近温暖的海水里时,突然觉得全身晕乎
乎懒洋洋的,就像人类感觉春天要到了一个样。他
记起了七千英里外诺瓦斯托西纳那儿又舒服又结实
的海滩,记起了他和同伴们玩过的游戏,记起了海
草的气味、海豹的咆哮和扭打。就在那一刻,他扭
转头,不停地向北方游去。他一路上遇见了几十个
同伴,他们都和他游向同一个地方,他们说道:
"你好,柯蒂克!今年我们全都是霍卢斯契基了,我
们可以在卢坎龙那边的激浪上跳火焰舞了,还可以

bound for

驶往

can dance the Fire-dance in the breakers off Lukannon and play on the new grass. But where did you get that coat?"

Kotick's fur was almost pure white now, and though he felt very proud of it, he only said, "Swim quickly! My bones are aching for the land." And so they all came to the beaches where they had been born, and heard the old seals, their fathers, fighting in the rolling mist.

That night Kotick danced the Fire-dance with the **yearling** seals. The sea is full of fire on summer nights all the way down from Novastoshnah to Lukannon, and each seal leaves a wake like burning oil behind him and a flaming flash when he jumps, and the waves break in great **phosphorescent streaks** and swirls. Then they went inland to the holluschickie grounds and rolled up and down in the new wild wheat and told stories of what they had done while they had been at sea. They talked about the Pacific as boys would talk about a wood that they had been **nutting** in, and if anyone had understood them he could have gone away and made such a chart of that ocean as never was. The three-and four-year-old holluschickie **romped** down from Hutchinson's Hill crying: "Out of the way, youngsters! The sea is deep and you don't know all that's in it yet. Wait till you've rounded the Horn. Hi, you yearling, where did you get that white coat?"

"I didn't get it," said Kotick. "It grew." And just as he was going to roll the speaker over, a couple of black-haired men with flat red faces came from behind a sand dune, and Kotick, who had never seen a man before, coughed and lowered his head. The holluschickie just **bundled off** a few yards and sat staring stupidly. The men were no less than Kerick Booterin, the chief of the seal-hunters on the island,

在嫩草地上玩了。可是，你这身毛皮是从哪儿搞来的呀？"

柯蒂克的毛皮现在差不多成了纯白色的，他对这身毛皮十分自豪，可是只说了句："快游！我想陆地想得骨头都疼了。"于是他们全都回到了他们出生的海滩。他们听见他们的父辈老海豹们正在起伏流动的雾气里战斗。

那天晚上，柯蒂克和一岁的海豹们一块儿跳起了火焰舞。在夏天的夜晚，从诺瓦斯托西纳直到卢坎龙，大海里充满了熠熠发光的火焰，每一头海豹身后都留下了一道亮痕，像是燃烧着的油。每当他们跳跃的时候就迸发出一道闪亮的火光，波浪碎成了无数片发着磷光的条纹和漩涡。后来他们进入内陆，来到霍卢斯契基的地盘上，他们在青嫩的野麦子地里滚来滚去，互相讲着他们在海里做过些什么。他们讲起太平洋，就像男孩子们讲起他们去采干果的那个树林一样。要是有人能听懂他们的话，他回去一定可以画出一幅从来没有人画过的大洋地图。一群三四岁的霍卢斯契基从哈钦森山上蹦跳下来，喊道："让开道，小家伙们！海水深着呢！海里还有好多东西是你们不知道的呢。等你们绕过了合恩角再说吧。嗨，你，一岁的小家伙，你从哪儿搞来的那件白外衣？"

"我没有搞来，"柯蒂克说，"它是自己长出来的。"他正要把说话的那家伙掀一个跟头，从沙丘后面走出来两个有着黑头发和扁平的红脸盘的人，柯蒂克从来没有见过人，他呛咳起来，低下了头。那些霍卢斯契基只是慌慌张张地往旁边躲开几码远，然后呆呆地坐在那里瞪着。这两人不是别人，

yearling
['jiəliŋ]
n. 一岁或还未满两岁的小动物

phosphorescent
[ˌfɔsfə'resənt]
adj. 发出磷光的, 熠熠发光的

streak
[stri:k]
n. 条纹

nut
[nʌt]
v. 采干果, 拾坚果

romp
[rɔmp]
v. 顽皮嬉戏

bundle off
匆匆离开

and Patalamon, his son. They came from the little village not half a mile from the seal nurseries, and they were deciding what seals they would drive up to the killing pens—for the seals were driven just like sheep—to be turned into seal-skin jackets later on.

"Ho!" said Patalamon. "Look! There's a white seal!"

Kerick Booterin turned nearly white under his oil and smoke, for he was an **Aleut**, and Aleuts are not clean people. Then he began to mutter a prayer. " Don't touch him, Patalamon. There has never been a white seal since—since I was born. Perhaps it is old Zaharrof's ghost. He was lost last year in the big gale."

" I'm not going near him, " said Patalamon. " He's unlucky. Do you really think he is old Zaharrof come back? I **owe him for** some **gulls'** eggs."

"Don't look at him," said Kerick. "Head off that drove of four-year-olds. The men ought to skin two hundred to-day, but it's the beginning of the season and they are new to the work. A hundred will do. Quick!"

Patalamon rattled a pair of seal's shoulder bones in front of a herd of holluschickie and they stopped dead, puffing and blowing. Then he stepped near and the seals began to move, and Kerick headed them inland, and they never tried to get back to their companions. Hundreds and hundreds of thousands of seals watched them being driven, but they went on playing just the same. Kotick was the only one who asked questions, and none of his companions could tell him anything, except that the men always drove seals in that way for six weeks or two months of every year.

" I am going to follow, " he said, and his eyes nearly

他们是岛上捕海豹的猎人首领克里克·布特林和他的儿子帕塔拉蒙。他们是从一个离小海豹窝不到半英里远的小村庄里来的。他们正在考虑把哪些海豹赶到屠场去（因为海豹是被赶着走的，和赶羊一个样），以后便把他们变成海豹皮外套。

"嗬！"帕塔拉蒙说，"瞧，有只白海豹！"

尽管皮肤上蒙着一层油腻和煤烟，克里克·布特林的脸色还是一下子变得惨白。他是阿留申岛民，阿留申岛的居民都不爱干净。接着他嘴里喃喃地念起了祷词。"别碰他，帕塔拉蒙。打从——打从我出生以来，还从来没有出现过一只白海豹。它也许是老扎哈罗夫的鬼魂。他是在去年那场大风暴里失踪的。"

"我不打算到他跟前去，"帕塔拉蒙说，"他是不吉利的。你真的认为这是老扎哈罗夫回来了吗？我还欠他几只海鸥蛋呢。"

"别瞧他，"克里克说，"赶那群四岁的海豹吧。工人们今天该剥出二百只海豹的皮，不过季节刚开始，他们还都是新手。剥一百只就够了。快些！"

帕塔拉蒙在一群霍卢斯契基面前敲起了一对海豹的肩胛骨，他们都呆住了，呼哧呼哧地直喘气。后来他往前逼近一些，海豹们便开始移动，于是克里克就领着他们朝内陆走去，他们根本没有想回到他们的同伴那里去。好几十万只海豹眼睁睁看着他们被赶着离开，却不闻不问，只管照样玩下去。柯蒂克是唯一提出问题的海豹，可是他的同伴什么也没法告诉他，他们只知道每年有六个星期或者两个月的时间，人们总是这样来赶走海豹。

"我要跟踪他们。"他说道。他就跟在那群海豹

Aleut
['æliu:t]
n. （爱斯基摩人中的）阿留申人

owe sb. for
对…负有义务，欠某人…

gull
[gʌl]
n. 海鸥

popped out of his head as he **shuffled** along **in the wake of** the herd.

"The white seal is coming after us," cried Patalamon. "That's the first time a seal has ever come to the killing-grounds alone."

"Hsh! Don't look behind you," said Kerick. "It is Zaharrof's ghost! I must speak to the priest about this."

The distance to the killing-grounds was only half a mile, but it took an hour to cover, because if the seals went too fast Kerick knew that they would get heated and then their fur would come off in patches when they were skinned. So they went on very slowly, past Sea Lion's Neck, past Webster House, till they came to the Salt House just beyond the sight of the seals on the beach. Kotick followed, panting and wondering. He thought that he was at the world's end, but the roar of the seal nurseries behind him sounded as loud as the roar of a train in a tunnel. Then Kerick sat down on the moss and pulled out a heavy **pewter** watch and let the drove cool off for thirty minutes, and Kotick could hear the fog-dew dripping off the **brim** of his cap. Then ten or twelve men, each with an **iron-bound club** three or four feet long, came up, and Kerick pointed out one or two of the drove that were bitten by their companions or too hot, and the men kicked those aside with their heavy boots made of the skin of a **walrus**'s throat, and then Kerick said, "Let go!" and then the men clubbed the seals on the head as fast as they could.

Ten minutes later little Kotick did not recognize his friends any more, for their skins were ripped off from the nose to the hind flippers, **whipped off** and thrown down on the ground in a pile.

后面爬过去，他的眼睛都差点儿要掉到脑袋外面了。

"那只白海豹跟在我们后面来了，"帕塔拉蒙喊了起来，"这是第一回有头海豹自己独自去屠宰场。"

"嗤！别往后看，"克里克说，"那是扎哈罗夫的鬼魂！我一定得把这事告诉神父。"

到屠宰场去有半英里路，但是他们却要花上一个小时才能走到，因为克里克知道，海豹们要是走得太快了，他们就会发热，剥了皮以后他们的毛就会一簇簇地脱落下来。于是，他们慢吞吞地朝前走，经过海狮颈、韦伯斯特邸宅，直到他们来到海滩上的海豹看不见的撒尔特邸宅。柯蒂克气喘吁吁、满怀好奇地跟在后面。他以为他已经到了世界的尽头，可是他背后哺育小海豹的营地的吼叫声仍然那么响亮，就像一列火车隆隆地穿过隧道一样。接着克里克在苔藓上坐了下来，拿出一只沉重的锡镴怀表，等了三十分钟，好让这群海豹凉快下来。柯蒂克都能听见清晨的露珠从他的帽檐上滴下的声音。然后有十到十二个人走了过来，手里都拿着三四英尺长、包着铁皮的木棒。克里克把海豹群里一两只被同伴咬伤或是赶路赶得太热的海豹指给他们看，那些人便抬起他们用海象脖颈皮制成的厚靴子，把这几只海豹踢到一边去。接着克里克说了声："干吧！"于是那些人举起棍棒朝海豹的头上敲去。

十分钟后，小柯蒂克再也不认识他的朋友们了，因为人们已经把他们的皮从鼻尖一直撕开到后鳍，然后猛地扯了下来，扔到地上，堆成了一堆。

shuffle
[ˈʃʌf(ə)l]
v. 拖曳，搅乱，慢吞吞地走
in the wake of
尾随，紧跟，仿效

pewter
[ˈpjuːtə(r)]
n. 白蜡，锡镴
brim
[brim]
n. 突出的边沿或边缘
iron-bound
adj. 用铁捆缚的，坚硬的
club
[klʌb]
n. 棍棒
walrus
[ˈwɔːlrəs]
n. 海象，海象胡须
whip off
猛地移动、扯下

That was enough for Kotick. He turned and **galloped** (a seal can gallop very swiftly for a short time) back to the sea; his little new mustache bristling with horror. At Sea Lion's Neck, where the great sea lions sit on the edge of the surf, he flung himself flipper-overhead into the cool water and rocked there, gasping miserably. "What's here?" said a sea lion gruffly, for as a rule the sea lions keep themselves to themselves.

"Scoochnie! Ochen scoochnie!" ("I'm lonesome, very lonesome!") said Kotick. "They're killing all the holluschickie on all the beaches!"

The Sea Lion turned his head inshore. "Nonsense!" he said. "Your friends are making as much noise as ever. You must have seen old Kerick **polishing off** a drove. He's done that for thirty years."

"It's horrible," said Kotick, backing water as a wave went over him, and steadying himself with a screw stroke of his flippers that brought him all standing within three inches of a jagged edge of rock.

"Well done for a yearling!" said the Sea Lion, who could **appreciate** good swimming. "I suppose it is rather awful from your way of looking at it, but if you seals will come here year after year, of course the men get to know of it, and unless you can find an island where no men ever come you will always be driven."

"Isn't there any such island?" began Kotick.

"I've followed the poltoos [the halibut] for twenty years, and I can't say I've found it yet. But look here—you seem to have a fondness for talking to your betters—suppose you go to Walrus **Islet** and talk to Sea Vitch. He may know something.

gallop

['gæləp]

v. 飞驰,急速进行

对于柯蒂克,这已经够了。他掉转身就狂奔起来(一头海豹只能狂奔很短的时间),一直奔回海里,他那刚长出来的小胡须恐惧得一根根竖了起来。他跑到海狮颈,巨大的海狮坐在那里的浅海滩边缘上。他抬起双鳍举过头顶,跳进清凉的海水里,在水里摇晃着,痛苦地喘着气。"那儿是什么?"有个海狮粗声粗气地说。因为海狮们一般都待在一起,不跟外人往来。

"斯库奇尼!欧钦·斯库奇尼!(我寂寞呀!我太寂寞了!)"柯蒂克说,"他们把所有的海滩上所有的霍卢斯契基都杀死了!"

海狮扭转头朝向内陆。"胡说八道!"他说,

polish off

草草做完,打败

"你的朋友们还在像往常那样大声嚷嚷呢。你一定是看见了老克里克干掉一群海豹了吧。他那么干已经三十年了。"

"太可怕了。"柯蒂克说。一个浪头打了过来,他一面向后退,一面划动双鳍打了个旋子,正好在离一块锯齿形岩石边上只有三英寸远的地方停住了身体。

appreciate

[ə'pri:ʃieit]

v. 赏识,欣赏

"干得不错,一岁的小伙子!"海狮说,他很能欣赏高超的游泳技术。"我想,从你的角度看,这的确是可怕的;不过,你们海豹们每年总是到这里来,人们当然会知道啦,除非你能找到一个人们从来没到过的岛,否则人们总是要来赶你们的。"

"有这样的岛吗?"柯蒂克开口问道。

Islet

['ailit]

n. 小岛

"我跟在波尔图(大比目鱼)后面游了二十年,还从来没有找到过这样的岛。不过,你似乎特别喜欢找比你身份高的人说话,你可以到海象小岛去找西威奇谈谈,他也许知道点儿什么。别那么拔脚就

Don't flounce off like that. It's a six-mile swim, and if I were you I should haul out and take a nap first, little one."

Kotick thought that that was good advice, so he swam round to his own beach, hauled out, and slept for half an hour, twitching all over, as seals will. Then he headed straight for Walrus Islet, a little low sheet of rocky island almost due northeast from Novastoshnah, all **ledges** and rock and gulls' nests, where the walrus herded by themselves.

He landed close to old Sea Vitch—the big, ugly, **bloated**, **pimpled**, fat-necked, long-tusked walrus of the North Pacific, who has no manners except when he is asleep—as he was then, with his hind flippers half in and half out of the surf.

"Wake up!" barked Kotick, for the gulls were making a great noise.

"Hah! Ho! Hmph! What's that?" said Sea Vitch, and he struck the next walrus a blow with his tusks and waked him up, and the next struck the next, and so on till they were all awake and staring in every direction but the right one.

"Hi! It's me," said Kotick, **bobbing** in the surf and looking like a little white **slug**.

"Well! May I be—skinned!" said Sea Vitch, and they all looked at Kotick as you can fancy a club full of drowsy old gentlemen would look at a little boy. Kotick did not care to hear any more about skinning just then; he had seen enough of it. So he called out:

"Isn't there any place for seals to go where men don't ever come?"

跑呀，你得游六海里才到呢。要是我的话，我就上岸去，先打个盹儿再说，小家伙。"

柯蒂克认为这主意很不错，所以他游回自己的海滩，上岸去睡了半个小时。他睡的时候周身不住地抽动，海豹们睡觉都是这个样的。接着他就直接出发到海象小岛去了。那是一块几乎正好位于诺瓦斯托西纳东北方的低矮多岩的小岛，岛上全是岩石台阶和海鸥窝，只有海象们成群结伙地在那里生活。

他在离老西威奇很近的地方上了岸，老西威奇是一只北太平洋的丑陋的大海象。他长着粗脖根和长长的牙齿，身躯肥胖，长满了疙瘩。除了睡觉的时候之外，他对人毫无礼貌，而这时他正好在睡觉，他的前鳍一半浸在浅浅的海水里，一半露在外边。

"醒醒！"柯蒂克喊道，因为这时海鸥的叫声震耳欲聋。

"咳！嗬！哼！什么事？"西威奇说，他用长牙敲了旁边的海象一下，把那只海象敲醒了，旁边那只海象又敲他旁边的海象一下，如此下去，直到所有的海象都醒了过来。他们向四面八方望来望去，偏偏不望那该望的地方。

"嗨！是我呀。"柯蒂克就像一条白色的小鼻涕虫似的在水里漂上漂下。

"哎，让老天……剥了我的皮吧！"西威奇说，于是他们一齐紧盯着柯蒂克瞧。你可以想象出那种景象，就跟一所俱乐部里那些打瞌睡的老绅士围着一个小男孩瞧那样。柯蒂克可不愿意再听什么剥皮不剥皮的话，他已经瞧够了剥皮的事，所以他喊了起来：

"请问有没有人从来没有到过的地方，可以让海豹去住？"

"Go and find out," said Sea Vitch, shutting his eyes. "Run away. We're busy here."

Kotick made his dolphin-jump in the air and shouted as loud as he could: "Clam-eater! Clam-eater!" He knew that Sea Vitch never caught a fish in his life but always rooted for clams and seaweed; though he pretended to be a very terrible person. Naturally the Chickies and the Gooverooskies and the Epatkas—the Burgomaster Gulls and the Kittiwakes and the Puffins, who are always looking for a chance to be rude, took up the cry, and—so Limmershin told me—for nearly five minutes you could not have heard a gun fired on Walrus Islet. All the population was yelling and screaming "Clam-eater! Stareek [old man]!" while Sea Vitch rolled from side to side grunting and coughing.

"Now will you tell?" said Kotick, all out of breath.

"Go and ask Sea Cow," said Sea Vitch. "If he is living still, he'll be able to tell you."

"How shall I know Sea Cow when I meet him?" said Kotick, **sheering off**.

"He's the only thing in the sea uglier than Sea Vitch," screamed a Burgomaster gull, wheeling under Sea Vitch's nose. "Uglier, and with worse manners! Stareek!"

Kotick swam back to Novastoshnah, leaving the gulls to scream. There he found that no one sympathized with him in his little attempt to discover a quiet place for the seals. They told him that men had always driven the holluschickie—it was part of the day's work—and that if he did not like to see ugly things he should not have gone to the killing grounds. But none of the other seals had seen the killing, and that made the difference between him and his friends. Besides, Kotick

"你自己去找吧，"西威奇闭上眼睛说道，"快走开。我们这儿正忙着呢。"

柯蒂克像海豚一样一下子腾空跃起，拼命放大嗓门嚷了起来："吃蛤蜊的家伙！吃蛤蜊的家伙！"他知道，虽说西威奇装作是个很吓人的角色，其实他一辈子从来没逮住过一条鱼，他只会用鼻子挖些蛤蜊和海草吃。那些随时都在等待机会欺负人的市长鸥、三趾鸥和海鹦们当然马上就响应起了这样的叫骂，于是——利默欣是这样告诉我的——几乎在五分钟之内，如果朝海象小岛开一炮，你也会听不见炮声。岛上的居民全都狂喊乱叫："吃蛤蜊的家伙！斯塔列克（老头儿）！"而西威奇则一面翻动着身体，一面哼哼着，呛咳着。

"这下你肯告诉我了吧？"喊叫得喘不过气来的柯蒂克问道。

"去问海牛吧，"西威奇说，"他要是还活着，一定能告诉你。"

"我怎么知道他是海牛呢？"柯蒂克在转身走开的时候问道。

"他是大海里面唯一比西威奇还丑的家伙，"一只市长鸥在西威奇鼻子底下盘旋着，尖叫道，"丑得多，更没有礼貌！斯塔列克！"

柯蒂克游回了诺瓦斯托西纳，留下海鸥在那里尖叫。他发现，虽说他尽了自己有限的力量给海豹找块安静地方，却没有一个海豹对他表示同情。海豹们告诉他说，人们总要把霍卢斯契基赶走的——这样的事儿一点儿不稀奇——他如果不愿看见这种丑恶的事，他就不该到屠宰场去。但是没有一只海豹亲眼见过屠杀，这就使他没法和他的朋友们得出

clam
[klæm]
n. 蛤，蛤蜊

sheer off
避开，转向

127

was a white seal.

"What you must do," said old Sea Catch, after he had heard his son's adventures, "is to grow up and be a big seal like your father, and have a nursery on the beach, and then they will leave you alone. In another five years you ought to be able to fight for yourself." Even gentle Matkah, his mother, said: "You will never be able to stop the killing. Go and play in the sea, Kotick." And Kotick went off and danced the Fire-dance with a very heavy little heart.

That autumn he left the beach as soon as he could, and set off alone because of a notion in his **bullet-head**. He was going to find Sea Cow, if there was such a person in the sea, and he was going to find a quiet island with good firm beaches for seals to live on, where men could not get at them. So he explored and explored by himself from the North to the South Pacific, swimming as much as three hundred miles in a day and a night. He met with more adventures than can be told, and narrowly escaped being caught by the Basking Shark, and the Spotted Shark, and the Hammer-head, and he met all the untrustworthy **ruffians** that **loaf** up and down the seas, and the heavy polite fish, and the scarlet spotted **scallops** that are **moored** in one place for hundreds of years, and grow very proud of it; but he never met Sea Cow, and he never found an island that he could fancy.

If the beach was good and hard, with a slope behind it for seals to play on, there was always the smoke of a whaler **on the horizon**, boiling down **blubber**, and Kotick knew what that meant. Or else he could see that seals had once visited the island and been killed off, and Kotick knew that where

一致的意见。况且，柯蒂克还是只白色的海豹呢。

"你一定得快点儿长大，长成你父亲一样的大海豹，"老西卡奇听了儿子的冒险经历后这样对他说，"到那时，你在海滩上也有一个哺育小海豹的窝，他们就不会来招惹你了。再过五年，你就该能独立地战斗了。"就连他的母亲，温柔的玛特卡也说："你永远也没法制止屠杀。到海里去玩吧，柯蒂克。"于是柯蒂克去了，他怀着一颗小小的、十分沉重的心，跳起了火焰舞。

那年秋天，他尽早地离开了海滩，独自出发了，因为他那顽固的脑袋瓜里有了一个主意。他一定要找到海牛，只要海里有这么个家伙的话。他还要找到一个海豹可以居住的、有出色的结实的沙滩的安静海岛，那里是人们找不到的地方。于是他独自去寻找了。他找了又找，从北太平洋找到南太平洋，有时一天一夜游了三百英里。他经历了说不完的冒险，他差点儿被晒鲨、斑点鲨和双髻鲨抓住，他遇见了所有那些在海里游荡的不可靠的恶棍，还有那些身体笨重、彬彬有礼的鱼，还有带着红色斑点的扇贝，它们居留在一个地方，已有几百年了，所以它们对此非常自豪。但是他从来没有遇见海牛，也没有找到一个使他中意的海岛。

如果他找到一处又好又结实的海滩，后面还有斜坡，可以让海豹们在上面戏耍，那么，在远方的天边总是有一艘捕鲸船在冒着黑烟，煮着鲸油，柯蒂克完全懂得它意味着什么。有时他看出海豹曾经来过某个海岛，但后来被捕杀光了。柯蒂克明白，

bullet-head
['bulithed]
n. 圆头者，笨蛋

ruffian
['rʌfiən]
n. 流氓，恶棍，无赖
loaf
[ləuf]
v. 混日子，游手好闲
scallop
['skɔləp]
n. 扇贝，干贝
moor
['muə(r),mɔː(r)]
v. 停泊，固定
on the horizon
在地平线上
blubber
['blʌbə(r)]
n. 鲸脂，鲸油

129

men had come once they would come again.

He picked up with an old stumpy-tailed albatross, who told him that Kerguelen Island was the very place for peace and quiet, and when Kotick went down there he was all but **smashed** to pieces against some wicked black cliffs in a heavy **sleet**-storm with lightning and thunder. Yet as he pulled out against the gale he could see that even there had once been a seal nursery. And it was so in all the other islands that he visited.

Limmershin gave a long list of them, for he said that Kotick spent five seasons exploring, with a four months' rest each year at Novastoshnah, when the holluschickie used to make fun of him and his imaginary islands. He went to the Gallapagos, a **horrid** dry place on the Equator, where he was nearly baked to death; he went to the Georgia Islands, the Orkneys, Emerald Island, Little Nightingale Island, Gough's Island, Bouvet's Island, the Crossets, and even to a little speck of an island south of the Cape of Good Hope. But everywhere the People of the Sea told him the same things. Seals had come to those islands once upon a time, but men had killed them all off. Even when he swam thousands of miles out of the Pacific and got to a place called Cape Corrientes (that was when he was coming back from Gough's Island), he found a few hundred mangy seals on a rock and they told him that men came there too.

That nearly broke his heart, and he headed round the Horn back to his own beaches; and on his way north he hauled out on an island full of green trees, where he found an old, old seal who was dying, and Kotick caught fish for him and told him all his sorrows. "Now," said Kotick, "I am

只要人们来过一次，他们以后还会再来的。

他认识了一只短尾巴的老信天翁，信天翁对他说，克圭伦岛是最平安最清静的地方，可是柯蒂克到了那儿，却遇到了一场夹着闪电雷鸣的大冻雨。在那里，他差点儿在黑乎乎的险恶的悬崖上被撞得粉身碎骨。可是当他顶着风暴离开这块地方的时候，他看出这里也曾有过一块哺育小海豹的营地。他去过的所有其他海岛也都是这样。

利默欣列举了一长串海岛的名字，因为他说柯蒂克花了五个季节的时间来寻找，每年只在诺瓦斯托西纳休息四个月，每到这时，那些霍卢斯契基们常常取笑他和他幻想中的岛屿。他去过加拉帕戈斯群岛，那是赤道线上一块干燥到极点的地方，他在那儿几乎被烤焦了；他到过乔治亚群岛、南奥克尼群岛、埃默腊尔德岛、小南丁格尔岛、果夫岛、布维岛、克罗泽群岛，甚至到过好望角以南的一个小不点儿的岛子。可是不管到哪儿，海里的百姓告诉他的，全是同样的事。从前海豹曾经来到这些岛上，但是人们把他们都杀绝了。甚至当他游了几千英里，游出了太平洋，到了一个名叫科连特斯角的地方（那是他刚从果夫岛回来的时候），他发现有几百头毛皮脏乱的海豹待在一块岩石上头，他们对他说，人们也到过这里。

这话伤透了他的心，他绕过合恩角回到了故乡的海滩；在北上的途中，他在一个长满苍翠树木的小岛上了岸，看见一头奄奄一息的、老极了的老海豹。柯蒂克替他捕鱼，向他倾诉了自己的苦恼。柯蒂克说："现在我就要回到诺瓦斯托西纳去了，以

smash
[smæʃ]
v. 打碎，粉碎
sleet
[sli:t]
n. 冰雨，雨夹雪

horrid
['hɔrid]
adj. 恐怖的，可怕的

131

going back to Novastoshnah, and if I am driven to the killing-pens with the holluschickie I shall not care."

The old seal said, "Try once more. I am the last of the Lost Rookery of Masafuera, and in the days when men killed us by the hundred thousand there was a story on the beaches that some day a white seal would come out of the North and lead the seal people to a quiet place. I am old, and I shall never live to see that day, but others will. Try once more."

And Kotick **curled** up his mustache (it was a beauty) and said, "I am the only white seal that has ever been born on the beaches, and I am the only seal, black or white, who ever thought of looking for new islands."

This cheered him **immensely**; and when he came back to Novastoshnah that summer, Matkah, his mother, begged him to marry and settle down, for he was no longer a holluschick but a full-grown sea-catch, with a curly white mane on his shoulders, as heavy, as big, and as fierce as his father. "Give me another season," he said. "Remember, Mother, it is always the seventh wave that goes farthest up the beach."

Curiously enough, there was another seal who thought that she would **put off** marrying till the next year, and Kotick danced the Fire-dance with her all down Lukannon Beach the night before he set off on his last exploration.

This time he went westward, because he had fallen on the trail of a great **shoal** of halibut, and he needed at least one hundred pounds of fish a day to keep him in good condition. He chased them till he was tired, and then he curled himself up and went to sleep on the hollows of the ground swell that sets in to Copper Island. He knew the coast

后哪怕我和霍卢斯契基一块儿被赶到屠宰场去，我也无动于衷了。"

老海豹说："再试一次吧。我是已经灭绝了的玛撒弗埃拉海豹家族里最后一个。当年人们成十万头地杀死我们，那时海滩上曾经流传过一个故事，说是有一天，一只白海豹会从北方来，他会引着海豹们到一个平安的地方。我老了，看不到那一天了，但是别的海豹还能看到的。再试一次吧。"

curl
[kə:l]
v.（使）卷曲,翘起

于是柯蒂克翘起他的胡须（它漂亮极了），说道："我是自古以来海滩上诞生的唯一的白海豹，而且我是在黑的和白的海豹里唯一想要去寻找新海岛的海豹。"

immensely
[i'mensli]
adv. 非常好地,无限地

这想法大大地鼓舞了他。那年夏天他回到诺瓦斯托西纳以后，他的母亲玛特卡恳求他结婚成家，因为他不再是个霍卢斯契基，他已经成了一个成年海豹了，他的肩头长着鬈曲的白色鬃毛，他像父亲一样高大魁梧、威风凛凛。"再让我等一个季度吧，"他说，"妈妈，要记住，第七个浪头总是最靠近海滩里面的。"

put off
推迟,拖延

说也奇怪，另外有一头海豹也认为她可以再等一年才结婚，柯蒂克出发去进行最后一次探索的前夕，就和她在卢坎龙海滩上跳了一整夜火焰舞。

shoal
[ʃəul]
n. 一大群鱼,鱼群,大量,许多

这次他动身向西方去，因为他跟踪上了一大群大比目鱼，而他一天至少需要一百磅鱼才能使他的身体保持良好的状态。他追逐他们，直到他感到困倦了，然后他蜷起身来，躺在涌向科珀岛的巨浪窝里睡着了。他非常熟悉这里的海岸，因此，当午夜

perfectly well, so about midnight, when he felt himself gently **bumped** on a weed-bed, he said, "Hm, tide's running strong tonight," and turning over under water opened his eyes slowly and stretched. Then he jumped like a cat, for he saw huge things nosing about in the shoal water and **browsing on** the heavy **fringes** of the weeds. "By the Great Combers of Magellan!" he said, beneath his mustache. "Who in the Deep Sea are these people?"

They were like no walrus, sea lion, seal, bear, whale, shark, fish, **squid**, or scallop that Kotick had ever seen before. They were between twenty and thirty feet long, and they had no hind flippers, but a shovel-like tail that looked as if it had been **whittled** out of wet leather. Their heads were the most foolish-looking things you ever saw, and they balanced on the ends of their tails in deep water when they weren't grazing, **bowing** solemnly to each other and waving their front flippers as a fat man waves his arm.

"Ahem!" said Kotick. "Good sport, gentlemen?" The big things answered by bowing and waving their flippers like the Frog Footman. When they began feeding again Kotick saw that their upper lip was split into two pieces that they could twitch apart about a foot and bring together again with a whole **bushel** of seaweed between the splits. They tucked the stuff into their mouths and **chumped** solemnly.

"**Messy** style of feeding, that," said Kotick. They bowed again, and Kotick began to lose his temper. "Very good," he said. "If you do happen to have an extra joint in your front flipper you needn't show off so. I see you bow gracefully, but I should like to know your names." The split lips moved and twitched; and the glassy green eyes stared, but they did not

bump
[bʌmp]
v. 碰撞,冲撞

browse on
吃草,嚼食

fringe
[frindʒ]
n. 须边,穗,边缘

squid
[skwid]
n. 鱿鱼,乌贼

whittle
['wit(ə)l]
v. 削制,削成

bow
[bəu]
v. 鞠躬,弯腰

bushel
['buʃ(ə)l]
n. 蒲式耳(容量等于八加仑)

chump
[tʃʌmp]
v. 咀嚼

messy
['mesi]
adj. 邋遢的,凌乱的

时分他觉得自己轻柔地撞在一块海草丛生的海床上时，他说："哼，今晚的潮水真猛呀。"他在水底下翻了个身，慢慢睁开眼睛，伸了个懒腰。这时，他突然像只猫一样地跳了起来，因为他看见在海滩的浅水里有些巨大的家伙在探头探脑，并且嚼食着浓密的海草丛边缘上的草。"用麦哲伦的巨浪起誓！"他在胡须的掩盖下悄声说："这到底是什么深海里的族类？"

他们不像柯蒂克见过的任何生物，不像海象，也不像海狮、海豹、熊、鲸、鲨、鱼、乌贼或者扇贝。他们有二十到三十英尺长，没有后鳍，却有一条铲子形的尾巴，看来像是用潮湿的皮革削成的。他们的脑袋是你从没见过的那种奇蠢无比的样子，他们不吃草的时候，便用尾巴顶端作支柱，支撑着身体，彼此庄严地躬身行礼，并且像个肥胖的男人挥舞手臂一样，摇晃着他们的前鳍。

"嗨！"柯蒂克说，"打食顺利吧，先生们？"那些硕大的生物鞠躬作答，并像青蛙跟班一样，摆动着他们的前鳍。当他们又开始吞吃起食物来时，柯蒂克看出，他们的上唇是裂成两半的，所以他们可以把上唇扯开一英尺长，在裂口里装进整整一蒲式耳的海草，再把裂口并拢。他们把这些海草统统塞进嘴里，一本正经地嚼啊嚼啊。

"这种吃法可够邋遢的，"柯蒂克说。他们再次鞠起躬来，柯蒂克开始按捺不住火气了。"好吧，"他说，"就算你们的前鳍比别人多出一节来，你们也用不着这么卖弄它呀。我看出你们会优雅地鞠躬，可是我想知道你们的尊姓大名。"裂开的上唇嚅动着，开合着，呆滞的绿眼睛瞪着，可是他们就

135

speak.

"Well!" said Kotick. "You're the only people I've ever met uglier than Sea Vitch—and with worse manners."

Then he remembered in a flash what the Burgomaster gull had screamed to him when he was a little yearling at Walrus Islet, and he tumbled backward in the water, for he knew that he had found Sea Cow at last.

The sea cows went on schlooping and grazing and chumping in the weed, and Kotick asked them questions in every language that he had picked up in his travels; and the Sea People talk nearly as many languages as human beings. But the sea cows did not answer because Sea Cow cannot talk. He has only six bones in his neck where he ought to have seven, and they say under the sea that prevents him from speaking even to his companions. But, as you know, he has an extra joint in his foreflipper, and by waving it up and down and about he makes what answers to a sort of **clumsy** telegraphic code.

By daylight Kotick's mane was standing on end and his temper was gone where the dead crabs go. Then the Sea Cow began to travel northward very slowly, stopping to hold **absurd** bowing councils from time to time, and Kotick followed them, saying to himself, "People who are such idiots as these are would have been killed long ago if they hadn't found out some safe island. And what is good enough for the Sea Cow is good enough for the Sea Catch. All the same, I wish they'd hurry."

It was weary work for Kotick. The herd never went more than forty or fifty miles a day, and stopped to feed at night, and kept close to the shore all the time; while Kotick swam

是不说话。

"好吧!"柯蒂克说,"你们是我所见过的唯一一比西威奇还丑的动物,而且你们比他更没有礼貌。"

突然,在一瞬间他想起了当他还是个小小的一岁海豹时,在海象岛上那只市长鸥向他尖叫的话。他赶忙又爬回到海水里,因为他知道他终于找到了海牛。

海牛继续在海草丛中撕扯着、吞咽着,柯蒂克用他在漫游途中学来的所有的各种语言向他们提出问题。海族们使用的语言种类和人类的几乎一样多。但是海牛总是不回答,因为海牛是不会说话的。他们的脖子上本该有七块骨头,可是实际上只有六块,因此,据说他们在海底甚至于都无法和同伴们交谈。不过,你要知道,他的前鳍上多了一节骨头,因此他们上下挥动前鳍,也可以勉强算是发出一种电报信号。

clumsy
['klʌmzi]
adj. 笨拙的

到天亮时,柯蒂克的鬃毛已气得竖了起来,他的克制力飞到了死螃蟹呆着的地方。这时海牛开始缓慢地向北旅行,不时停下来用可笑的鞠躬方式进行商讨,柯蒂克跟在他们后头,他对自己说:"像这类白痴似的家伙,如果没有找到某个安全的海岛,他们早就被杀光了;对于海牛有好处的地方,对于海豹也一定是够好的。不过,我真希望他们快点赶路。"

absurd
[əb'sə:d]
adj. 荒谬的,可笑的

这种旅行对柯蒂克来说实在是太腻烦了。海牛们一天的行程从不超过四五十英里,他们到晚上就停下来吃食,而且一直停留在离海岸很近的地方;不论柯蒂克是绕着他们转圈子,在他们头顶上游,

round them, and over them, and under them, but he could not hurry them up one-half mile. As they went farther north they held a bowing council every few hours, and Kotick nearly bit off his mustache with impatience till he saw that they were following up a warm current of water, and then he respected them more.

One night they sank through the shiny water—sank like stones—and for the first time since he had known them began to swim quickly. Kotick followed, and the pace astonished him, for he never dreamed that Sea Cow was anything of a swimmer. They headed for a cliff by the shore—a cliff that ran down into deep water, and plunged into a dark hole at the foot of it, twenty fathoms under the sea. It was a long, long swim, and Kotick badly wanted fresh air before he was out of the dark **tunnel** they led him through.

"My wig!" he said, when he rose, gasping and puffing, into open water at the farther end. "It was a long dive, but it was worth it."

The sea cows had separated and were browsing lazily along the edges of the finest beaches that Kotick had ever seen. There were long stretches of smooth-worn rock running for miles, exactly fitted to make seal-nurseries, and there were play-grounds of hard sand sloping inland behind them, and there were rollers for seals to dance in, and long grass to roll in, and sand dunes to climb up and down, and, best of all, Kotick knew by the feel of the water, which never deceives a true sea catch, that no men had ever come there.

The first thing he did was to assure himself that the fishing was good, and then he swam along the beaches and counted up the **delightful** low sandy islands half hidden in the beautiful

还是在他们身子底下游，都没法促使他们快走半英里路。他们到了北边，每隔几小时便凑在一块儿鞠着躬商量一次，柯蒂克不耐烦得差点把胡须都咬掉了。后来他发现他们是在追随一股温暖的水流，这才使他增加了对他们的尊敬。

一天晚上，他们沉进了闪闪发光的海水里，像石头一样沉下去。自从柯蒂克认识他们以来，他们第一次迅速地游了起来。柯蒂克跟着他们，他们的速度使他感到惊讶，因为他从来不认为海牛是什么出色的游泳家。他们朝岸边的一座峭壁游去，峭壁的底部深深地埋进水底，他们钻进了峭壁底部离海面二十英寻的一个黑沉沉的洞穴。他们游了很久很久，柯蒂克跟着他们，早在钻出那黑暗的隧道之前很久，他就觉得缺乏新鲜空气了。

tunnel
['tʌn(ə)l]
n. 隧道，地道

"我的脑袋！"他浮出另一头的水面，呼哧呼哧地大口喘着气说，"这趟潜游虽说不短，可也真值得。"

海牛们已经散开，正沿着一条条柯蒂克从来没见过的最出色的海滩边缘吃着草。这儿有一望无际的、磨得光溜溜的岩石，伸延到许多英里外，正适合做海豹的哺育营地。在岩石后面，有一片坚实的沙地嬉游场，倾斜着伸向内陆。这里还有可以让海豹在上面跳舞的大浪头，有让海豹打滚的茂密的野草，还有可以爬上爬下的沙丘。最叫人满意的是，柯蒂克从海水的味道知道，人从来没有到过这里。这一点，真正的海豹是从不会弄错的。

delightful
[di'laitful]
adj. 令人愉快的，快乐的

他做的第一件事就是弄清楚这儿是否可以捕到大量的鱼，然后他沿着海滩游过去，数一数在起伏

rolling fog. Away to the northward, out to sea, ran a line of bars and shoals and rocks that would never let a ship come within six miles of the beach, and between the islands and the mainland was a stretch of deep water that ran up to the **perpendicular** cliffs, and somewhere below the cliffs was the mouth of the tunnel.

"It's Novastoshnah over again, but ten times better," said Kotick. "Sea Cow must be wiser than I thought. Men can't come down the cliffs, even if there were any men; and the shoals to seaward would knock a ship to **splinters**. If any place in the sea is safe, this is it."

He began to think of the seal he had left behind him, but though he was in a hurry to go back to Novastoshnah, he **thoroughly** explored the new country, so that he would be able to answer all questions.

Then he dived and made sure of the mouth of the tunnel, and raced through to the southward. No one but a sea cow or a seal would have dreamed of there being such a place, and when he looked back at the cliffs even Kotick could hardly believe that he had been under them.

He was six days going home, though he was not swimming slowly; and when he hauled out just above Sea Lion's Neck the first person he met was the seal who had been waiting for him, and she saw by the look in his eyes that he had found his island at last.

But the holluschickie and Sea Catch, his father, and all the other seals laughed at him when he told them what he had discovered, and a young seal about his own age said, "This is all very well, Kotick, but you can't come from no one knows where and order us off like this. Remember we've been

流动的美妙雾气中，那半隐半现的、妙不可言的低洼多沙的小岛到底有多少个。北边出海的地方是一连串的沙洲、浅滩和暗礁，使得任何船只都没法开到离海滩六英里以内。在小岛群和这片陆地之间有一条深水区，一直延伸到那垂直的峭壁脚下，在悬崖下面某个地方便是那条隧道的出口。

perpendicular
[pə:pən'dikjulə(r)]
adj. 垂直的

"这儿简直跟诺瓦斯托西纳一模一样，不过比它还要好上十倍，"柯蒂克说，"海牛肯定比我想的要聪明得多。哪怕这儿有人的话，他们也没法从峭壁上下来，而且在这里，海边的沙洲会把一条船撞成碎片。如果说大海里有什么安全的地方，那就是这儿了。"

splinter
['splintə(r)]
n. 裂片，碎片

他开始想念留在家里的海豹，但是，虽说他急于要回到诺瓦斯托西纳，他还是彻底巡视了一番这块新地方，以便回答所有向他提出的问题。

thoroughly
['θʌrəli]
adv. 彻底地，完全地

然后他潜进海水里，摸清楚了隧道的出口，便迅速向南游去。除了海牛和海豹，别人做梦也不会想到有这样一块地方。当柯蒂克回头望着悬崖时，他自己也很难相信，他曾经游到过悬崖下面。

虽然他游得并不慢，但还是用了六天工夫才赶回家里。当他恰好从海狮颈下面露出水面来时，他遇见的第一个人就是那个一直在等待着他的海豹。她从他眼里看出，他终于找到了他的岛。

但是当他把他的发现告诉那些霍卢斯契基和他的父亲西卡奇，还有所有其他的海豹的时候，他们全都嘲笑他。一头年龄和他相仿的年轻海豹说："这些话听起来倒不错，柯蒂克，可是你不能像这样从谁也不知道的地方钻出来，就这么命令我们出发。

fighting for our nurseries, and that's a thing you never did. You preferred **prowling** about in the sea."

"I've no nursery to fight for," said Kotick. "I only want to show you all a place where you will be safe. What's the use of fighting?"

"Oh, if you're trying to back out, of course I've no more to say," said the young seal with an ugly chuckle.

"Will you come with me if I win?" said Kotick. And a green light came into his eye, for he was very angry at having to fight at all.

"Very good," said the young seal carelessly. "If you win, I'll come."

He had no time to change his mind, for Kotick's head was out and his teeth sunk in the blubber of the young seal's neck. Then he threw himself back on his haunches and hauled his enemy down the beach, shook him, and knocked him over. Then Kotick roared to the seals: "I've done my best for you these five seasons past. I've found you the island where you'll be safe, but unless your heads are **dragged** off your silly necks you won't believe. I'm going to teach you now. Look out for yourselves!"

Limmershin told me that never in his life—and Limmershin sees ten thousand big seals fighting every year—never in all his little life did he see anything like Kotick's charge into the nurseries. He flung himself at the biggest sea catch he could find, caught him by the throat, choked him and bumped him and banged him till he grunted for mercy, and then threw him aside and attacked the next. You see, Kotick had never fasted for four months as the big seals did every year, and his deep-sea swimming trips kept him in perfect condition,

prowl

[praul]

v. 巡游

drag

[dræg]

v. 拖,拖曳,缓慢而费力地行动

记着,我们曾为我们的哺养营地战斗过,可你从来也没有。你只愿意在海里荡来荡去。"

"可是我没有哺育海豹的窝需要我为它战斗呀," 柯蒂克说,"我只想指给你们看一块儿你们在那里会很安全的地方。打架有什么用处?"

"哦,假如你想缩回去,我当然没有什么话可说了。"那头年轻的海豹恶意地嘻嘻笑着说。

"假如我打赢了,你同意跟我一块儿去吗?"柯蒂克问道。他的眼里射出绿幽幽的光来,因为他不得不打一架,所以非常生气。

"很好,"年轻的海豹毫不在意地说,"假如你打赢了,我一定去。"

他没有时间改变主意了,因为柯蒂克的头已经伸了过来,牙齿埋进了年轻海豹颈项的那块肥肉里。接着他朝后一歪,蹲了下来,把他的对手拽到海滩上,使劲摇晃他,把他打翻在地。接着,柯蒂克对海豹们吼叫道:"五个季度来,我为你们费尽了力气,我给你们找到了一个安全的海岛。可如果不把你们的脑袋拽得跟你们的傻脖子分了家,你们硬是不相信。我现在就教训你们一顿。你们小心点儿吧!"

利默欣告诉我,他这辈子——利默欣每年都能见到一万头大海豹进行战斗——他这短短的一辈子里,从没见过像柯蒂克那样对海豹哺育营地发起的冲锋。他对着他能找到的个头最大的海豹扑了上去,咬住他的喉咙,弄得对方出不了气,噼里啪啦地把这头海豹打得直叫饶命,然后他甩开这头海豹,再向下一头海豹进攻。你要知道,柯蒂克从来没有像大海豹那样每年禁食四个月,而他的深海旅行又使得他的身体状况保持得非常良好,而最妙的

and, best of all, he had never fought before. His curly white mane stood up with rage, and his eyes flamed, and his big dog teeth **glistened**, and he was splendid to look at.

Old Sea Catch, his father, saw him tearing past, hauling the **grizzled** old seals about as though they had been halibut, and **upsetting** the young **bachelors** in all directions; and Sea Catch gave a roar and shouted: "He may be a fool, but he is the best fighter on the beaches! Don't tackle your father, my son! He's with you!"

Kotick roared in answer, and old Sea Catch **waddled** in with his mustache on end, blowing like a **locomotive**, while Matkah and the seal that was going to marry Kotick cowered down and admired their men-folk. It was a gorgeous fight, for the two fought as long as there was a seal that dared lift up his head, and when there were none they **paraded** grandly up and down the beach side by side, bellowing.

At night, just as the Northern Lights were winking and flashing through the fog, Kotick climbed a bare rock and looked down on the scattered nurseries and the torn and bleeding seals. "Now," he said, "I've taught you your lesson."

"My wig!" said old Sea Catch, **boosting** himself up stiffly, for he was fearfully **mauled**. "The Killer Whale himself could not have cut them up worse. Son, I'm proud of you, and what's more, I'll come with you to your island—if there is such a place."

"Hear you, fat pigs of the sea. Who comes with me to the Sea Cow's tunnel? Answer, or I shall teach you again," roared Kotick.

There was a murmur like the **ripple** of the tide all up and

是，他从来没有打过架。他一生起气来，那鬈曲的白色鬃毛就一根根竖了起来，眼睛冒出火焰，大犬牙白生生地发着光，样子确实神气极了。

他的父亲老西卡奇看着他猛冲过来，把那些灰色的老海豹像大比目鱼似的推过来拽过去，把那些年轻的单身汉们撞得东歪西倒。于是西卡奇大吼一声，喊道："他也许是个傻瓜，可是他却是海滩上最出色的斗士。别跟你父亲交手啦，我的儿子！他是站在你这边的！"

柯蒂克吼了一声作为回答。于是老西卡奇便摇摇摆摆地参加到战斗中去了，他的胡须直竖起来，吼声像个火车头，玛特卡和那个要和柯蒂克结婚的海豹退到一边，欣赏着她们的男子汉。这是一场了不起的决斗，父子两人一直揍到没有一只海豹敢抬起头来为止，于是他们父子俩便大声吼叫着，肩并肩地在海滩上神气十足地踱来踱去。

天黑了，北极光刚刚在雾气中闪烁发亮的时候，柯蒂克爬上了一块光秃秃的岩石，低头看着打得七零八落的海豹营地和被咬得皮开肉绽遍体鳞伤的海豹们。"瞧吧，"他说，"我已经教训了你们一顿。"

"哎唷！"老西卡奇吃力地挺起腰来说道，因为他身上也给咬得伤痕斑斑了。"就连逆戟鲸也没法把他们教训得更狠。儿子啊，我真为你骄傲，不止是骄傲，我还要和你一块儿到你的那个岛上去——要是真的有这么个地方的话。"

"嗨，你们这些海里的肥猪！谁跟我到海牛的隧道里去？回答呀，不然我又要教训你们了。"柯蒂克吼道。

沿着长长的海滩，响起了像潮水拍打海岸般的

down the beaches. "We will come," said thousands of tired voices. "We will follow Kotick, the White Seal."

Then Kotick dropped his head between his shoulders and shut his eyes proudly. He was not a white seal any more, but red from head to tail. All the same he would have **scorned** to look at or touch one of his wounds.

A week later he and his army (nearly ten thousand holluschickie and old seals) went away north to the Sea Cow's tunnel, Kotick leading them, and the seals that stayed at Novastoshnah called them idiots. But next spring, when they all met off the fishing banks of the Pacific, Kotick's seals told such tales of the new beaches beyond Sea Cow's tunnel that more and more seals left Novastoshnah.

Of course it was not all done at once, for the seals are not very clever, and they need a long time to turn things over in their minds, but year after year more seals went away from Novastoshnah, and Lukannon, and the other nurseries, to the quiet, sheltered beaches where Kotick sits all the summer through, getting bigger and fatter and stronger each year, while the holluschickie play around him, in that sea where no man comes.

嗬嗬声。"我们跟你去，"成千个疲倦的声音说道，"我们愿意跟随白海豹柯蒂克。"

于是柯蒂克把脑袋垂到双肩里，骄傲地闭上了眼睛。他不再是一只白色的海豹了，他从头到尾全身都染成了红色。可是，他却一点儿也不屑于去看一看或者碰一碰他的伤口。

一星期以后，他和他的那支大军（将近一万头霍卢斯契基和老海豹）便浩浩荡荡地向北方海牛的隧道出发了。柯蒂克率领着他们，而那些留在诺瓦斯托西纳的海豹把他们叫作白痴。但是到了下一年的春天，他们全体在太平洋上的捕鱼场碰头了。柯蒂克的那伙海豹讲了许多关于海牛隧道尽头的新海滩的故事，使得以后每年都有更多的海豹离开了诺瓦斯托西纳。

当然，事情不是一下子就一帆风顺的，因为海豹们总是爱花很长的时间盘算来盘算去。不过年复一年，每年都有更多的海豹离开诺瓦斯托西纳，离开卢坎龙，离开其他的哺育营地，去到那安静的、隐蔽的海滩。每个夏天，柯蒂克都坐在那些海滩上，一年比一年更高大、更肥胖、更壮实。而那些霍卢斯契基们都在他四周，在人类从没有到过的海里嬉戏玩耍。

scorn
[skɔːn]
v. 轻蔑，不屑做

The King's Ankus

国王的象叉

These are the Four that are never content, that have never been filled since the Dews began—Jacala's mouth, and the glut of the Kite, and the hands of the Ape, and the Eyes of Man.

Jungle Saying

Kaa, the big Rock **Python**, had changed his skin for perhaps the two-hundredth time since his birth; and Mowgli, who never forgot that he owed his life to Kaa for a night's work at Cold Lairs, which you may perhaps remember, went to congratulate him. Skin-changing always makes a snake **moody** and depressed till the new skin begins to shine and look beautiful. Kaa never made fun of Mowgli any more, but accepted him, as the other Jungle People did, for the Master of the Jungle, and brought him all the news that a python of his size would naturally hear. What Kaa did not know, about the Middle Jungle, as they call it, —the life that runs close to the earth or under it, the boulder, burrow, and the tree-**bole** life, —might have been written upon the smallest of his scales.

That afternoon Mowgli was sitting in the circle of Kaa's great coils, fingering the **flaked** and broken old skin that lay all **looped** and twisted among the rocks just as Kaa had left it.

ankus

['æŋkəs]

n.（印度的）驯象刺
棒,象叉

有四样最最贪得无厌的东西,

　　自古以来从没有感到满足;

　　茄卡那鸟的嘴巴,

　　　　鸢的胃口,

　　无尾猿的手和人的眼睛。

　　　　　　　　　——丛林谚语

python

['paiθ(ə)n]

n. 大蟒,巨蟒

　　这是大蟒蛇卡阿出生以来大约第二百次蜕皮。
莫格里从来没有忘记陷进"寒穴"那个夜晚,幸亏
卡阿救了他一命——这件事你也许还记得——于是
这次莫格里便去祝贺他蜕皮。蛇在蜕皮时总是情绪

moody

['mu:di]

adj. 阴沉的,忧郁的

低沉,闷闷不乐,一直要到新的蛇皮变得光亮美观
的时候为止。现在卡阿再也不拿莫格里取笑了,而
是像丛林里的其他兽族一样,把他奉为丛林的大王,
他经常把像自己这么大的身躯的蟒蛇自然而然能打

bole

[bəul]

n. 树干,树身

flake

[fleik]

v. 成薄片或片剥落

loop

[lu:p]

v. 使成圈状

听到的消息都告诉莫格里。卡阿对人们所谓的中部
丛林可说是了如指掌——凡是有关地面上跑的、地
底下跑的、石头上待着的、地洞里住着的,还有在
树上住着的那些生物的事情,他都知道——他不知
道的事,满可以全部写在他身上最小的一块鳞片上。

　　那天下午,莫格里正坐在卡阿蜷成一团的身体
中间,抚摸着卡阿刚换下的那身破破烂烂、碎成一
片片的旧蛇皮。这块蛇皮还像卡阿蜕掉它的时候那

Kaa had very **courteously** packed himself under Mowgli's broad, bare shoulders, so that the boy was really resting in a living arm-chair.

"Even to the scales of the eyes it is perfect," said Mowgli, under his breath, playing with the old skin. "Strange to see the covering of one's own head at one's own feet!"

"Ay, but I lack feet," said Kaa; "and since this is the custom of all my people, I do not find it strange. Does thy skin never feel old and harsh?"

"Then go I and wash, Flathead; but, it is true, in the great heats I have wished I could **slough** my skin without pain, and run skinless."

"I wash, and also I take off my skin. How looks the new coat?"

Mowgli ran his hand down the **diagonal checkerings** of the immense back. "The Turtle is harder-backed, but not so gay," he said judgmatically. "The Frog, my name-bearer, is more gay, but not so hard. It is very beautiful to see—like the **mottling** in the mouth of a lily."

"It needs water. A new skin never comes to full colour before the first bath. Let us go bathe."

"I will carry thee," said Mowgli; and he stooped down, laughing, to lift the middle section of Kaa's great body, just where the barrel was thickest. A man might just as well have tried to heave up a two-foot **water-main**; and Kaa lay still, puffing with quiet amusement. Then the regular evening game began—the Boy in the flush of his great strength, and the Python in his **sumptuous** new skin, standing up one against the other for a **wrestling** match—a trial of eye and strength. Of

样，纠结在一块，扭得乱七八糟，扔在岩石中间。卡阿非常殷勤地把自己的身躯垫在莫格里光裸的宽肩膀后面，所以这个少年简直就像靠在一张活躺椅里一样舒服。

"连眼睛上的鳞片也是十全十美的，"莫格里抚弄着旧蛇皮，悄声说道，"看见自己脑袋上的皮躺在自己脚底下，真有点不可思议！"

"是呀，不过我没有脚，"卡阿说，"而且蜕皮既然是我们这族的规矩，我也就不觉得有什么奇怪了。你的皮难道从来没有感到破旧和粗糙的时候吗？"

"要是那样，我就去洗洗，扁脑袋。不过，在热极了的暑天里，我倒真的希望我能一点儿不觉得疼地把皮脱下来，光溜溜地到处跑。"

"我洗自己，可是同时也脱掉我的皮。你瞧我这身新外衣怎么样？"

莫格里顺着他巨大脊背上的垂直的方格花纹摸下去。"乌龟的背比你更硬，可是没你的鲜艳，"他精明地说，"和我同名的青蛙比你鲜艳，可是没有你坚硬。你的外皮看上去真美——就像百合花蕊边缘上的斑纹。"

"它还缺点水。一张新皮不洗一次澡是不会把全部颜色都显出来的。我们去洗个澡吧。"

"我抱你去吧。"莫格里说。于是他乐呵呵地俯下身子，想把卡阿那巨大的躯体的中间那一段，正好是最粗的那一段身子抱起来。这就好比一个人想抬起一根两英尺长的总水管一样。卡阿纹丝不动地躺在那里，鼓起双颊，暗自觉得有趣。接着，他们每天傍晚都要玩的游戏开始了——一个是充溢着巨大精力的男孩子，另一个是换了一身华丽新皮的蟒蛇，他们开始交手，进行一场摔跤比赛，这是眼力

153

course, Kaa could have crushed a dozen Mowglis if he had let himself go; but he played carefully, and never loosed one-tenth of his power. Ever since Mowgli was strong enough to endure a little rough handling, Kaa had taught him this game, and it **suppled** his limbs as nothing else could. Sometimes Mowgli would stand lapped almost to his throat in Kaa's shifting coils, striving to get one arm free and catch him by the throat. Then Kaa would give way limply, and Mowgli, with both quick-moving feet, would try to cramp the purchase of that huge tail as it flung backward feeling for a rock or a stump. They would rock to and fro, head to head, each waiting for his chance, till the beautiful, statue-like group melted in a whirl of black-and-yellow coils and struggling legs and arms, to rise up again and again. "Now! now! now!" said Kaa, making **feints** with his head that even Mowgli's quick hand could not turn aside. "Look! I touch thee here, Little Brother! Here, and here! Are thy hands numb? Here again!"

The game always ended in one way—with a straight, driving blow of the head that knocked the boy over and over. Mowgli could never learn the guard for that lightning lunge, and, as Kaa said, there was not the least use in trying.

"Good hunting!" Kaa grunted at last; and Mowgli, as usual, was shot away half a dozen yards, gasping and laughing. He rose with his fingers full of grass, and followed Kaa to the wise snake's pet bathing-place—a deep, **pitchy**-black pool surrounded with rocks, and made interesting by sunken tree-stumps. The boy slipped in, Jungle-fashion, without a sound, and dived across; rose, too, without a

supple
['sʌp(ə)l]
v. 使柔软，使顺从

feint
[feint]
n. 假象

pitchy
['pitʃi]
adj. 漆黑的

和劲头的较量。当然，只要卡阿使足了劲头，他完全能把哪怕是十二个莫格里压成肉泥；但是他玩得很小心，从来不把劲头使出十分之一来。自从莫格里长大了，能承受得了一点点粗暴待遇时起，卡阿就教会了他这种游戏，这比什么其他办法都更能锤炼他的四肢。有时，莫格里几乎被卡阿绕成一圈圈的滑动的躯体团团围住，直到嗓子眼那里。他使劲想松出一只手臂，好抓住卡阿的喉咙。接着，卡阿突然变软了，松开了，莫格里就会趁着卡阿巨大的蛇尾向后摆动，去找一块石头或者树桩撑住身体的时候，飞快地移动脚步，不让它找到支撑点。这时他们便互相抱着头滚来滚去，相互窥伺着时机，于是这一对像雕塑般健美的对手就变成了一团黄黑色的蛇圈和胡乱挣扎的胳臂和腿，一次又一次地倒下，然后又竖立起来。"嗨！嗨！嗨！"卡阿说道，他伸出脑袋一次次佯装进攻的样子，快得连莫格里那样敏捷的手也无法把它推开。"瞧吧！我碰着你这儿啦，小兄弟！这儿，还有这儿！你的手麻木了吗？这儿又是一下！"

游戏总是以同一种方式结束——蛇脑袋一记笔直有力的打击，把男孩打翻在地。莫格里始终没学会如何对付那一记闪电似的袭击，而卡阿说，他根本用不着想去对付它。

"祝你打猎顺利！"卡阿最后咕噜道。而莫格里像往常一样，一下子被摔到了六码以外的地方。他一面喘着气，一面大笑。他抓了满满一手的青草，从地上站起来，跟在卡阿后面，来到这条聪明的蛇最喜爱的洗澡的地方——这是一汪围在岩石中间的黑洞洞的深水潭，旁边散布着沉入地里的树桩，给这地方添加了一些情趣。小伙子照丛林的方式，静悄悄地溜进水里，潜水到了对岸，然后同样静悄悄

sound, and turned on his back, his arms behind his head, watching the moon rising above the rocks, and breaking up her reflection in the water with his toes. Kaa's diamond-shaped head cut the pool like a **razor**, and came out to rest on Mowgli's shoulder. They lay still, **soaking** luxuriously in the cool water.

"It is very good," said Mowgli at last, sleepily. "Now, in the Man-Pack, at this hour, as I remember, they laid them down upon hard pieces of wood in the inside of a mud-trap, and, having carefully shut out all the clean winds, drew foul cloth over their heavy heads and made evil songs through their noses. It is better in the Jungle."

A hurrying cobra slipped down over a rock and drank, gave them "Good hunting!" and went away.

" Sssh! " said Kaa, as though he had suddenly remembered something. "So the Jungle gives thee all that thou hast ever desired, Little Brother?"

"Not all," said Mowgli, laughing; "else there would be a new and strong Shere Khan to kill once a moon. Now, I could kill with my own hands, asking no help of buffaloes. And also I have wished the sun to shine in the middle of the Rains, and the Rains to cover the sun in the deep of summer; and also I have never gone empty but I wished that I had killed a goat; and also I have never killed a goat but I wished it had been buck; nor buck but I wished it had been **nilghai**. But thus do we feel, all of us."

"Thou hast no other desire?" the big snake demanded.

" What more can I wish? I have the Jungle, and the favour of the Jungle! Is there more anywhere between sunrise

razor
['reizə(r)]
n. 剃刀

soak
[səuk]
v. 浸泡,浸透

地冒出水面，仰面躺着，两只胳臂交叉在脑袋后面，望着升起在岩石上面的月亮，用脚丫子把月亮映在水里的影子搅碎。卡阿钻石形状的脑袋像一把剃刀划开了湖水，他浮出水面，正好躺在莫格里的肩头上。他们就这样静静地躺着，舒舒服服地浸泡在沁凉的水里。

"真棒呀，"莫格里终于睡意蒙眬地说道，"这会儿，在'人群'里，我记得每到这个时候，他们就把一些坚硬的木头片放进一个泥做的陷阱里，他们仔细地把清新空气都关在门外以后，便用一块臭气扑鼻的布蒙住他们的笨脑袋，鼻子里哼呀咳地唱起邪恶的歌来。丛林里可比他们那里好得多。"

一条匆忙赶路的眼镜蛇从一块岩石背后出溜下来，饮了水后，对他们说了声"打猎顺利"，便走开了。

"嗤！"卡阿说，他仿佛刚刚想起了什么事。"丛林满足了你的一切愿望，是吗，小兄弟？"

"并不是一切愿望都满足了，"莫格里笑着说道，"否则每个月都得再出生一头新的强壮的谢尔汗，好让我把他杀死。现在，我可以用自己的手杀死他了，不用请水牛们帮忙。另外，我曾经希望在雨季里能够阳光普照，而在夏天最酷热的时候，我希望雨水能盖住阳光。还有，我每次饿着肚子的时候，总是希望我能杀死一头山羊；每次我杀了一头山羊的时候，又总是希望它是一头公鹿；而当我杀了一头公鹿的时候，我又希望它是一头大羚羊。不过，人心不知足，我们全都这样。"

nilgai
['nilgai]
n. 大羚羊

"你没有别的愿望了吗？"大蛇问道。

"我还能有什么更多的愿望呢？我有丛林，还有丛林赐给我的一切恩惠！在日出和日落之间，还有

157

and sunset?"

"Now, the Cobra said..." Kaa began.

"What cobra? He that went away just now said nothing. He was hunting."

"It was another."

"Hast thou many dealings with the Poison People? I give them their own path. They carry death in the fore-tooth, and that is not good—for they are so small. But what hood is this thou hast spoken with?"

Kaa rolled slowly in the water like a steamer in a **beam sea**. "Three or four moons since," said he, "I hunted in Cold Lairs, which place thou hast not forgotten. And the thing I hunted fled shrieking past the tanks and to that house whose side I once broke for thy sake, and ran into the ground."

"But the people of Cold Lairs do not live in burrows." Mowgli knew that Kaa was telling of the Monkey People.

"This thing was not living, but seeking to live," Kaa replied, with a quiver of his tongue. "He ran into a burrow that led very far. I followed, and having killed, I slept. When I waked I went forward."

"Under the earth?"

"Even so, coming at last upon a White Hood [white cobra], who spoke of things beyond my knowledge, and showed me many things I had never before seen."

"New game? Was it good hunting?" Mowgli turned quickly on his side.

"It was no game, and would have broken all my teeth; but the White Hood said that a man—he spoke as one that knew the **breed**—that a man would give the breath under his

什么地方的东西比这儿更丰富呢？"

"喂，那条眼镜蛇说……"卡阿开口说道。

"哪条眼镜蛇？是那条刚才没说什么就走开的眼镜蛇吗？他正在打猎。"

"我说的是另一条。"

"你和那些有毒的兽族有很多来往吗？我总是让他们走自己的路。他们的门牙里携带着死亡，那可不是件好事——因为他们是那么小。不过，和你说话的那条蛇的头兜是什么样的？"

beam sea
n. 横浪

卡阿在水里慢吞吞地翻了个身，就像在横浪里前进的一艘火轮船一样。"三四个月以前，"他说，"我在'寒穴'那儿狩猎，那地方你大概没忘记吧。我捕猎的那家伙尖叫着逃过蓄水池，逃进那所房子——就是我曾经为了救你而砸破它的墙的那所房子——钻进地洞里去了。"

"可是'寒穴'里的兽族并不是生活在地洞里的，"莫格里明白卡阿指的是猴子。

"这家伙并不是在'生活'，倒是想要'生活'下去，"卡阿回答说，他的舌头颤动了一下，"他钻进一条很深很长的地洞里。我跟踪上去，捕杀了他以后，我就睡了。醒来以后我向前走去。"

"在地底下吗？"

"正是。后来我遇见了一条'白头兜'（白眼镜蛇），他告诉了我一些我不知道的事，还带我看了许多我从来没有见过的东西。"

"是新的猎物吗？你的狩猎成功吗？"莫格里迅速地侧过身来。

breed
[bri:d]
n. 品种,种类

"那不是猎物，而且它们会把我所有的牙齿都咬断的。可是'白头兜'说，人——他对人类是很了解的——人为了能看一眼这些东西，哪怕舍出命

ribs for only the sight of those things."

"We will look," said Mowgli. "I now remember that I was once a man."

"Slowly—slowly. It was haste killed the Yellow Snake that ate the sun. We two spoke together under the earth, and I spoke of thee, naming thee as a man. Said the White Hood (and he is indeed as old as the Jungle) : "It is long since I have seen a man. Let him come, and he shall see all these things, for the least of which very many men would die."

"That must be new game. And yet the Poison People do not tell us when game is **afoot**. They are an unfriendly folk."

"It is not game. It is...it is...I cannot, say what it is."

"We will go there. I have never seen a White Hood, and I wish to see the other things. Did he kill them?"

"They are all dead things. He says he is the keeper of them all."

"Ah! As a wolf stands above meat he has taken to his own lair. Let us go."

Mowgli swam to bank, rolled on the grass to dry himself, and the two set off for Cold Lairs, the deserted city of which you may have heard. Mowgli was not the least afraid of the Monkey People in those days, but the Monkey People had the liveliest horror of Mowgli. Their tribes, however, were **raiding** in the jungle, and so Cold Lairs stood empty and silent in the moonlight. Kaa led up to the ruins of the queens" pavilion that stood on the terrace, slipped over the rubbish, and dived down the half-choked **staircase** that went underground from the centre of the **pavilion**. Mowgli gave the snake-call, —"We be of one blood, ye and I," —and followed on his hands and knees. They crawled a long distance down a sloping passage

来也肯干的。"

"我们去看一看吧，"莫格里说，"我现在记起了，我也曾经是人。"

"慢些——慢些。那条吃掉了太阳的黄蛇，就是因为匆忙才送了命。我们在地下谈了起来，我提到了你，说你是一个人。'白头兜'说（他的确和丛林一样老了），'我有很久没见到一个人了。叫他来吧，他会看见所有这些东西的。许多人为了这里最小的一件东西也愿意舍掉性命。'"

"那肯定是什么新的猎物。可是那些有毒的兽族遇到猎物时是从来不通知我们的。他们是很不友好的一族。"

"它们不是猎物。它是……它是……我说不出它是什么。"

"我们到那里去吧。我还从没见过一条'白头兜'，另外我还想看看那些东西。他捕杀它们吗？"

"它们是没有生命的东西。他说，他是那所有东西的看守人。"

"噢！就像一头狼看守着他拖回自己巢穴里去的肉那样。我们走吧。"

莫格里游向岸边，在草地上滚干了身体，他们两个便出发到"寒穴"去了。这是一个荒无人迹的城市遗址，你大概听说过它。莫格里那时一点儿也不怕猴群了，可是猴群却对莫格里怕得要命。不过，他们一族全到丛林劫掠去了，所以在月光下，"寒穴"是空旷寂静的。卡阿带路来到阳台上王妃亭的废墟，他从一堆垃圾上溜了过去，钻进了亭子中心通往地下的那座堵住了一半的楼梯。莫格里先是发出了一声蛇的呼喊："你和我，我们是同胞。"然后手脚并用，跟在后面。他们爬进一个长长的倾

afoot
[əˈfut]
adj. 准备中，进行中的

raid
[reid]
v. 袭击，劫掠

staircase
[ˈstɛəkeis]
n. 楼梯

pavilion
[pəˈviljən]
n. 亭子，阁

161

that turned and twisted several times, and at last came to where the root of some great tree, growing thirty feet overhead, had forced out a solid stone in the wall. They crept through the gap, and found themselves in a large **vault**, whose **domed** roof had been also broken away by tree-roots so that a few streaks of light dropped down into the darkness.

"A safe lair," said Mowgli, rising to his firm feet, "but over-far to visit daily. And now what do we see?"

"Am I nothing?" said a voice in the middle of the vault; and Mowgli saw something white move till, little by little, there stood up the hugest cobra he had ever set eyes on—a creature nearly eight feet long, and **bleached** by being in darkness to an old ivory-white. Even the spectacle-marks of his spread hood had faded to faint yellow. His eyes were as red as **rubies**, and altogether he was most wonderful.

"Good hunting!" said Mowgli, who carried his manners with his knife, and that never left him.

" What of the city? " said the White Cobra, without answering the greeting. "What of the great, the walled city—the city of a hundred elephants and twenty thousand horses, and cattle past counting—the city of the King of Twenty Kings? I grow deaf here, and it is long since I heard their **war-gongs**."

"The Jungle is above our heads," said Mowgli. "I know only Hathi and his sons among elephants. Bagheera has **slain** all the horses in one village, and what is a King?"

"I told thee," said Kaa softly to the Cobra, "I told thee, four moons ago, that thy city was not."

斜的通道。通道拐来拐去，拐了好几个弯，最后他
们爬到一个地方，那里有一棵离地三十英尺的巨大
的树，树根把墙上一块实心的石头顶了出来。他们
就从这个窟窿里爬了过去，爬进了一间很大的地下
洞窟，洞窟的圆顶也被树根顶破了，因此有几条光
线从洞顶射进黑暗中。

"这是个很安全的窝，"莫格里稳稳站起身来说，
"可惜太远了，没法天天来。好吧，我们来看的那些
东西在哪里？"

"难道我不值得看吗？"洞窟正中有个声音说道。
莫格里看见有个白色的东西在移动，一条他所见过
的最大的眼镜蛇慢慢地直立起来——这条蛇足有八
英尺长，由于长期待在黑暗里，身体的颜色已经褪
成了陈旧的象牙般的白色，就连蛇的头兜也褪成了
淡黄色。他的眼睛像红宝石一样鲜红。总而言之，
这条蛇简直奇妙极了。

"祝你打猎顺利！"莫格里说，他从不忘记对人
要有礼貌，就跟他从不忘记带上他的小刀一样。

"关于那座城市有什么消息吗？"白眼镜蛇没有
回答他的问候，却这样问道，"就是那座有围墙的
巨大的城市——那个拥有一百头象、两千匹马和不
计其数的牛羊的城市——那个统率着二十个国王的
王中之王的城市？我的耳朵在这里已经变聋了，我
很久没听见他作战的锣声了。"

"我们的头顶上是丛林，"莫格里说，"我只认
识象群里的哈蒂和他的儿子们。巴希拉把一个村庄
里所有的马都杀死了，而且，什么是国王呀？"

"我告诉过你了，"卡阿温和地对眼镜蛇说，"四
个月以前我就告诉过你，你的城市已经不存在了。"

vault
[vɔːlt]
n. 拱顶
dome
[dəum]
v. 隆成穹顶形

bleach
[bliːtʃ]
v. 使褪色，漂白
ruby
['ruːbi]
n. 红宝石

war-gong
n. 战争的锣鼓

slay
[slei]
v. 宰杀，杀死

163

"The city—the great city of the forest whose gates are guarded by the King's towers—can never pass. They builded it before my father's father came from the egg, and it shall endure when my son's sons are as white as I! Salomdhi, son of Chandrabija, son of Viyeja, son of Yegasuri, made it in the days of Bappa Rawal. Whose cattle are ye?"

"It is a lost trail," said Mowgli, turning to Kaa. "I know not his talk."

"Nor I. He is very old. Father of Cobras, there is only the jungle here, as it has been since the beginning."

"Then who is he," said the White Cobra, "sitting down before me, unafraid, knowing not the name of the King, talking our talk through a man's lips? Who is he with the knife and the snake's tongue?"

"Mowgli they call me," was the answer. "I am of the jungle. The wolves are my people, and Kaa here is my brother. Father of Cobras, who art thou?"

"I am the **Warden** of the King's Treasure. Kurrur Raja builded the stone above me, in the days when my skin was dark, that I might teach death to those who came to steal. Then they let down the treasure through the stone, and I heard the song of the **Brahmins** my masters."

"Umm!" said Mowgli to himself. "I have dealt with one Brahmin already, in the Man-Pack, and—I know what I know. Evil comes here in a little."

"Five times since I came here has the stone been lifted, but always to let down more, and never to take away. There are no riches like these riches—the treasures of a hundred

"那座城市——那座森林中的巨大城市，它所有的城门都由国王的塔楼把守着——它是永远不会消灭的。还在我父亲的父亲从蛇卵里孵化出来以前，他们就建立了那座城市，它会一直存在，直到我的儿子们的儿子也变得像我一样白！它是由叶迦苏里的儿子维叶加，维叶加的儿子昌德拉比加，昌德拉比加的儿子萨洛姆狄在巴帕·拉瓦文时代建造起来的。你是属于谁家的牲口?"

　　"此路不通，"莫格里转过脸对卡阿说道，"我听不懂他说的话。"

　　"我也听不懂。他太老了。眼镜蛇的父亲呵，这里只有丛林，自古以来它就在这里。"

　　"那么，他是谁，"白眼镜蛇说道，"那个坐在我面前，毫不害怕，不知道国王是什么，用人的嘴说着我们的话的人是谁? 那个佩带小刀，会讲蛇的语言的人是谁?"

　　"他们叫我莫格里，"回答是这样的，"我来自丛林。狼是我的同胞，这里的卡阿是我的兄弟。眼镜蛇的父亲呵，你是谁?"

　　"我是国王宝藏的看守人。当我的皮肤还是黑色的时候，库伦王公建造了我头顶上这座石窟，命令我用死亡来教训那些前来盗宝的人。然后他们从上面把珠宝放进石窟里，那时我听见了我们的主人婆罗门的歌声。"

　　"嗯!" 莫格里自言自语，"我在'人群'里的时候，已经跟一个婆罗门打过了交道，我心里有数。邪恶也会来到这里。"

　　"自从我待在这儿以后，上面的石头已经被掀起过五次，每次都是为了放进更多的珍宝，从来没有取出去过。不论在哪儿都没有这样的宝藏，这是

warden
['wɔ:d(ə)n]
n. 典狱官,看守人

Brahmin
['brɑ:min]
n. 婆罗门

165

kings. But it is long and long since the stone was last moved, and I think that my city has forgotten."

"There is no city. Look up. **Yonder** are roots of the great trees tearing the stones apart. Trees and men do not grow together," Kaa insisted.

"Twice and **thrice** have men found their way here," the White Cobra answered savagely; "but they never spoke till I came upon them **groping** in the dark, and then they cried only a little time. But ye come with lies, Man and Snake both, and would have me believe the city is not, and that my wardship ends. Little do men change in the years. But I change never! Till the stone is lifted, and the Brahmins come down singing the songs that I know, and feed me with warm milk, and take me to the light again, I...I...I, and no other, am the Warden of the King's Treasure! The city is dead, ye say, and here are the roots of the trees? Stoop down, then, and take what ye will. Earth has no treasure like to these. Man with the snake's tongue, if thou canst go alive by the way that thou hast entered at, the lesser Kings will be, thy servants!"

"Again the trail is lost," said Mowgli coolly. "Can any jackal have burrowed so deep and bitten this great White Hood? He is surely mad. Father of Cobras, I see nothing here to take away."

"By the Gods of the Sun and Moon, it is the madness of death upon the boy!" hissed the Cobra. "Before thine eyes close I will allow thee this favour. Look thou, and see what man has never seen before!"

"They do not well in the Jungle who speak to Mowgli of favours," said the boy, between his teeth; "but the dark

yonder
['jɔndə(r)]
adv. 在那边

thrice
[θrais]
adv. 三次

grope
[grəup]
v. 摸索

属于一百个国王的珍宝。可是在最后一次石盖被掀起以后，已经过去了很久很久了，我还以为我的城市把我们忘了呢。"

"城市已经没有了。抬头看看吧，在你头顶上，大树的树根把石头都掀开了。树和人是不会在一块儿长大的，"卡阿坚持道。

"有两三回，人们找到了这个地方，"白眼镜蛇恶狠狠地说，"他们在黑暗里摸索，可是他们一直没有出声，接着，他们只短短地喊叫了一声。可是你们却带着谎话来到这里，你们两个——人和蛇，你们要使我相信城市已经不存在了，我的看守职责也就结束了。多少年来，人的变化不大。可是我是绝不改变的！我要一直等到石盖被掀起，婆罗门教徒们唱着我知道的歌走下地窖，用热牛奶喂我，把我带到明亮的地方去的时候，否则我……我……我，而不是别人，仍然是国王宝藏的看守官！你们说城市已经死亡了，你们说，树根长到了这里？那么，你们弯下腰随便拿吧。天下没有这样的珍宝。那个会说蛇的语言的人，你要是能从你进来的地方活着出去，那么那些小国王们就都要听从你的命令了！"

"还是此路不通，"莫格里泰然自若地说道，"难道真有一头豺钻到这么深的地方，咬了这位伟大的'白头兜'一口吗？他肯定是疯了。眼镜蛇的父亲呵，我看不见这儿有什么东西可以拿走。"

"我以太阳和月亮的神明的名字起誓，这孩子犯了疯病，是在找死啊！"眼镜蛇咝声说道，"在叫你合上眼以前，我赐给你这个恩惠。瞧吧，瞧瞧从来没有人看见过的东西！"

"还没有哪个丛林里的生物敢说什么赐给莫格里恩惠的话呢，"男孩子低声说道，"不过，我想，

changes all, as I know. I will look, if that please thee."

He stared with puckered-up eyes round the vault, and then lifted up from the floor a handful of something that glittered.

"Oho!" said he, "this is like the stuff they play with in the Man-Pack: only this is yellow and the other was brown."

He let the gold pieces fall, and move forward. The floor of the vault was buried some five or six feet deep in coined gold and silver that had burst from the sacks it had been originally stored in, and, in the long years, the metal had packed and settled as sand packs at low tide. On it and in it, and rising through it, as wrecks lift through the sand, were jewelled elephant-**howdahs** of **embossed** silver, **studded** with plates of hammered gold, and **adorned** with carbuncles and turquoises. There were palanquins and **litters** for carrying queens, framed and braced with silver and **enamel**, with jade-handled poles and **amber** curtain-rings; there were golden candlesticks hung with **pierced emeralds** that quivered on the branches; there were studded images, five feet high, of forgotten gods, silver with jewelled eyes; there were coats of mail, gold **inlaid** on steel, and fringed with rotted and blackened seed-pearls; there were helmets, crested and beaded with pigeon's-blood rubies; there were shields of lacquer, of tortoise-shell and rhinoceros-hide, strapped and bossed with red gold and set with emeralds at the edge; there were sheaves of diamond-hilted swords, daggers, and hunting-knives; there were golden sacrificial bowls and ladles, and portable altars of a shape that never sees the light of day; there were jade cups and bracelets; there were incense-burners, combs, and pots for perfume, henna, and eye-powder, all in embossed gold;

howdah

['haudə]

n. 象轿（象背上设置有篷盖的座席）

emboss

[im'bɔs]

v. 装饰,饰以凸物

stud

[stʌd]

v. 用饰纽装饰

adorn

[ə'dɔ:n]

v. 装饰,使美观

litter

['litə(r)]

n. 暖轿,担架

enamel

[i'næm(ə)l]

n. 珐琅,瓷釉

amber

['æmbə(r)]

n. 琥珀

pierce

[piəs]

v. 穿孔于,打眼于

emerald

['emərəld]

n. 祖母绿，翡翠，绿宝

inlaid

[in'leid]

adj. 嵌入的,镶嵌的

在这片黑暗的地方大概谁都会变样的。好吧，我就看看，如果这会使你高兴的话。"

他眯起双眼朝洞窟四周望去，然后从地上拾起一把闪闪发亮的东西。

"啊哈！"他说道，"这很像在'人群'里他们常常玩的那种东西。不过这是黄色的，他们玩的都是褐色的。"

他扔下了手里那些金币，向前走去，洞窟的地上堆积的金币和银币足有五六英尺深。它们已经挣破了原来包装它们的麻袋而滚落出来，由于年深日久，这些金属就像在退潮时滞留下来的砂砾一样，压得紧紧的，形成一堆。一些镶着珠宝的、有浮雕花样的银制象轿散落在金币和银币上面，或是从金币里面露出来，就像沉船在砂砾中显露出来一样，它们外面点缀着锤得薄薄的金片，上面还装饰着红宝石和绿松石。这里还有女王使用的肩舆和暖轿，它们的骨架是用银和上釉的珐琅制作的，轿杠的把手是翡翠做的，窗帘的吊环是琥珀做的；这儿还有装饰着绿宝石的金烛台，穿了孔的绿宝石在烛台支架上晃动；这儿还有已被人遗忘的神的银制神像，它们有五英尺高，装饰着饰钉，眼睛是用宝石做的；这儿还有嵌金的锁子钢甲，边缘上缀着乌黑的、已经朽坏的细粒珍珠；这里还有顶上饰以一串串深红色红宝石的头盔；这儿还有用龟甲和水牛皮制作的漆盾牌，上面饰以镏金片，边缘上嵌了绿宝石；这儿还有一捆捆柄上镶着钻石的宝剑、匕首和猎刀；这儿还有祭祀用的金碗和金勺以及设在地下从没见过天日的轻便祭坛；这儿还有玉杯和玉镯；这儿还有香炉，梳子，装香水、染指甲水和眼膏的

there were nose-rings, **armlets**, head-bands, finger-rings, and girdles past any counting; there were belts, seven fingers broad, of square-cut diamonds and rubies, and wooden boxes, trebly clamped with iron, from which the wood had fallen away in powder, showing the pile of uncut star-sapphires, opals, cat's-eyes, sapphires, rubies, diamonds, emeralds, and garnets within.

The White Cobra was right. No mere money would begin to pay the value of this treasure, the **sifted** pickings of centuries of war, **plunder**, trade, and taxation. The coins alone were priceless, leaving out of count all the precious stones; and the dead-weight of the gold and silver alone might be two or three hundred tons. Every native ruler in India to-day, however poor, has a **hoard** to which he is always adding; and though, once in a long while, some enlightened prince may send off forty or fifty bullock-cart loads of silver to be exchanged for Government securities, the bulk of them keep their treasure and the knowledge of it very closely to themselves.

But Mowgli naturally did not understand what these things meant. The knives interested him a little, but they did not balance so well as his own, and so he dropped them. At last he found something really fascinating laid on the front of a howdah half buried in the coins. It was a three-foot ankus, or elephant-goad—something like a small boathook. The top was one round, shining ruby, and eight inches of the handle below it were studded with rough turquoises close together, giving a most satisfactory grip. Below them was a rim of jade with a flower-pattern running round it—only the leaves were emeralds, and the blossoms were rubies sunk in the cool,

armlet
['ɑːmlit]
n. 臂章

带有浮雕的金瓶；这儿还有数不清的鼻环、臂箍、束发带、指环和腰带；这儿还有七指宽的嵌有四方形钻石和红宝石的皮腰带；还有箍了三层铁圈的木箱，箱子的木头已经朽烂成了粉末，露出里面装的一堆堆没有琢磨过的星形蓝宝石、蛋白石、猫眼石、蓝宝石、红宝石、钻石、祖母绿、石榴石。

"白头兜"说得不错，不论多少钱也买不到这些宝藏。这是经过多少个世纪的战乱、抢劫、贸易和税收，经过仔细筛选和淘汰而后挑选出来的宝物。不要说那些宝石，仅仅那些钱币，就是无价之宝。这里的金银大约净重两三百吨。现在印度的每个土著王公，不论怎么穷，都有窖藏的财宝，他们总是不断地往里面增加东西。虽说隔很久会出一个比较开明的王公，他也许会派四五十头水牛载着银子，去换取政府的债券，可是绝大多数王公都保存了他们的宝藏，并且秘而不宣，牢牢保守着自己的秘密。

sift
[sift]
v. 筛分,过滤
plunder
['plʌndə(r)]
n. 抢劫,战利品
hoard
[hɔːd]
n. 贮藏物,大量

莫格里当然不会懂得这些财宝的含义。其中那些匕首使他稍稍产生了一点兴趣，可是它们不像他自己那把刀有准头，因此他又把它们扔下了。最后，他在一只象轿前面，找到一样被钱币埋掉一半的东西，它可真正使他着了迷。那是根三英尺长的象叉，或者叫象刺——样子有些像一只小小的带钩的撑船篙子。把手的顶部有一块光彩夺目的圆形红宝石，把手约有八英寸长，密密麻麻嵌满了天然绿松石，握起来非常方便。接下来是一个翡翠环，上面雕着一朵花——红宝石做的花瓣，嵌在冰凉的绿宝石叶片之中。把手的其余部分是一根纯粹的象

green stone. The rest of the handle was a shaft of pure ivory, while the point—the **spike** and hook—was gold-inlaid steel with pictures of elephant-catching; and the pictures attracted Mowgli, who saw that they had something to do with his friend Hathi the Silent.

The White Cobra had been following him closely.

"Is this not worth dying to **behold**?" he said. "Have I not done thee a great favour?"

"I do not understand," said Mowgli. "The things are hard and cold, and by no means good to eat. But this" —he lifted the ankus—"I desire to take away, that I may see it in the sun. Thou sayest they are all thine? Wilt thou give it to me, and I will bring thee frogs to eat?"

The White Cobra fairly shook with evil light. "Assuredly I will give it," he said. "All that is here I will give thee—till thou goest away."

"But I go now. This place is dark and cold, and I wish to take the thorn-pointed thing to the jungle."

"Look by thy foot! What is that there?"

Mowgli picked up something white and smooth.

"It is the bone of a man's head," he said quietly. "And here are two more."

"They came to take the treasure away many years ago. I spoke to them in the dark, and they lay still."

"But what do I need of this that is called treasure? If thou wilt give me the ankus to take away, it is good hunting. If not, it is good hunting none the less. I do not fight with the Poison People, and I was also taught the Masterword of thy tribe."

"There is but one Master word here. It is mine!"

Kaa flung himself forward with blazing eyes. "Who **bade**

spike
[spaik]
n. 尖刺,大钉

behold
[bi'həuld]
v. 看,目睹

bid
[bid]
(过去式为 bade)
v. 命令,吩咐

牙。象叉的顶端是一根尖刺和一只钩子——都是钢的，外面镏金，刻有猎象的图画，这些图画吸引了莫格里，他看出这些图画和他的沉默的朋友大象哈蒂有些关系。

"白头兜"一直紧紧地跟在他身后。

"为了看看这些，难道不值得舍掉性命吗?"他说，"你瞧，我难道没有大大地帮你的忙吗?"

"我不懂，"莫格里说，"这些东西又硬又冷，一点也不好吃。不过这个，"他举起了象叉，"我想拿到太阳底下去瞧瞧。你说这些东西全都属于你吗? 你能不能把它送给我? 我会给你抓些青蛙来吃的。"

"白头兜"恶意地笑了，笑得全身都抖动起来。"我当然肯送给你，"他说道，"这儿的一切我都送给你，只要你能离开这个地方。"

"可是我现在就要离开。这里又黑暗又冰冷，我想把这个有尖刺的东西拿到丛林里去。"

"看看你的脚下。那儿是什么?"

莫格里拾起一块白白的光滑的东西。

"它是一个人的头骨，"他安然说道，"这儿还有另外两块头骨。"

"他们是许多年前想来拿走宝藏的人。我在黑暗里和他们说了话，于是他们就安安静静地躺下了。"

"可是我要这叫作宝藏的东西干什么? 你只要让我拿走象叉，我这次狩猎就算没有白来。就是不给我，也不要紧，我的狩猎仍然是成功的。我不爱跟有毒的兽族打架，人家也教过我你们这一族的密语。"

"这儿只有一句密语。它是属于我的!"

卡阿眼睛熠熠发光，挺身上前。"是谁叫我把

173

me bring the Man?" he hissed.

"I surely," the old Cobra lisped. "It is long since I have seen Man, and this Man speaks our tongue."

"But there was no talk of killing. How can I go to the Jungle and say that I have led him to his death?" said Kaa.

"I talk not of killing till the time. And as to thy going or not going, there is the hole in the wall. Peace, now, thou fat monkey-killer! I have but to touch thy neck, and the Jungle will know thee no longer. Never Man came here that went away with the breath under his ribs. I am the Warden of the Treasure of the King's City!"

"But, thou white worm of the dark, I tell thee there is neither king nor city! The Jungle is all about us!" cried Kaa.

"There is still the Treasure. But this can be done. Wait awhile, Kaa of the Rocks, and see the boy run. There is room for great sport here. Life is good. Run to and fro awhile, and make sport, boy!"

Mowgli put his hand on Kaa's head quietly.

"The white thing has dealt with men of the Man-Pack until now. He does not know me," he whispered. "He has asked for this hunting. Let him have it." Mowgli had been standing with the ankus held point down. He flung it from him quickly and it dropped crossways just behind the great snake's hood, pinning him to the floor. In a flash, Kaa's weight was upon the writhing body, paralysing it from hood to tail. The red eyes burned, and the six spare inches of the head struck furiously right and left.

"Kill!" said Kaa, as Mowgli's hand went to his knife.

"No," he said, as he drew the blade; "I will never kill

人带到这儿来的?"他咝声说道。

lisp

[lisp]

v. 口齿不清地说

"当然是我,"老眼镜蛇口齿不清地说道,"我很久没有看见人了,而且这个人还会说我们的语言。"

"可是我们没有说过要杀死他呀。你叫我怎么能回到丛林里去,让别人说是我害死他的?"

"不到时候,我不会说出杀他的话。至于你回不回去,那边墙上有个洞。住嘴吧,你这宰猴子的胖家伙!我只要碰一下你的脖子,丛林里就再也不会见到你了。到这里来的人还从来没有活着出去的。我是国王城市的宝藏看守人!"

"可是,你这个黑洞里的白蛆虫,我告诉你,国王和城市都不存在了!我们的四周全是丛林!"卡阿喊道。

"宝藏还在。不过,我们可以这样办。等一等,岩石里的卡阿,让那男孩跑吧。这儿地方很大,够我们好好玩玩的。生命是宝贵的。来回跑跑,玩一玩吧,孩子!"

莫格里悄悄地伸手摸摸卡阿的头顶。

"这个白家伙直到现在只跟'人群'里的人打过交道,他并不了解我。"他悄声耳语道,"这次狩猎是他自己要求的,就让他试试吧。"莫格里本来是刺尖朝下握着象叉的,他迅速地把它抛了出去,象叉斜着横飞出去,正好落在那条大蛇的头兜后面,把他牢牢钉在地上。一瞬间,卡阿便扑到了那扭曲的躯体上,使他从头到尾都无力动弹。他那红眼睛燃烧着,没有钉住的六英寸花脑袋狂怒地向左右扑打着。

"杀死他!"就在莫格里的手伸出去拔出小刀时,卡阿说道。

"不,"他抽出刀来说,"今后,除了找食物,

again save for food. But look you, Kaa!" He caught the snake behind the hood, forced the mouth open with the blade of the knife, and showed the terrible **poison-fangs** of the upper jaw lying black and withered in the gum. The White Cobra had **outlived** his poison, as a snake will.

"Thuu (It is dried up)", said Mowgli; and motioning Kaa away, he picked up the ankus, setting the White Cobra free.

"The King's Treasure needs a new Warden," he said gravely. "Thuu, thou hast not done well. Run to and fro and make sport, Thuu!"

"I am ashamed. Kill me!" hissed the White Cobra.

"There has been too much talk of killing. We will go now. I take the thorn-pointed thing, Thuu, because I have fought and worsted thee."

"See, then, that the thing does not kill thee at last. It is Death! Remember, it is Death! There is enough in that thing to kill the men of all my city. Not long wilt thou hold it, Jungle Man, nor he who takes it from thee. They will kill, and kill, and kill for its sake! My strength is dried up, but the ankus will do my work. It is Death! It is Death! It is Death!"

Mowgli crawled out through the hole into the **passage** again, and the last that he saw was the White Cobra striking furiously with his harmless fangs at the **stolid** golden faces of the gods that lay on the floor, and hissing, "It is Death!"

They were glad to get to the light of day once more; and when they were back in their own Jungle and Mowgli made the ankus glitter in the morning light, he was almost as pleased as though he had found a bunch of new flowers to stick in his hair.

poison-fang

n. 毒牙

outlive

[aut'liv]

v. 比…长命，比…活得长

我再也不杀生了。可是，你瞧瞧吧，卡阿！"他揪住蛇的头兜，用刀锋撬开他的嘴，显出了上颚里那对可怕的毒牙，它埋在牙床里，已经萎缩发黑了。像蛇类通常那样，这头白眼镜蛇已经老得没有毒汁了。

"苏（它已经干涸了）①。"莫格里说道，他挥手叫卡阿让开，拾起象叉，放了白眼镜蛇。

"国王的宝藏需要一个新的看守了，"他郑重地说道，"苏，你可没有干好自己的工作啊，还是来回跑跑，玩玩吧，苏！"

"我太惭愧了。杀死我吧！"白眼镜蛇咝咝地说。

"杀人的话已经说得太多了。我们现在要走了。我要拿走这个带尖刺的东西，苏，因为我和你交了手，打败了你。"

"好吧，瞧瞧到头来这东西会不会把你杀死。它就是死亡！记住，它就是死亡！这一种东西就足够杀死我的城市里所有的人。丛林里来的人，你占有它的时间不会长的，从你那儿抢走它的人，占有它的时间也不会长的。他们会为了它杀人，杀啊，杀个没完！我的力量已经干涸了，可是这根象叉会代替我干活的。它就是死亡！它就是死亡！它就是死亡！"

passage

['pæsidʒ]

n. 通道，通路

莫格里从那个洞里爬回到地道里，他最后一眼看见的是白眼镜蛇疯狂地用他无毒的毒牙啃着地上那些神像的坚硬的金脸，咝咝地说："它就是死亡！"

stolid

['stɔlid]

adj. 不动声色的，无动于衷的

他们又回到阳光下面，心里很痛快。回到自己的丛林以后，莫格里转动象叉，让它在晨曦中闪闪发光，高兴得就像他找到了一丛新的花朵，把它们插在头发里一样。

---

① "苏"的字面意思是"腐烂的树桩"。

" This is brighter than Bagheera's eyes, " he said delightedly, as he **twirled** the ruby. "I will show it to him; but what did the Thuu mean when he talked of death?"

"I cannot say. I am sorrowful to my tail's tail that he felt not thy knife. There is always evil at Cold Lairs—above ground or below. But now I am hungry. Dost thou hunt with me this dawn?" said Kaa.

" No; Bagheera must see this thing. Good hunting! " Mowgli danced off, flourishing the great ankus, and stopping from time to time to admire it, till he came to that part of the Jungle Bagheera chiefly used, and found him drinking after a heavy kill. Mowgli told him all his adventures from beginning to end, and Bagheera **sniffed** at the ankus between whiles. When Mowgli came to the White Cobra's last words, the Panther purred **approvingly**.

" Then the White Hood spoke the thing which is true? " Mowgli asked quickly.

"I was born in the King's cages at Oodeypore, and it is in my stomach that I know some little of Man. Very many men would kill thrice in a night for the sake of that one big red stone alone."

"But the stone makes it heavy to the hand. My little bright knife is better; and—see! the red stone is not good to eat. Then why would they kill?"

"Mowgli, go thou and sleep. Thou hast lived among men, and..."

"I remember. Men kill because they are not hunting—for idleness and pleasure. Wake again, Bagheera. For what use was this thorn-pointed thing made?"

Bagheera half opened his eyes—he was very sleepy—with

twirl

[twə:l]

v.（使）快速转动，
捻弄

sniff

[snif]

v. 嗅，闻

approvingly

[əˈpru:viŋli]

adv. 赞许地，满意地

"这比巴希拉的眼睛还亮，"他旋转着红宝石高兴地说，"我要把它拿去给他看看。可是那个苏说什么死亡，那是什么意思?"

"我也说不清。他没有挨你的刀子，我觉得非常可惜。在'寒穴'里总是有些邪恶的东西——不管是在地上还是地下。可是我现在觉得饿了，今天早晨你同我一块儿去打猎好吗?"卡阿说道。

"不，我一定得让巴希拉看看这东西。祝你狩猎顺利!"莫格里手舞足蹈地挥舞着象叉走开了。他不时停下来欣赏它，直到他来到巴希拉经常待的那块丛林里的地方。他看见巴希拉吃过丰盛的猎物以后正在饮水。莫格里把自己的冒险事从头到尾告诉了他，巴希拉一面听着，不时嗅嗅那根象叉。当莫格里讲到白眼镜蛇最后的话时，豹子呼噜呼噜地表示赞同。

"那么'白头兜'讲的是实话喽?"莫格里急忙问道。

"我是出生在奥德普尔国王的兽笼里的。我心里明白，我对人还是有点了解的。有好多人单是为了一大块红石头，就会一晚上杀掉三条性命的。"

"但是石头拿在手里多重啊。我那把发亮的小刀要好得多。而且，你瞧! 那红石头不能吃。那么他们究竟为什么要杀人呢?"

"莫格里，去睡觉吧。你在人当中生活过，而且……"

"我记得。人们杀生不是为了打猎——是为了无聊，为了取乐。醒醒吧，巴希拉。这个有尖刺的东西是做什么用的?"

巴希拉的眼睛半睁半闭——他太困了——眼里

a **malicious twinkle**.

"It was made by men to thrust into the head of the sons of Hathi, so that the blood should pour out. I have seen the like in the street of Oodeypore, before our cages. That thing has tasted the blood of many such as Hathi."

"But why do they thrust into the heads of elephants?"

"To teach them Man's Law. Having neither claws nor teeth, men make these things—and worse."

"Always more blood when I come near, even to the things the Man-Pack have made," said Mowgli **disgustedly**. He was getting a little tired of the weight of the ankus. "If I had known this, I would not have taken it. First it was Messua's blood on the **thongs**, and now it is Hathi's. I will use it no more. Look!"

The ankus flew sparkling, and buried itself point down thirty yards away, between the trees. "So my hands are clean of Death," said Mowgli, rubbing his palms on the fresh, moist earth. "The Thuu said Death would follow me. He is old and white and mad."

"White or black, or death or life, I am going to sleep, Little Brother. I cannot hunt all night and howl all day, as do some folk."

Bagheera went off to a hunting-lair that he knew, about two miles off. Mowgli made an easy way for himself up a convenient tree, **knotted** three or four creepers together, and in less time than it takes to tell was swinging in a hammock fifty feet above ground. Though he had no positive **objection** to strong daylight, Mowgli followed the custom of his friends, and used it as little as he could. When he waked among the very loud-voiced peoples that live in the trees, it was twilight

malicious
[mə'liʃəs]
adj. 怀恶意的，恶毒的

twinkle
['twiŋk(ə)l]
n. 闪烁，发光，眨眼

disgustedly
[dis'gʌstidli]
adv. 厌烦地，厌恶地

thong
[θɒŋ]
n. 皮带

knot
[nɒt]
v. 打结，使缠结或纠缠

objection
[əb'dʒekʃ(ə)n]
n. 反对的话，异议

发出恶意的闪光。

"它是人们造出来，用来扎哈蒂的儿子们的脑袋，好让它流出血来的。我在奥德普尔大街上，在兽笼前面，就见过这样的事。这玩意儿尝过许多哈蒂的同胞们的血。"

"可是他们为什么要用它扎象的脑袋呢？"

"为了教会他们遵守人的法律。人由于没有尖牙利爪，就造出这类东西来，而且有的东西比这更凶狠。"

"无论我走到什么地方，总是要流血，就连'人群'造出的东西也是这样，"莫格里厌恶地说。他对于沉重的象叉已经有点厌倦了。"我要是知道这些，绝不会拿走它。起先，是米苏阿染在皮带上的血，现在又是哈蒂的血，我再也不用它了。瞧！"

象叉闪着光芒飞了出去，插进三十码外的树丛中间。"我的双手再也不沾死亡的边了，"莫格里在清新潮湿的泥土上擦了擦他的巴掌说，"那个苏说死亡会跟随我。他老得变白了，他发疯了。"

"不管是白是黑，是死还是活，我可要睡觉了，小兄弟。我实在没法像有些人那样，打猎打了整晚上，接着又嚎叫一个白天。"

巴希拉到两英里外的一个狩猎用的巢穴去了。莫格里为图省事，爬上了附近的一棵树，把三四根藤蔓捆在一起，转眼间就已经在一张离地五十英尺的吊床里晃悠了。莫格里虽说对于强烈的日光没什么绝对的反感，但他还是按照他的朋友们的习惯，尽可能不去利用白天。当莫格里在林中那些喜欢喧闹的兽族中间醒来时，已经暮色重重了，他一直在

once more, and he had been dreaming of the beautiful pebbles he had thrown away.

"At least I will look at the thing again," he said, and slid down a creeper to the earth; but Bagheera was before him. Mowgli could hear him snuffing in the half light.

"Where is the thorn-pointed thing?" cried Mowgli.

"A man has taken it. Here is the trail."

"Now we shall see whether the Thuu spoke truth. If the pointed thing is Death, that man will die. Let us follow."

"Kill first," said Bagheera. "An empty stomach makes a careless eye. Men go very slowly, and the jungle is wet enough to hold the lightest mark."

They killed as soon as they could, but it was nearly three hours before they finished their meat and drink and buckled down to the trail. The Jungle People know that nothing makes up for being hurried over your meals.

"Think you the pointed thing will turn in the man's hand and kill him?" Mowgli asked. "The Thuu said it was Death."

"We shall see when we find," said Bagheera, trotting with his head low. "It is single-foot" (he meant that there was only one man), "and the weight of the thing has pressed his heel far into the ground."

"Hai! This is as clear as summer lightning," Mowgli answered; and they fell into the quick, choppy trail-trot in and out through the checkers of the moonlight, following the marks of those two bare feet.

"Now he runs swiftly," said Mowgli. "The toes are spread apart." They went on over some wet ground. "Now why does he turn aside here?"

"Wait!" said Bagheera, and flung himself forward with

梦着他扔掉的那些好看的鹅卵石。

"我至少得再去看一眼那件东西，"他说。于是他攀着一根藤蔓爬到地面上。但是巴希拉比他更快。莫格里听见他在昏暗的光线里嗅来嗅去。

"那个有尖刺的东西在哪儿？"莫格里喊道。

"有个人拿走了它。这是他的足迹。"

"这下我们可以知道苏说的是不是实话了。假如那个有刺的东西意味着死亡，那个人就会死。我们跟上他吧。"

"我们先去捕杀猎物吧，"巴希拉说，"空肚子的人眼力一定不济。反正人走起来很慢，丛林又够潮湿的，哪怕最轻微的痕迹也会留下来。"

他们尽快地捕杀了猎物，不过当他们吃完肉，饮过水，开始认真地跟踪足迹时，已经过去了将近三个小时。丛林的生物都知道，不管你急着去干什么，吃饭却不该匆忙。

"你认为那个有刺的东西会在那人的手里掉过头来把他杀死吗？"莫格里问道，"苏说它就是死亡。"

"我们找到他以后就会明白的，"巴希拉说，他正低着头在赶路。"这足迹是独脚（他的意思是说，只有一个人的足迹），这件东西的重量已经使他的脚后跟深深压进了地里。"

"嗨！这是明摆着的，就跟夏天的闪电一样。"莫格里回答说。于是他们重新跟着两只赤裸的脚留下的足迹迅速地追踪着，他们在月光洒下的斑斑点点的黑影里绕出绕进，不时改变着方向。

"现在他飞快地跑了起来，"莫格里说，"脚趾张得非常开。"他们走过一段潮湿的地面，"为什么他在这里拐了弯？"

"等一会儿！"巴希拉说，他使劲往前一跃，跳

slide
[slaid]
过去式为 slid
v. 滑动，滑行

buckle down to
认真干起来

choppy
['tʃɒpi]
adj. 多变的

one superb bound as far as ever he could. The first thing to do when a trail **ceases** to explain itself is to cast forward without leaving your own confusing foot-marks on the ground. Bagheera turned as he landed, and faced Mowgli, crying, "Here comes another trail to meet him. It is a smaller foot, this second trail, and the toes turn inward."

Then Mowgli ran up and looked. "It is the foot of a Gond hunter," he said. "Look! Here he dragged his bow on the grass. That is why the first trail **turned aside** so quickly. Big Foot hid from Little Foot."

"That is true," said Bagheera. "Now, lest by crossing each other's tracks we foul the signs, let each take one trail. I am Big Foot, Little Brother, and thou art Little Foot, the Gond."

Bagheera leaped back to the original trail, leaving Mowgli stooping above the curious narrow track of the wild little man of the woods.

"Now," said Bagheera, moving step by step along the chain of **footprints**, "I, Big Foot, turn aside here. Now I hide me behind a rock and stand still, not daring to shift my feet. Cry thy trail, Little Brother."

"Now, I, Little Foot, come to the rock," said Mowgli, running up his trail. "Now, I sit down under the rock, leaning upon my right hand, and resting my bow between my toes. I wait long, for the mark of my feet is deep here."

"I also," said Bagheera, hidden behind the rock. "I wait, resting the end of the thorn-pointed thing upon a stone. It slips, for here is a scratch upon the stone. Cry thy trail, Little Brother."

"One, two twigs and a big branch are broken here,"

得非常远。当你跟踪的痕迹变得不清楚的时候，首先就得朝前迈步，别让你自己乱七八糟的足迹留在地上。巴希拉落地以后，转过身对莫格里喊道："这儿有另一条足迹，是冲着他来的。这人脚板要小些，脚趾是朝里的。"

莫格里跑上去仔细察看。"这是一个冈德猎手的脚板，"他说，"瞧！他拖着弓在草地上走了过去。这就是为什么第一条足迹这么快地拐了个弯。大脚板在躲小脚板。"

"对，"巴希拉说，"我们最好别弄乱了痕迹，踩到了自己人的脚印上，我们还是每人跟踪一条脚印吧。我是大脚板，小兄弟，你是小脚板，那个冈德人。"

巴希拉跳回到原来的足迹那里，留下莫格里弯身考察森林里野蛮的矮人留下的奇特的狭小足迹。

"好啦，"巴希拉沿着一串脚印一步步地挪动着，"我，大脚板，在这儿拐了弯。现在我躲在一块岩石后头，死死地站住了，连脚也不敢挪动一下。把你的足迹说出来，小兄弟。"

"好，我，小脚板，已经来到岩石边了，"莫格里沿着痕迹跑了过来，"现在我在岩石下面坐了下来，倚在我的右手上，我的弓放在我的脚趾中间。我等了很久，因为我在这里留下了很深的脚印。"

"我也一样，"巴希拉躲在石头后边说，"我等待着，把那个有刺的东西的尖头靠在一块石头上。它滑了一下，因为石头上刮了一道痕迹。说说你的足迹吧，小兄弟。"

"这里有一根、两根小树枝和一根粗树干被折

cease
[si:s]
v. 停止,终止行动

turn aside
撇开,使转变方向

footprint
['futprint]
n. 足迹,脚印

said Mowgli, in an undertone. "Now, how shall I cry that? Ah! It is plain now. I, Little Foot, go away making noises and tramplings so that Big Foot may hear me." He moved away from the rock pace by pace among the trees, his voice rising in the distance as he **approached** a little **cascade**. "I...go... far...away...to...where...the...noise...of...falling...water...covers... my...noise; and...here...I...wait. Cry thy trail, Bagheera, Big Foot!"

The panther had been casting in every direction to see how Big Foot's trail led away from behind the rock. Then he gave tongue: "I come from behind the rock upon my knees, dragging the thorn-pointed thing. Seeing no one, I run. I, Big Foot, run swiftly. The trail is clear. Let each follow his own. I run!"

Bagheera swept on along the clearly-marked trail, and Mowgli followed the steps of the Gond. For some time there was silence in the jungle.

"Where art thou, Little Foot?" cried Bagheera, Mowgli's voice answered him not fifty yards to the right.

"Um!" said the Panther, with a deep cough. "The two run side by side, drawing nearer!"

They raced on another half-mile, always keeping about the same distance, till Mowgli, whose head was not so close to the ground as Bagheera's, cried: "They have met. Good hunting—look! Here stood Little Foot, with his knee on a rock—and **yonder** is Big Foot indeed!"

Not ten yards in front of them, stretched across a pile of broken rocks, lay the body of a villager of the district, a long, small-feathered Gond arrow through his back and breast.

"Was the Thuu so old and so mad, Little Brother?" said

断了，"莫格里压低了嗓子说，"喂，那条足迹我该怎么说呢？噢，现在明白了。我，小脚板，离开这里，发出声音，踩出脚步声，好让大脚板听见我。"他离开岩石一步一步在树丛中走着。到了一条小小的瀑布旁边，他的声音从远方传来。"我……走得……远远的……这儿……哗哗的……流水声……掩盖了我的……声音。我就……在这儿……等着。说说你的足迹吧，巴希拉，大脚板！"

豹子正在四下察看大脚板的足迹是怎样从岩石后边伸展开去的。然后他开口说："我跪着从岩石后边爬了出来，拖着那根带尖刺的东西。我看看四下没有人，就跑开了。我，大脚板，飞快地跑着，足迹很清楚。我们跟着自己追踪的那条足迹去吧。我跑啦！"

巴希拉沿着清晰的足印奔去，莫格里跟着那个冈德族人的足迹。丛林里寂静了片刻。

"你在哪儿，小脚板？"巴希拉喊道。莫格里的声音从右边不到五十码的地方回答了他。

"嗯！"豹子低沉地咳了一声说，"这两人是肩并肩地向前跑哩，他们越来越接近了。"

他们又跑了半英里路，中间一直保持着同样的距离，直到莫格里——他的头不像巴希拉那样低得俯到地上——喊了起来："他们碰头了！祝狩猎顺利——瞧！小脚板在这儿站过，他的膝盖曾经靠在这块岩石上——嗨，大脚板就在那儿呢！"

在他们前面不到十码远，一堆高低起伏的岩石堆上，躺着一个当地的村民。一支缀着小羽毛的冈德族长箭从他的后背一直刺到前胸。

"你瞧那个苏果真是老糊涂，是疯了吗，小兄

approach
[ə'prəutʃ]
v. 接近，靠近
cascade
[kæs'keid]
n. 小瀑布，喷流

yonder
['jɔndə]
adv. 在那边

187

Bagheera gently. "Here is one death, at least."

"Follow on. But where is the drinker of elephant's blood—the red-eyed thorn?"

"Little Foot has it—perhaps. It is single-foot again now."

The single trail of a light man who had been running quickly and bearing a burden on his left shoulder held on round a long, low spur of dried grass, where each footfall seemed, to the sharp eyes of the trackers, marked in hot iron.

Neither spoke till the trail ran up to the ashes of a camp-fire hidden in a ravine.

"Again!" said Bagheera, checking as though he had been turned into stone.

The body of a little **wizened** Gond lay with its feet in the ashes, and Bagheera looked **inquiringly** at Mowgli.

"That was done with a bamboo," said the boy, after one glance. "I have used such a thing among the buffaloes when I served in the Man-Pack. The Father of Cobras—I am sorrowful that I **made a jest of** him—knew the breed well, as I might have known. Said I not that men kill for idleness?"

"Indeed, they killed for the sake of the red and blue stones," Bagheera answered. "Remember, I was in the King's cages at Oodeypore."

"One, two, three, four tracks," said Mowgli, stooping over the ashes. "Four tracks of men with shod feet. They do not go so quickly as Gonds. Now, what evil had the little woodman done to them? See, they talked together, all five, standing up, before they killed him. Bagheera, let us go back. My stomach is heavy in me, and yet it heaves up and down like an **oriole**'s nest at the end of a branch."

弟？这儿至少已经死了一个。"

"我们继续跟下去吧。可是，那个喝过象血的东西，那根红眼睛的尖叉在哪儿？"

"也许是小脚板拿走了它。现在只剩下一个人的足迹了。"

一个个子瘦小，肩上背着什么东西正在飞快奔跑的人的足迹，沿着一块长着干草的低矮漫长的岩坡延伸下去。在追踪者锐利的目光下，每一步足迹都清晰得仿佛是用烙铁印下来似的。

他们谁也没有开口，直到足迹把他们引到山涧里一堆篝火的灰烬旁边。

"又是一个！"巴希拉收住了脚步，仿佛变成了石头，僵硬地说道。

一个瘦小干瘪的冈德人的尸体躺在那里，脚伸进火堆的灰烬里。巴希拉疑惑地看看莫格里。

"那是用一根竹棍儿干的，"男孩子看了一眼说，"我在'人群'里干活的时候，放牧水牛群时也使用过这样的东西，眼镜蛇的父亲——我很抱歉我取笑过他——很了解这个种族，我早该明白这一点。我不是说过吗？人们杀人完全是出于无聊。"

"他们其实是为了那些红色和蓝色的石头而杀人的，"巴希拉回答道，"你要记住，我曾经在奥德普尔国王的兽笼里生活过。"

"一、二、三、四，四条足迹，"莫格里俯身看着灰烬说，"四个穿鞋的人的足迹。他们不像冈德人走得那样快。唉，那个小个子樵夫干了什么对不起他们的事呀？瞧，他们在杀死他以前，五个人都站了起来，在一块儿谈过话。巴希拉，我们回去吧。我觉得胃里很沉重，可是同时它又在上下晃悠，就像挂在树梢头的一只黄鹂窝一样。"

wizen
['wizn]
adj. 消瘦的，干瘪的
inquiringly
[in'kwaiəriŋli]
adj. 咨询的，打听的
make a jest of
愚弄某人

oriole
['ɔːriəul]
n. 黄鹂，金莺

189

"It is not good hunting to leave game afoot. Follow!" said the panther. "Those eight shod feet have not gone far."

No more was said for fully an hour, as they worked up the broad trail of the four men with shod feet.

It was clear, hot daylight now, and Bagheera said, "I smell smoke."

"Men are always more ready to eat than to run." Mowgli answered, trotting in and out between the low scrub bushes of the new jungle they were exploring. Bagheera, a little to his left, made an **indescribable** noise in his throat.

"Here is one that has done with feeding." said he. A tumbled bundle of gay-coloured clothes lay under a bush, and round it was some spilt flour.

"That was done by the bamboo again," said Mowgli. "See! that white dust is what men eat. They have taken the kill from this one, —he carried their food, —and given him for a kill to Chil, the Kite."

"It is the third," said Bagheera.

"I will go with new, big frogs to the Father of Cobras, and feed him fat," said Mowgli to himself. "The drinker of elephant's blood is Death himself—but still I do not understand!"

"Follow!" said Bagheera.

They had not gone half a mile farther when they heard Ko, the Crow, singing the death-song in the top of a **tamarisk** under whose shade three men were lying. A half-dead fire smoked in the centre of the circle, under an iron plate which held a blackened and burned cake of **unleavened** bread. Close to the fire, and blazing in the sunshine, lay the ruby-and-turquoise ankus.

"丢下正在追逐的猎物，这种打猎习惯可不好。还是跟上去吧!"豹子说，"这八只穿鞋的脚走得不远。"

他们整整一个钟头没有说话，跟着那四个穿鞋的人的宽宽的足迹。

这时已经是炎热的大白天了。巴希拉说："我嗅到了烟味。"

"人们总是更喜欢吃饭而不喜欢跑路，"莫格里回答道。这是一片长着低矮的灌木丛的丛林地带。他就在这片灌木丛中一会儿穿出，一会儿又穿进。巴希拉走在略为靠左边的地方，从他喉咙里发出了一种难以形容的声音。

"这儿有一个人，他再也不会吃东西了。"在一丛矮树下，仿佛有堆花花哨哨的衣服乱七八糟地堆在那里，四周有些面粉撒在地上。

"这又是用竹棍儿干的，"莫格里说，"瞧，那白颜色的粉末就是人们的食物。他们从这个人手里夺走了猎物——他本来替他们背着食物——又把他作为猎物送给了鸢鹰朗恩。"

"这是第三个了，"巴希拉说。

"我要送些又肥又大的青蛙到眼镜蛇的父亲那里去，把他喂得胖胖的，"莫格里自言自语道，"那件喝象血的东西意味着死亡。可是我还是不懂!"

"跟踪上去吧!"巴希拉说。

他们还没有走出半英里，就听见乌鸦阿科在一棵柽柳顶上高唱着死亡之歌。树阴下躺着三个人。在他们中间，一堆即将熄灭的篝火在冒着烟，火上有个铁盘子，盘子里面有一块没有发过酵的饼，已经烤焦了。那只镶着红宝石和绿松石的象叉就扔在火堆旁边，在阳光下闪闪发光。

indescribable
[indi'skraibəb(ə)l]
adj. 难以形容的

tamarisk
['tæmərisk]
n. 撑柳,柽柳

unleavened
[ʌn'lev(ə)nd]
adj. 未经发酵的

"The thing works quickly; all ends here," said Bagheera. "How did these die, Mowgli? There is no mark on any."

A Jungle-dweller gets to learn by experience as much as many doctors know of poisonous plants and **berries**. Mowgli sniffed the smoke that came up from the fire, broke off a morsel of the blackened bread, tasted it, and spat it out again.

" 'Apple of Death,' " he coughed. "The first must have made it ready in the food for these, who killed him, having first killed the Gond."

" Good hunting, indeed! The kills follow close, " said Bagheera.

" Apple of Death" is what the jungle call thorn-apple or dhatura, the readiest poison in all India.

"What now?" said the panther. "Must thou and I kill each other for yonder red-eyed slayer?"

"Can it speak?" said Mowgli in a whisper. "Did I do it a wrong when I threw it away? Between us two it can do no wrong, for we do not desire what men desire: If it be left here, it will assuredly continue to kill men one after another as fast as nuts fall in a **high wind**. I have no love to men, but even I would not have them die six in a night."

" What matter? They are only men. They killed one another, and were well pleased, " said Bagheera. "That first little woodman hunted well."

" They are cubs none the less; and a cub will drown himself to bite the moon's light on the water. The fault was mine," said Mowgli, who spoke as though he knew all about everything. "I will never again bring into the Jungle strange things—not though they be as beautiful as flowers. This" —he

berry
['beri]
n. 浆果
morsel
['mɔːs(ə)l]
n. (食物)一口,少量

"这东西干起活来真快呀,他们都完蛋了。"巴希拉说,"这些人是怎么死的,莫格里?他们身上没有伤痕呀。"

生活在丛林的生物,是凭着经验辨别有毒的植物和果实的,他们跟许多医生知道的一样多。莫格里嗅了一下篝火上升起的烟气,掰开一小块发黑的饼,尝了一口,把它吐了出来。

"'死亡苹果',"他呛咳着说道,"刚才那个人一定是把它放进食物里给这几个人吃,这几个人一起先杀了那个冈德人,后来又杀了他。"

"打猎的成绩真不错呀!一个猎物紧接着另一个。"巴希拉说道。

丛林里的生物把刺苹果或者"达图拉"称作"死亡苹果",它是全印度药效最快的毒药。

"现在该怎么办?"豹子说,"我和你是不是也该为了争夺那儿的那只红眼睛杀人凶器而彼此残杀呢?"

"它会说话吗?"莫格里低声说,"我扔掉它是不是冒犯了它?它是没法引诱我们做坏事的,因为我们不想要那些人想要的东西。我们要是把它留在这儿,它一定会继续一个接一个地杀人,就像大风刮下树上的坚果一样。我并不喜欢人,可是我也不愿让他们一晚上就死掉六个。"

"那有什么关系?他们只是人。他们自相残杀,还觉得很满意,"巴希拉说,"那第一个矮小的樵夫很会打猎。"

"可是他们全都是些小崽子。小崽子们想去咬水里的月亮,结果自己就淹死了。这都是我的过错,"莫格里说,他那神气仿佛什么都懂了似的,"我以后再也不把新奇的东西带到丛林来了——哪怕

handled the ankus **gingerly**—" goes back to the Father of Cobras. But first we must sleep, and we cannot sleep near these sleepers. Also we must bury him, lest he run away and kill another six. Dig me a hole under that tree."

"But, Little Brother," said Bagheera, moving off to the spot, "I tell thee it is no fault of the blood-drinker. The trouble is with the men."

"All one," said Mowgli. "Dig the hole deep. When we wake I will take him up and carry him back."

Two nights later, as the White Cobra sat mourning in the darkness of the vault, ashamed, and robbed, and alone, the **turquoise** ankus whirled through the hole in the wall, and clashed on the floor of golden coins.

"Father of Cobras," said Mowgli (he was careful to keep the other side of the wall), "get thee a young and ripe one of thine own people to help thee guard the King's Treasure, so that no man may come away alive any more."

"Ah-ha! It returns, then. I said the thing was Death. How comes it that thou art still alive?" the old Cobra **mumbled, twining** lovingly round the ankus-haft.

"By the Bull that bought me, I do not know! That thing has killed six times in a night. Let him go out no more."

gingerly

['ʤinʤəli]

adv. 小心翼翼地,谨慎地,极为小心地

turquoise

['tə:kwɔiz]

n. 绿宝石,绿松石色

mumble

['mʌmb(ə)l]

v. 喃喃而语,咕哝

twine

[twain]

v. 围绕或缠绕,包裹某物

它像花儿一样美。这玩意儿,"他小心翼翼地掂起象叉说,"得送回眼镜蛇父亲那里去,但是我们首先要睡觉,而且我们不能在这些长眠不醒的人旁边睡觉。还有,我们得把它埋起来,不然它会跑掉,去杀死另外六个人。你给我在那棵树下面挖一个洞。"

"可是小兄弟,"巴希拉往树那里挪动着身子说,"我告诉你,这并不是那个喝血的东西的错儿。麻烦是出在那些人身上。"

"全都是一回事,"莫格里说,"挖一个深一点的洞。等我睡醒以后再把它挖出来送回去。"

两夜以后,白眼镜蛇正独自一人坐在黑暗的地窖里自怨自艾,他的宝物被抢走了,他心里感到十分羞愧。突然那个镶着绿松石的象叉呼的一声穿过墙洞被扔了进来,砸在盛满金币的地上。

"眼镜蛇的父亲,"莫格里说(他小心翼翼地待在墙的那一边),"你去找一个年轻力壮的同族,来帮你看守国王的宝藏吧,免得再有人活着离开这里。"

"啊哈!它回来了。我说过,这东西就是死亡。你怎么还活着呢?"老眼镜蛇喃喃地说,亲热地用身体裹住了叉柄。

"我拿赎买我的那头公牛起誓,我也不知道为什么!那东西一晚上杀了六个人。再也别放它出去了。"

In the Rukh

在丛林里

The Only Son lay down again and dreamed that he dreamed a dream.

The last ash dropped from the dying fire with the click of a falling spark,

And the Only Son woke up again and called across the dark:

"Now, was I born of womankind and laid in a mother's breast?

For I have dreamed of a **shaggy** hide whereon I went to rest.

And was I born of womankind and laid on a father's arm?

For I have dreamed of long white teeth that guarded me from harm.

Oh, was I born of womankind and did I play alone?

For I have dreamed of playmates **twain** that bit me to the bone.

And did I break the **barley** bread and steep it in the tyre?

For I have dreamed of a **youngling** kid new riven from the byre.

An hour it lacks and an hour it lacks to the rising of the moon...

But I can see the black roof-beams as plain as it were noon!

"Tis a league and a league to the Lena Falls where the trooping Sambur go,

But I can hear the little fawn that bleats behind the **doe**!

"Tis a league and a league to the Lena Falls where the crop and the upland meet,

独生子又躺下了，他梦见他做了一个梦。

炉火即将熄灭，随着一声唑响，火光四溅，

　　最后一星灰烬落了下来。

独生子又醒了，他在黑暗中喊道：

"我是女人生的吗？我曾经躺在母亲的怀抱里吗？

因为，我梦见我曾经躺在一张毛茸茸的皮上。

我是女人生的吗？我曾经躺在父亲的手臂上吗？

因为我梦见白花花的长牙齿保护着我的安全。

啊，我是女人生的，我曾经独自玩耍吗？

因为我梦见了一对游伴，他们一口咬穿到我的骨头。

我是不是掰过大麦面包，把它泡在凝乳里？

因为我梦见一只刚刚从畜棚抓来的小山羊。

还有一个小时，还有一个小时月亮才会升起

　　……

可是我能清清楚楚地看见那黑色的房梁，

　　就好像在正午时分一样！

离这儿一里格①远，离这儿一里格远，是连纳

　　瀑布，一群群大麋鹿在那儿聚集，我能听见小

　　鹿咩咩叫，它就躲在那母鹿身后！

离这儿一里格远，离这儿一里格远，是连纳瀑

　　布，庄稼地和山坡在那儿汇合，

shaggy

['ʃægi]

adj. 蓬松的，毛茸茸的

twain

[twein]

n. 一对,两个

barley

['bɑːli]

n. 大麦

youngling

['jʌŋliŋ]

adj. 年轻的,年幼的

doe

[dəu]

n. 母鹿

①里格，长度单位，约合三英里。

199

But I can smell the warm wet wind that whispers through the wheat!"

The Only Son

Of the wheels of public service that turn under the Indian Government, there is none more important than the Department of Woods and Forests. The **reboisement** of all India is in its hands; or will be when Government has the money to spend. Its servants wrestle with wandering sand-torrents and shifting dunes wattling them at the sides, **damming** them in front, and **pegging** them down atop with coarse grass and spindling pine after the rules of Nancy. They are responsible for all the **timber** in the State forests of the **Himalayas**, as well as for the **denuded** hillsides that the **monsoons** wash into dry gullies and aching ravines; each cut a mouth crying aloud what carelessness can do. They experiment with **battalions** of foreign trees, and **coax** the blue gum to take root and, perhaps, dry up the Canal fever. In the plains the chief part of their duty is to see that the belt fire-lines in the forest reserves are kept clean, so that when **drought** comes and the cattle starve, they may throw the reserve open to the villager's herds and allow the man himself to gather sticks. They poll and **lop** for the stacked railway-fuel along the lines that burn no coal; they calculate the profit of their plantations to five points of decimals; they are the doctors and midwives of the huge teak forests of Upper Burma, the rubber of the Eastern Jungles, and the gall-nuts of the South; and they are always **hampered** by lack of funds. But since a Forest Officer's business takes him far from the beaten roads and the regular

reboisement

[ri'bɔismənt]

n. 重新绿化，重新
植树造林

dam

[dæm]

v. 筑坝

peg

[peg]

v. 钉木钉,固定,限制

timber

['timbə(r)]

n. 木材

Himalayas

[,himə'leiəz]

n. 喜马拉雅山脉

denude

[di'nju:d;di'nu:d]

v. 使裸露，剥下，
剥夺

monsoon

[mɔn'su:n]

n.（印度等地的）雨
季,季风

battalion

[bə'tæliən]

n. 军营,军队

coax

['kəuks]

v. 用好话相劝,哄

drought

[draut]

n. 干旱,缺乏

lop

[lɔp]

v. 修剪,砍伐

hamper

['hæmpə]

v. 妨碍,牵制

在印度政府治下运转的公用事业机器里，没有一个部门比森林部更为重要。重新绿化全印度的事业就掌握在它的手里。或者不如说，等到政府有了足够的经费以后，这番事业就全靠它来完成了。森林部的职员们跟那些到处游荡的沙流作斗争，和不断移动的沙丘作斗争：在它们两边拦上篱笆，正面修起堤坝，沙丘上头则根据生态法则，种上粗劣稀疏的杂草和长成了细长条的松树。他们要为喜马拉雅山国家森林里的所有木材负责，也要为那些光秃秃的山坡负责，它们一到雨季就被冲刷成干涸的溪谷和令人痛心的深涧。每个职员都大声疾呼，谴责漠不关心的现象，直到喊得声嘶力竭。他们大量引进了外国树种做试验，想哄着桉树在这里生根，盼望它治好运河区的热病。在平原上，他们的职责则是保护森林保护区的环形防火线，使之畅通无阻，以便当旱季到来，牲畜挨饿的时候，可以向村民的畜群开放禁伐区，并且容许村民去拾些柴禾。他们修剪树梢，伐去树杈，在一条不用烧煤的铁路线上积攒下了堆积如山的燃料供铁路使用；他们仔细地计算着他们种植园的盈利，一直算到小数点后面第五位数；他们是上缅甸巨大的柚木森林、东部丛林的橡胶树和南方五倍子果树的医生和产婆；他们永远由于缺乏资金而手头困窘。既然林务官常常要因公出差到距离大路和正规驻地很远的地方，他就变

stations, he learns to grow wise in more than wood-lore alone; to know the people and the polity of the jungle; meeting tiger, bear, leopard, wild-dog, and all the deer, not once or twice after days of beating, but again and again in the execution of his duty. He spends much time in saddle or under **canvas**— the friend of newly-planted trees, the associate of **uncouth rangers** and hairy trackers—till the woods, that show his care, in turn set their mark upon him, and he ceases to sing the **naughty** French songs he learned at Nancy, and grows silent with the silent things of the underbrush.

Gisborne of the Woods and Forests had spent four years in the service. At first he loved it without comprehension, because it led him into the open on horseback and gave him authority. Then he hated it furiously, and would have given a year's pay for one month of such society as India affords. That crisis over, the forests took him back again, and he was content to serve them, to deepen and widen his fire-lines, to watch the green mist of his new plantation against the older **foliage**, to **dredge** out the choked stream, and to follow and strengthen the last struggle of the forest where it broke down and died among the long pig-grass. On some still day that grass would be burned off, and a hundred beasts that had their homes there would rush out before the pale flames at **high noon**. Later, the forest would creep forward over the blackened ground in orderly lines of **saplings**, and Gisborne, watching, would be well pleased. His bungalow, a thatched white-walled cottage of two rooms, was set at one end of the great rukh and overlooking it. He made no pretence at keeping a garden, for the rukh swept up to his door, curled over in a

得聪明世故，而且不仅仅只是知道一些森林的歌谣传说而已；他还学会了识别人和识别丛林里的政体；他会碰上老虎、熊、豹子、野狗和所有的鹿，不是在经过许多天的搜寻后偶尔有一两次遇见它们，而是在执行公务时一再地看见它们。他把大量时间花费在马鞍上和帐篷里——他是新栽下的树苗的朋友，他和粗野的森林看守人和多毛的猎人为伍——直到树林报答了他的操劳，反过来又在他身上打下了它们的印记，于是他不再唱在南锡学来的轻佻的法国歌曲，并且和矮树丛里那些沉默的生物一样，也变得沉默起来。

森林部的吉斯博恩在英国驻印度的行政部门里已经工作了四年。他起初对这种生活并不理解，但却喜欢它，因为这种生活要求他经常骑马外出，并且给予了他一些权力。后来他却狂热地仇恨起这种生活来了，他宁可拿出一年的工资来享受一个月印度所能提供的社交生活。等他度过这一段危机以后，森林又把他吸引回去，他也满足于为森林卖力：把他的防火线加宽和加深，注视着他新开辟的种植园在老树丛中展现出一片雾般的新绿，疏通堵塞的小溪，当森林埋进了又高又深的蒺藜草中间快要死掉的时候，他就来把森林最后的斗争继续进行下去。在一个平静的日子里，那些蒺藜草被烧掉了，在里面做窝的上百头野兽，就在大白天的中午时刻，从苍白的火焰里冲了出去。在这以后，森林慢慢地向前伸展，在烧黑的土地上长起了一排排整齐的树苗，吉斯博恩在一边儿瞧着，不禁觉得心满意足。他住的是一幢平房，它只有两间居室，墙壁是白色的，屋顶是茅草铺的，坐落在大森林尽头，居高临下俯瞰着大森林。他从来不想开辟一块菜园子，因为森林一直侵犯到他的门口，紧挨着房子前

canvas
['kænvəs]
n. 帆布
uncouth
[ʌn'ku:θ]
adj. 粗俗的,粗野的
ranger
['reindʒə(r)]
n. 森林看守人,护林员
naughty
['nɔ:ti]
adj. 下流的,轻佻的
foliage
['fəuliidʒ]
n. 树叶,植物
dredge
[dredʒ]
v. 挖掘,疏浚,疏通

high noon
正午
sapling
['sæpliŋ]
n. 小树苗

thicket of bamboo, and he rode from his verandah into its heart without the need of any carriage-drive.

Abdul Gafur, his fat Mohammedan **butler**, fed him when he was at home, and spent the rest of the time gossiping with the little band of native servants whose huts lay behind the bungalow. There were two grooms, a cook, a water-carrier, and a sweeper, and that was all. Gisborne cleaned his own guns and kept no dog. Dogs **scared** the game, and it pleased the man to be able to say where the **subjects** of his kingdom would drink at moonrise, eat before dawn, and lie up in the day's heat. The rangers and forest-guards lived in little huts far away in the rukh, only appearing when one of them had been injured by a falling tree or a wild beast. There Gisborne was alone.

In spring the rukh put out few new leaves, but lay dry and still untouched by the finger of the year, waiting for rain. Only there was then more calling and roaring in the dark on a quiet night; the **tumult** of a battle-royal among the tigers, the bellowing of arrogant buck, or the steady wood-chopping of an old boar sharpening his tushes against a bole. Then Gisborne laid aside his little-used gun altogether, for it was to him a sin to kill. In summer, through the furious May heats, the rukh **reeled** in the **haze**, and Gisborne watched for the first sign of curling smoke that should betray a forest fire. Then came the Rains with a roar, and the rukh was **blotted** out in fetch after fetch of warm mist, and the broad leaves drummed the night through under the big drops; and there was a noise of running water, and of juicy green stuff crackling where the wind struck it, and the lightning wove patterns behind the dense matting of the foliage, till the sun broke loose again

面就是一丛竹林，他在游廊上上了马以后，一步就跨进了森林的心脏，门口根本不需要修什么马车道。

　　他在家里的时候，他的那个肥胖的穆斯林男仆阿布杜尔·加福尔给他做饭吃。在其余的时间加福尔就和住在平房后面的草屋里的土著仆人闲聊。那里住了两名马夫，一名厨子，一名挑水夫，还有一名清扫夫，这就是吉斯博恩的所有仆人。吉斯博恩自己收拾他的枪支，他没有养狗，狗会惊走猎物。而吉斯博恩最得意的是，他能说出他的王国的臣民们在月亮升起的时候会到什么地方去饮水，黎明前它们会在什么地方吃食，而在炎热的白天里，它们又会在哪里躺下休息。看林人和护林警察住在森林里面很远的小屋里，他们只是在被一棵倒下的树压伤或者被一头野兽咬伤时才到这里来。因此吉斯博恩总是独自一人呆着。

　　到了春天，森林里长出了几片稀稀拉拉的嫩叶，然而到处都是干旱，都在等待着雨水，并没有因为新的一年到来而有所改变。只不过，在寂静的夜晚，黑暗里传来更多的叫唤声和怒吼声。其中有老虎们为争夺霸权进行战斗的骚乱声，有高傲的公鹿呦呦的吼叫声，还有一头老野猪不停地在树干上磨他的獠牙时发出的伐木般的声音。这时吉斯博恩索性收拾起了他很少使用的枪，因为他觉得杀害生灵是犯罪的。到了夏天，在暑气灼人的五月高温里，森林仿佛在雾气里旋转，这时吉斯博恩特别注意监视刚刚升起的一缕黑烟，它表示有个地方发生了森林火灾。接着，雨季呼啸而来，森林一块一块地淹没在温暖的水雾里，巨大的雨点整夜打在阔叶片上，叮叮咚咚，直到天明。这时只听见哗哗的流水声，充满汁液的绿色植物被风吹得噼啪噼啪地

butler
['bʌtlə(r)]
n. 男仆，男管家

scare
['skeə(r)]
v. 惊吓，使恐慌

subject
['sʌbdʒikt]
n. 臣服者，臣民

tumult
['tju:mʌlt]
n. 吵闹，骚动，混乱

reel
[ri:l]
v. 使旋转

haze
[heiz]
n. 薄雾，阴霾

blot
[blɔt]
v. 玷污，弄脏

and the rukh stood with hot flanks smoking to the newly-washed sky. Then the heat and the dry cold **subdued** everything to tiger-colour again. So Gisborne learned to know his rukh and was very happy. His pay came month by month, but he had very little need for money. The **currency** notes **accumulated** in the drawer where he kept his home letters and the **recapping**-machine. If he drew anything, it was to make a purchase from the Calcutta Botanical Gardens, or to pay a ranger's widow a sum that the Government of India would never have **sanctioned** for her man's death.

Payment was good, but **vengeance** was also necessary, and he took that when he could. One night of many nights a runner, breathless and gasping, came to him with the news that a forest-guard lay dead by the Kanye stream, the side of his head smashed in as though it had been an eggshell. Gisborne went out at dawn to look for the murderer. It is only travellers and now and then young soldiers who are known to the world as great hunters. The Forest Officers take their shikar as part of the day's work, and no one hears of it. Gisborne went on foot to the place of the kill: the widow was wailing over the **corpse** as it lay on a bedstead, while two or three men were looking at footprints on the moist ground. "That is the Red One," said a man. "I knew he would turn to man in time, but surely there is game enough even for him. This must have been done for **devilry**."

"The Red One lies up in the rocks at the back of the sal trees," said Gisborne. He knew the tiger under **suspicion**.

"Not now, Sahib, not now. He will be raging and ranging to and fro. Remember that the first kill is a triple kill always. Our blood makes them mad. He may be behind us even as

subdue
[səb'dju:]
v. 征服

currency
['kʌrənsi]
n. 货币

accumulate
[ə'kju:mjuleit]
v. 积聚,堆积,累积

recap
['ri:kæp]
v. 翻新胎面

sanction
['sæŋkʃ(ə)n]
v. 批准,同意

vengeance
['venʤəns]
n. 惩罚,报仇

corpse
[kɔ:ps]
n. 尸体

devilry
['devilri]
n. 恶行,残暴

suspicion
[sə'spiʃ(ə)n]
n. 猜疑,怀疑

响。而闪电在纠结成一团的浓密枝叶后面织出种种花纹，一直要到雨过天晴，阳光重新照耀大地，森林才再一次将自己雾气腾腾的灼热身躯迎向洗刷得一尘不染的天空。然后，接踵而来的暑热和干冷天气又把一切染成了老虎身上的花斑色。吉斯博恩就这样学会了识别他的森林，这使他感到十分幸福。他的工资每月送来，但他很少需要花钱。那些纸币就堆在他放家信和换轮胎工具的抽屉里，越积越多。他要是取出一些来，不是为了到加尔各答植物园去买点什么，就是为了付给某个看林人寡妇一笔钱，而印度政府是绝不会为了她丈夫的死批付给她这笔款子的。

薪金是丰厚的，但有时也必须进行惩罚。凡是需要加以惩罚的，他就给予惩罚。许多天以前的一个晚上，有个上气不接下气的信差前来向他报信，说有个森林警察死在坎叶河边，他的脑袋像个鸡蛋壳似的被打烂了。黎明时吉斯博恩出发去寻找凶手。大家都知道，只有旅游者喜欢打猎，偶尔还有些年轻的兵士。森林部的职员们把打猎当作毫不稀奇的平常事，从没有人把它当回事。吉斯博恩步行到了杀人的地点。被害者的寡妇正在尸体旁边号哭，尸体放在一张床板上，有两三个人正在察看湿地上的脚印。"这是'红家伙'干的,"一个人说，"我知道他总有一天会杀人的，可他确实有足够的猎物呀。这肯定是他在故意捣蛋。"

"'红家伙'就埋伏在那些娑罗双树后面的岩石堆里。"吉斯博恩说。他知道大家怀疑的那只老虎。

"现在不在那儿了，先生，现在不在了。他现在一定是在跑来跑去，到处转悠。俗话说，头次杀人总是连杀三个。人的鲜血会使他发狂。也许我们正

we speak."

"He may have gone to the next hut," said another. "It is only four koss. Wallah, who is this?"

Gisborne turned with the others. A man was walking down the dried bed of the stream, naked except for the **loin-cloth**, but crowned with a **wreath** of the **tasselled** blossoms of the white **convolvulus** creeper. So noiselessly did he move over the little pebbles, that even Gisborne, used to the soft-footedness of trackers, started.

"The tiger that killed," he began, without any **salute**, "has gone to drink, and now he is asleep under a rock beyond that hill." His voice was clear and bell-like, utterly different from the usual whine of the native, and his face as he lifted it in the sunshine might have been that of an angel strayed among the woods. The widow ceased wailing above the corpse and looked round-eyed at the stranger, returning to her duty with double strength.

"Shall I show the **Sahib**?" he said simply.

"If thou art sure..." Gisborne began.

"Sure indeed. I saw him only an hour ago—the dog. It is before his time to eat man's flesh. He has yet a dozen sound teeth in his evil head."

The men kneeling above the footprints slunk off quietly, for fear that Gisborne should ask them to go with him, and the young man laughed a little to himself.

"Come, Sahib." he cried, and turned on his heel, walking before his companion.

"Not so fast. I cannot keep that pace," said the white man. "**Halt** there. Thy face is new to me."

"That may be. I am but newly come into this forest."

说话的时候，他正在我们背后呢。"

"他也许到附近那间茅屋那里去了，"另一个人说，"那间茅屋离这儿只有四'柯斯'远。瓦拉，这是谁呀？"

吉斯博恩跟大家一块儿转过脸来。有个人正从干涸的河床上走来，他全身赤裸，只在腰间缠了块布，头上却戴了一束用爬藤的白色旋花的穗状花朵编成的花环。他无声无息地踩着小鹅卵石走过来，连习惯了猎人轻柔脚步的吉斯博恩也吃了一惊。

"那只咬死人的老虎，"他没有打招呼，就开口说了起来，"已经饮过水了，他现在在小山那边的一块岩石下面睡着了。"他的声音非常悦耳，清脆得像铃声一般，跟当地人说话时稍带哼哼的腔调完全不同。当他仰起脸来面对着阳光时，简直像是一位在森林里迷了路的天使。那个寡妇在尸体边停止了哭泣，瞪大眼睛看着这个陌生人，然后更加起劲地哭了起来。

"要我给先生带路吗？"他直率地问道。

"假如你敢肯定……"吉斯博恩开口说道。

"当然敢肯定！我在一小时以前还见过他呢！——那狗家伙。他还不到吃人肉的岁数。在他那邪恶的脑袋里还长着十二颗上好的牙齿。"

那些跪着察看脚印的人悄悄地溜走了，因为他们害怕吉斯博恩要他们一块儿去。年轻人淡淡地笑了。

"来吧，先生。"他喊道，接着便转过身，带头走在他的同伴前面。

"别那么快，我跟不上，"那个白人说道，"等一下。我从来没有见过你。"

"很有可能是这样的。我最近才到这块森林里来。"

loin-cloth
['lɔinkləθ]
n. 缠腰带, 缠腰布

wreath
[ri:θ;ri:ð]
n. 花圈, 圈状物

tassel
['tæs(ə)l]
n. 穗, 缨

convolvulus
[kən'vɔlvjuləs]
n. 旋花植物

salute
[sə'lu:t]
n. 问候, 打招呼

Sahib
['sɑ:hib]
n. （旧时印度对欧洲人的尊称）先生, 老爷, 大人

halt
['hɔ:lt]
v. 立定, 停止

"From what village?"

"I am without a village. I came from over there." He flung out his arm towards the north.

"A gipsy then?"

"No, Sahib. I am a man without caste, and for matter of that without a father."

"What do men call thee?"

"Mowgli, Sahib. And what is the Sahib's name?"

"I am the warden of this rukh—Gisborne is my name."

"How? Do they number the trees and the **blades** of grass here?"

"Even so; lest such gipsy fellows as thou set them afire."

"I! I would not hurt the jungle for any gift. That is my home."

He turned to Gisborne with a smile that was irresistible, and held up a warning hand.

"Now, Sahib, we must go a little quietly. There is no need to wake the dog, though he sleeps heavily enough. Perhaps it were better if I went forward alone and drove him down wind to the Sahib."

"**Allah!** Since when have tigers been driven to and fro like cattle by naked men?" said Gisborne, **aghast** at the man's **audacity**.

He laughed again softly. "Nay, then, come along with me and shoot him in thy own way with the big English rifle."

Gisborne stepped in his guide's track, twisted, crawled, and **clomb** and stooped and suffered through all the many agonies of a jungle-stalk. He was purple and dripping with

"从哪个村庄来的?"

"我不属于哪个村庄。我是从那边来的。"他摊开手臂,指着北方。

"那么,你是吉卜赛人?"

"不,先生,我是个没有种姓的人,而且,我连父亲也没有。"

"你叫什么名字?"

"莫格里,先生。请问先生叫什么名字?"

"我是这片森林的总监,我的名字叫吉斯博恩。"

"怎么?难道他们要给这儿的树和草都编上号码?"

blade
[bleid]
n. 扁平或薄的一段

"对的,不然有些像你这样的吉卜赛流浪汉会把它们放火烧掉的。"

"我!不论给我多大好处,我也不会伤害丛林里的一根草。这儿就是我的家。"

他带着迷人的微笑转脸朝着吉斯博恩,举起一只手表示警告。

"好了,先生,我们得稍稍安静一点前进了。虽说这狗家伙睡得很死,我们也不用惊醒他。也许最好还是让我一个人往前走,把他从下风方向赶到先生这儿来吧。"

Allah
['ælə]
n. 阿拉,真主
aghast
[ə'gɑ:st]
adj. 惊骇的,吓呆的
audacity
[ɔ:'dæsiti]
n. 大胆,鲁莽的行为,放肆的言语
clomb
[kləum]
v. climb 的过去式及过去分词

"真主安拉!从什么时候开始,老虎居然像牲口一样被赤身裸体的人赶来赶去?"吉斯博恩被这人的大胆放肆吓坏了,这样说道。

他又一次淡淡地笑了笑。"不同意吗,那么,跟我来吧,就照你自己的方式,用那支英国式的大来复枪打死他吧。"

吉斯博恩紧跟着他的向导的足迹,低着头,弯着腰,拐弯抹角地匍匐前进,总之,他受够了追踪森林中的猎物时的辛苦。最后,当莫格里叫他抬起

211

sweat when Mowgli at the last bade him raise his head and peer over a blue baked rock near a tiny hill pool. By the waterside lay the tiger extended and at ease, lazily licking clean again an **enormous** elbow and fore paw. He was old, yellow-toothed, and not a little mangy, but in that setting and sunshine, imposing enough.

Gisborne had no false ideas of sport where the man-eater was concerned. This thing was **vermin**, to be killed as speedily as possible. He waited to recover his breath, rested the rifle on the rock and whistled. The **brute**'s head turned slowly not twenty feet from the rifle-mouth, and Gisborne planted his shots, business-like, one behind the shoulder and the other a little below the eye. At that range the heavy bones were no guard against the **rending** bullets.

"Well, the skin was not worth keeping at any rate," said he, as the smoke cleared away and the beast lay kicking and gasping in the last agony.

"A dog's death for a dog," said Mowgli quietly. "Indeed there is nothing in that **carrion** worth taking away."

"The whiskers. Dost thou not take the whiskers?" said Gisborne, who knew how the rangers valued such things.

"I? Am I a **lousy shikarri** of the jungle to paddle with a tiger's muzzle? Let him lie. Here come his friends already."

A dropping kite whistled shrilly overhead, as Gisborne snapped out the empty shells, and wiped his face.

"And if thou art not a shikarri, where didst thou learn thy knowledge of the tiger-folk?" said he. "No tracker could have done better."

"I hate all tigers," said Mowgli **curtly**. "Let the Sahib give

enormous
[i'nɔ:məs]
adj. 巨大的,庞大的

vermin
['və:min]
n. 害虫,害兽

brute
[bru:t]
n. 畜生,野兽

rend
[rend]
v. 穿透

carrion
['kæriən]
n. 死肉,腐肉

lousy
['lauzi]
adj. 下贱的,污秽的,恶心的

shikarri
[ʃikɑ:'ri:]
n. 狩猎人,打猎人

curtly
['kə:tli]
adv. 简略地,草率地

头来，趴在靠近一汪小小的水塘旁边的一块被阳光烤灼得发蓝的岩石后面窥视的时候，他的脸已经涨得通红，浑身都被汗湿透了。那只老虎伸展开了四肢，正舒舒服服地躺在水塘边，懒洋洋地一次又一次地把一只巨大的虎肘和前掌舔个干净。这只虎已经老了，牙齿发黄，身上毛皮乱糟糟的，可是在四周的环境和阳光衬托下，他仍然显得很威风。

对付吃人的老虎，吉斯博恩一点也不讲什么虚伪的狩猎道德。这家伙是害人虫，必须尽快地杀死它。他歇了一会儿，等到缓过气来，便把来复枪架在岩石上，吹了一声口哨。那只野兽的头慢慢地转了过来，离来复枪不到二十英尺。吉斯博恩不慌不忙地射出他的子弹，一发射进老虎肩胛，另一发打在眼睛下面。在这么近的距离，老虎那粗大的骨骼是挡不住穿透力很强的子弹的。

"好啦，反正这张皮不值得保留下来。"烟雾散开了，那只垂死的野兽正又踢腿又喘气地折腾着。

"这只狗也死得像只狗，"莫格里沉着地说道，"那堆臭肉上确实没什么值得留下的。"

"还有胡须呢。难道你不要胡须吗?"吉斯博恩问道。他很了解，守林人都非常看重这类东西。

"我吗? 难道我是个喜欢摆弄老虎嘴巴的下贱猎人? 让他躺在那里吧，他的朋友们已经到场了。"

就在吉斯博恩取出空子弹壳并且擦把脸的工夫，一只鸢鹰降了下来，在他们头顶上发出尖利的呼啸声。

"如果你不是猎人，那么你又从哪里学会关于老虎的事情呢?"他说，"没有一个追踪的人比你干得更出色。"

"我恨所有的老虎，"莫格里简短地说道，"先

me his gun to carry. Arre, it is a very fine one. And where does the Sahib go now?"

"To my house."

"May I come? I have never yet looked within a white man's house."

Gisborne returned to his bungalow, Mowgli striding noiselessly before him, his brown skin glistening in the sunlight.

He stared curiously at the verandah and the two chairs there, fingered the split bamboo shade curtains with suspicion, and entered, looking always behind him. Gisborne loosed a curtain to keep out the sun. It dropped with a **clatter**, but almost before it touched the flagging of the verandah Mowgli had leaped clear, and was standing with heaving chest in the open.

"It is a trap," he said quickly.

Gisborne laughed. "White men do not trap men. Indeed thou art altogether of the jungle."

"I see," said Mowgli, "it has neither catch nor fall. I...I never beheld these things till to-day."

He came in on **tiptoe** and stared with large eyes at the furniture of the two rooms. Abdul Gafur, who was laying lunch, looked at him with deep disgust.

"So much trouble to eat, and so much trouble to lie down after you have eaten!" said Mowgli with a grin. "We do better in the jungle. It is very wonderful. There are very many rich things here. Is the Sahib not afraid that he may be robbed? I have never seen such wonderful things." He was staring at a dusty Benares brass plate on a **rickety bracket**.

"Only a thief from the jungle would rob here," said Abdul

生，把枪交给我背吧。哈，这是支非常好的枪。现在先生想到什么地方去呢?"

"回我的住宅去。"

"我可以去吗? 我还从来没有进过一个白人的屋子看看呢。"

吉斯博恩回到了他的平房。莫格里在他前面无声无息地迈开大步走着，他的棕色皮肤在阳光下闪闪发亮。

他好奇地看着游廊和放在那儿的两把椅子，不放心地摸了摸裂了缝的竹帘子，然后他一面注意着背后，一面走进了屋子。吉斯博恩随手放下一扇竹帘，好挡住阳光。竹帘落下时"咣"的一下发出了响声，竹帘子还没有落在走廊的石板地上，莫格里就迅速地跳开了，只在一瞬间他已经站在屋子外面，胸脯不停地起伏着。

clatter
['klætə(r)]
n. 咔嗒，哗啦声

"这是个陷阱吧?"他急促地说。

吉斯博恩笑了。"白人是不对别人设陷阱的。你的确是丛林里来的。"

"我明白了，"莫格里说，"它没有机关，也没有陷坑。我……我从来没有见过这类东西。"

他踮着脚尖进了屋子，睁大了眼睛端详着两间屋子里的摆设。正在摆放午餐餐具的阿布杜尔·加福尔极端厌恶地瞧着他。

tiptoe
['tiptəu]
n. 脚尖，趾尖
rickety
['rikiti]
adj. 摇摇晃晃的，东倒西歪的
bracket
['brækit]
n. 支架

"你们吃一顿饭要费这么多事，吃完了又要费那么多事躺下睡觉!"莫格里咧开嘴笑着说，"我们在丛林里就省事得多。啊，真美呀。这里有这么多贵重的东西。先生难道不怕人家来抢劫你吗? 我从来没有见过这么多迷人的东西。"他正在注视着一个蒙满了灰尘的贝纳列斯铜盘，它是放在一个东歪西倒的支架上的。

"只有丛林里来的小偷才会抢劫这儿的东西。"

Gafur, setting down a plate with a clatter. Mowgli opened his eyes wide and stared at the white-bearded **Mohammedan**.

"In my country when goats bleat very loud we cut their throats," he returned cheerfully. "But have no fear, thou. I am going."

He turned and disappeared into the rukh. Gisborne looked after him with a laugh that ended in a little sigh. There was not much outside his regular work to interest the Forest Officer, and this son of the forest, who seemed to know tigers as other people know dogs, would have been a **diversion**.

"He's a most wonderful chap," thought Gisborne; "he's like the **illustrations** in the Classical Dictionary. I wish I could have made him a gunboy. There's no fun in shikarring alone, and this fellow would have been a perfect shikarri. I wonder what in the world he is."

That evening he sat on the verandah under the stars smoking as he wondered. A puff of smoke curled from the pipebowl. As it cleared he was aware of Mowgli sitting with arms crossed on the verandah edge. A ghost could not have **drifted** up more noiselessly. Gisborne started and let the pipe drop.

"There is no man to talk to out there in the rukh," said Mowgli; "I came here, therefore." He picked up the pipe and returned it to Gisborne.

"Oh," said Gisborne, and after a long pause, "What news is there in the rukh? Hast thou found another tiger?"

"The nilghai are changing their feeding-ground against the new moon, as is their custom. The pig are feeding near the Kanye river now, because they will not feed with the nilghai, and one of their sows has been killed by a leopard in the long

Mohammedan
[məu'hæmidən]
n. 伊斯兰教徒，回
教徒

阿布杜尔·加福尔哗啦一声把一个盘子放下，说道。莫格里睁大了眼睛，盯着这个白胡子的穆斯林教徒。

"在我的家乡，要是一头山羊咩咩叫得太响了，我们就割断他的喉咙，"他乐呵呵地反击道，"不过你不用害怕。我要走了。"

他转过身，消失在森林中。吉斯博恩目送着他，乐呵呵地笑了。不久，笑声就变成了一声轻叹。除了日常公务以外，没有多少能引起这位林务官兴趣的事物。而这个了解老虎就像人们了解狗那样的丛林之子，本来是可以给他提供一些消遣的。

diversion
[dai'və:ʃ(ə)n]
n. 解闷，娱乐
illustration
[ilə'streiʃ(ə)n]
n. 插图，图解

"他真是个了不起的家伙，"吉斯博恩想道，"他就像古典文学辞典里的插图。我真希望我能让他当个扛枪手。独自打猎真没意思，这家伙可以成为一个最完美的猎手。我真奇怪他到底是什么人。"

当天傍晚，满天星斗，他坐在游廊上抽着烟，心里还在纳闷儿。一缕轻烟从他的烟斗袅袅升起。当烟雾散开以后，他发现莫格里正叉着手臂坐在游廊边上，就是鬼魂也没法比他更悄无声息。吉斯博恩吃了一惊，烟斗落在地上。

drift
[drift]
v. 漂流，随意移动

"我在森林里没有人可以谈话，"莫格里说，"所以，我就到这里来了。"他拾起了烟斗，递还给吉斯博恩。

"噢，"吉斯博恩说，停了好久，他问道，"森林里有什么新闻？你又发现了一只老虎吗？"

"大羚羊换了牧场，他们每逢新月出来的时候总是这么做的。现在猪群都到坎叶河附近去觅食了，因为他们不肯跟大羚羊在一块儿吃食，结果猪群里有头母猪被一只藏在上游河边深草丛里的豹子

grass at the water-head. I do not know any more."

" And how didst thou know all these things? " said Gisborne, leaning forward and looking at the eyes that glittered in the starlight.

"How should I not know? The nilghai has his custom and his use, and a child knows that pig will not feed with him."

"I do not know this," said Gisborne.

"Tck! Tck! And thou art in charge—so the men of the huts tell me—in charge of all this rukh." He laughed to himself.

" It is well enough to talk and to tell child's tales, " Gisborne **retorted, nettled** at the chuckle. "To say that this and that goes on in the rukh. No man can deny thee."

"As for the sow's carcase, I will show thee her bones to-morrow," Mowgli returned, absolutely unmoved. "Touching the matter of the nilghai, if the Sahib will sit here very still I will drive one nilghai up to this place, and by listening to the sounds carefully, the Sahib can tell **whence** that nilghai has been driven."

"Mowgli, the jungle has made thee mad," said Gisborne. "Who can drive nilghai?"

"Still—sit still, then. I go."

"Gad, the man's a ghost!" said Gisborne; for Mowgli had faded out into the darkness and there was no sound of feet. The rukh lay out in great **velvety** folds in the uncertain **shimmer** of the stardust—so still that the least little wandering wind among the tree-tops came up as the sigh of a child sleeping equably. Abdul Gafur in the cook-house was clicking plates together.

" Be still there! " shouted Gisborne, and composed

捕杀了。除此以外，我没有什么别的新闻了。"

"你怎么会知道所有这些事的呢？"吉斯博恩向前低下身去，注视着他那在星光下闪烁的眼睛说道。

"我怎么会不知道？大羚羊有他的生活习惯，而且就连小娃娃也知道，猪群是不愿意跟大羚羊一块儿吃食的。"

"可是我偏偏不知道这些，"吉斯博恩说。

"唉！唉！你可是掌管着——草屋里的人对我这么说——掌管着这片森林啊。"他对自己微微一笑。

retort
[ri'tɔ:t]
v. 反驳，反击

"随口胡说，编些哄孩子的故事是很容易的，"吉斯博恩被笑声惹恼了，反驳说，"你说什么森林里发生了这样那样的事，反正没有人能反驳你。"

nettle
['netl]
v. 激怒，使烦恼

"关于那头被咬死的母猪，明天我就可以带你去看看她的骨头，"莫格里丝毫不动声色地回答道，"至于那些大羚羊，只要先生安安静静地坐在这儿，我可以去赶一头来，先生只要仔细听听声音，就可以听出那头羚羊是从哪个方向赶来的。"

whence
['(h)wens]
n. 来处，根源

"莫格里，难道丛林把你弄疯了吗？"吉斯博恩说，"谁能赶来一头大羚羊呢？"

"可是——你静静地坐着吧，我去了。"

"天哪，这人简直是个鬼魂！"吉斯博恩说道，因为莫格里已经消失在黑暗中，一点儿没有弄出声音。群星发出闪烁不定的微光，森林像一层层丝绒一样伸延到远方。它是那么寂静，一丝从树梢掠过的游荡的轻风，听起来就像一个睡得很熟的娃娃的一声叹息。阿布杜尔·加福尔在厨房里正弄得盘子叮当直响。

velvety
['velviti]
adj. 像天鹅绒的，柔软的

shimmer
['ʃimə(r)]
n. 微光

"别闹了！"吉斯博恩喊道，然后他像一个习惯

219

himself to listen as a man can who is used to the stillness of
the rukh. It had been his custom, to preserve his self-respect
in his **isolation**, to dress for dinner each night, and the stiff
white **shirtfront** creaked with his regular breathing till he shifted
a little sideways. Then the tobacco of a somewhat foul pipe
began to purr, and he threw the pipe from him. Now, except
for the nightbreath in the rukh, everything was dumb.

From an **inconceivable** distance, and drawled through
immeasurable darkness, came the faint, faint echo of a wolf's
howl. Then silence again for, it seemed, long hours. At last,
when his legs below the knees had lost all feeling, Gisborne
heard something that might have been a crash far off through
the **undergrowth**. He doubted till it was repeated again and yet
again.

" That's from the west, " he muttered; " there's
something on foot there." The noise increased—crash on
crash, plunge on plunge—with the thick grunting of a hotly
pressed nilghai, flying in panic terror and taking no heed to
his course.

A shadow **blundered** out from between the tree-trunks,
wheeled back, turned again grunting, and with a clatter on
the bare ground dashed up almost within reach of his hand. It
was a bull nilghai, dripping with dew—his **withers** hung with a
torn trail of creeper, his eyes shining in the light from the
house. The creature checked at sight of the man, and fled
along the edge of the rukh till he melted in the darkness. The
first idea in Gisborne's bewildered mind was the **indecency** of
thus dragging out for inspection the big blue bull of the rukh—
the putting him through his paces in the night which should
have been his own.

于森林里的寂静的人那样，静下心来倾听。在他孤独的生活中，他为了保持住个人的自尊心，每天总是穿上晚礼服进晚餐。这时，那硬挺的白衬衫前胸随着他有规律的呼吸吱吱嘎嘎地响了起来，他侧了一下身子，响声才止住了，接着，他的烟斗有点堵塞不通，于是，烟草便开始呜呜地响了起来，他把烟斗扔掉了。现在，除了森林里的夜风，一切都哑然无声。

从难以想象的距离外，透过无边无际的黑暗，传来了一声狼嚎的低微回声，回声被拉得长长的。然后又是寂静。仿佛已经寂静了好几个小时。最后，当吉斯博恩的小腿仿佛完全失去了知觉的时候，他听见远处矮树丛中仿佛发出了碰撞的声音。他怀疑自己听错了，但声音又响了起来，接着又响了一次。

"那是在西边，"他喃喃说道，"那儿正在发生什么事情。"声音越来越响——碰撞，再碰撞，横冲直撞——伴随着一头被紧紧追逼的大羚羊沉重的哼哼声。他惊惶恐惧地飞奔着，根本没有注意他跑到什么地方来了。

一条黑影从树干中间冲了出来，转了回去，又哼哼着回过身来，蹄子在光秃的泥地上敲得嗒嗒地响，几乎冲到他的手够得着的地方。那是头公羚羊，浑身都被露水打湿了，他隆起的肩头上挂着一根被撕扯下来的藤蔓，屋里射出的灯光照得他的眼睛闪闪发亮。这头羚羊一看见人，便止住了脚步，沿着森林边缘逃开了，消失在黑暗里。在吉斯博恩弄糊涂了的头脑里出现的第一个想法是，把森林里巨大的蓝色公羚羊拖出来供人参观——而夜晚本来是应该完全属于他的——让他在夜晚里这样奔跑，实在太不应该了。

221

Then said a smooth voice at his ear as he stood staring:

"He came from the **water-head** where he was leading the herd. From the west he came. Does the Sahib believe now, or shall I bring up the herd to be counted? The Sahib is in charge of this rukh."

Mowgli had reseated himself on the verandah, breathing a little quickly. Gisborne looked at him with open mouth. "How was that **accomplished**?" he said.

The Sahib saw. The bull was driven—driven as a buffalo is. Ho! ho! He will have a fine tale to tell when he returns to the herd."

"That is a new trick to me. Canst thou run as swiftly as the nilghai, then?"

"The Sahib has seen. If the Sahib needs more knowledge at any time of the movings of the game, I, Mowgli, am here. This is a good rukh, and I shall stay."

"Stay then, and if thou hast need of a meal at any time my servants shall give thee one."

"Yes, indeed, I am fond of cooked food," Mowgli answered quickly. "No man may say that I do not eat boiled and roast as much as any other man. I will come for that meal. Now, **on my part**, I promise that the Sahib shall sleep safely in his house by night, and no thief shall break in to carry away his so rich treasures."

The conversation ended itself on Mowgli's abrupt **departure**. Gisborne sat long smoking, and the **upshot** of his thoughts was that in Mowgli he had found at last that ideal ranger and forest-guard for whom he and the Department were always looking.

water-head
n. 水源

当他站在那里瞪眼瞧着的时候，耳边有个娓娓动听的声音说道：

"他是从水源那儿来的，他在那儿率领着一群羚羊，他是从西边来的。先生现在相信了吧？还要不要我把那群羚羊一个个地赶来让你数一数呢？先生是这片森林的父母官呀。"

莫格里重新在游廊上坐了下来，呼吸有点儿急促。吉斯博恩惊奇得张大了嘴，注视着他。"你是怎么干成功的？"他问道。

accomplish
[ə'kʌmpliʃ]
v. 完成，达到，实现

"先生已经看见了。这头公羚羊是被赶来的——就像赶一头水牛那样。哈！哈！等他回到羚羊群里，他一定会对他们讲一个了不起的故事。"

"对我来说，这可是新的一招。那么你能够跑得像大羚羊一样快喽？"

"先生不是看见了吗？不论什么时候，先生如果想知道猎物的活动情况，我莫格里就在这里。这是一片很好的森林，我打算留下来。"

"那么你就留下吧。不论什么时候，你需要一顿饭的话，我的仆人会给你的。"

"好的。说真的，我很喜欢吃煮熟的食物。"莫格里马上回答道，"谁也不会说，我跟别人不一样，不爱吃煮的和烤的食物。我一定来吃饭。至于我嘛，我答应先生，你可以晚上平安地睡在自己的屋子里，没有一个贼能破门进来，偷走你那些值钱的珍宝。"

on one's part
就某人而言

departure
[di'pɑ:tʃə(r)]
n. 启程，出发，离开
upshot
['ʌpʃɔt]
n. 结果

莫格里说完就立刻走开了。吉斯博恩抽着烟，坐了很久，他考虑的结果是，他终于找到了他和森林部一直在寻找的理想的看林人和森林警察，那就是莫格里。

"I must get him into the Government service somehow. A man who can drive nilghai would know more about the rukh than fifty men. He's a **miracle**—a lusus natur? —but a forest-guard he must be if he'll only settle down in one place," said Gisborne.

Abdul Gafur's opinion was less favourable. He **confided** to Gisborne at bedtime that strangers from God-knew-where were more than likely to be professional thieves, and that he personally did not approve of naked **outcastes** who had not the proper manner of **addressing** white people. Gisborne laughed and bade him go to his **quarters**, and Abdul Gafur retreated growling. Later in the night he found occasion to rise up and beat his thirteen-year-old daughter. Nobody knew the cause of dispute, but Gisborne heard the cry.

Through the days that followed Mowgli came and went like a shadow. He had established himself and his wild house-keeping close to the bungalow, but on the edge of the rukh, where Gisborne, going out on to the verandah for a breath of cool air, would see him sometimes sitting in the moonlight, his forehead on his knees, or lying out along the **fling** of a branch, closely pressed to it as some beast of the night. **Thence** Mowgli would throw him a **salutation** and bid him sleep at ease, or descending would weave prodigious stories of the manners of the beasts in the rukh. Once he wandered into the stables and was found looking at the horses with deep interest.

"That," said Abdul Gafur **pointedly**, "is sure sign that some day he will steal one. Why, if he lives about this house, does he not take an honest employment? But no, he must wander up and down like a loose camel, turning the heads of

miracle
['mirək(ə)l]
n. 奇迹,奇事

confide
[kən'faid]
（与 to 连用）吐露
（心事、秘密等）

outcaste
['autkɑːst]
n.（印度）被剥夺种姓者,贱民

address
[ə'dres]
v. 与…说话，向…致辞

quarters
['kwɔːtə(r)s]
n. 住处,岗位

fling
[fliŋ]
n. 伸出的部分

thence
[ðens]
adv. 从此,从那时起

salutation
[sælju:'teiʃ(ə)n]
n. 招呼

pointedly
['pɔintidli]
adv. 尖锐地,尖刻地

"我得想办法让政府雇他做职员。一个能驱赶大羚羊的人要比五十个别的人更加了解森林。他是个奇迹——天然的畸形物。不过，他一定得担任森林警察，只要他能够在一个地方待下去。"吉斯博恩说道。

阿布杜尔·加福尔对莫格里的看法可没有那么好。他在睡觉时对吉斯博恩推心置腹地说，这个陌生人天晓得是从什么地方钻出来的，他很可能是个惯偷。他本人根本不赞成收留赤身裸体的流浪汉，他们连应该怎样对白种人说话都不会。吉斯博恩笑了，叫他回自己屋里去。阿布杜尔·加福尔嘟嘟囔囔地退了下去。那天夜里，他爬起床来，把他的十三岁的女儿揍了一顿。没有人知道他为什么要揍女儿，但是吉斯博恩听见了哭声。

在后来的那些天里，莫格里像个影子一样独来独往。他在平房旁边住了下来，按他那种未开化的方式安了家，不过，他安家的地方是在森林的边缘上。每当吉斯博恩出来到游廊上呼吸一点儿清凉空气时，往往会看见他坐在月光下面，脑袋低低地埋在膝盖上，或是他躺在一根伸出的树干上，像某些夜间活动的动物一样紧紧贴着树干。莫格里会从树上向他送来一声问候，并且请他放心睡觉，有时还爬下来为他编造出许多神奇的故事，对他讲述森林里各种动物的生活方式。有一次他溜达进了马厩，人们发现他正以浓厚的兴趣注视着马匹。

阿布杜尔·加福尔尖刻地说："这件事非常明确地证明，他总有一天会偷走一匹马的。既然他住在这幢房屋附近，他为什么不找一件实实在在的差事干呢？他偏偏什么也不干，一定要像个没有系笼

225

fools and opening the jaws of the unwise to folly." So Abdul Gafur would give harsh orders to Mowgli when they met, would bid him fetch water and **pluck** fowls, and Mowgli, laughing **unconcernedly**, would obey.

"He has no caste," said Abdul Gafur. He will do anything. Look to it, Sahib, that he does not do too much. A snake is a snake, and a jungle-gipsy is a thief till the death."

" Be silent, then, " said Gisborne. " I allow thee to correct thy own household if there is not too much noise, because I know thy customs and use. My custom thou dost not know. The man is without doubt a little mad."

"Very little mad indeed, " said Abdul Gafur. "But we shall see what comes thereof."

A few days later on his business took Gisborne into the rukh for three days. Abdul Gafur being old and fat was left at home. He did not approve of lying up in rangers" huts, and was inclined to levy contributions in his master's name of grain and oil and milk from those who could ill afford such **benevolences**. Gisborne rode off early one dawn a little **vexed** that his man of the woods was not at the verandah to accompany him. He liked him—liked his strength, **fleetness**, and silence of foot, and his ever-ready open smile; his ignorance of all forms of ceremony and salutations, and the childlike tales that he would tell (and Gisborne would credit now) of what the game was doing in the rukh. After an hour's riding through the **greenery**, he heard a rustle behind him, and Mowgli trotted at his **stirrup**.

"We have a three days" work toward, " said Gisborne, "among the new trees."

pluck

[plʌk]

v. 拔去（鸡、鸭等的）毛

unconcernedly

[ˈʌnkənˈsəːndli]

adv. 不在乎地，漠不关心地

头的骆驼一样到处游荡，弄得一些傻瓜晕头晕脑，害得那些笨家伙张着大嘴，把他的蠢话全吞了下去。"因此阿布杜尔·加福尔一见到莫格里就很粗暴地命令他干这干那，派他去提水，去拔家禽的毛，而莫格里总是毫不在乎地笑着听从他的指挥。

"他是没有种姓的，"阿布杜尔·加福尔说，"他什么都干得出来。老爷，你可要小心，别让他干得太过火。蛇总归是蛇，丛林里的吉卜赛流浪汉到死也是贼。"

"好了，住嘴吧，"吉斯博恩说，"我可以容许你管教你自己家里的人，只要你不弄出太大的声音，因为我了解你们的习惯和方式。可是你并不了解我的习惯。那人显然有点疯病。"

"有点疯病，确实不错，"阿布杜尔·加福尔说，"我们等着瞧瞧，看看以后会出什么事吧。"

benevolence

[biˈnevələns]

n. 仁爱心，善行

vex

[veks]

v. 使烦恼，恼怒

fleetness

[ˈfliːtnis]

n. 快速，无常

greenery

[ˈɡriːnəri]

n. 温室，草木

stirrup

[ˈstirəp]

n. 马镫，镫形物

几天以后，吉斯博恩因公要到森林里去三天。由于阿布杜尔·加福尔人老了，又长得肥胖，就被留在家里。每到这种时刻，他总不满足于躺在看林人的小屋里睡大觉，而偏偏要以他主人的名义，向那些承受不了这种关怀的人征收谷物、食油和牛奶。这天天刚亮，吉斯博恩就骑马离开了住处。他有点闷闷不乐，因为他那个林中人没有在游廊上等着陪他出门。他喜欢这个小伙子，喜欢他的力气、敏捷和静悄悄的脚步声，以及他常常挂在脸上的坦率的微笑，喜欢他对于一切礼节和恭维话的无知，以及他讲的关于猎物们正在森林里做什么的孩子气的故事（现在吉斯博恩对这些故事已经深信不疑了）。他在树丛里骑马前进了一个小时以后，听见背后有点响动。接着，莫格里快步出现在他的马镫旁边。

"我们大概得干三天的活，"吉斯博恩说，"是在那些新栽的树苗那儿。"

"Good," said Mowgli. "It is always good to cherish young trees. They make cover if the beasts leave them alone. We must shift the pig again."

"Again? How?" Gisborne smiled.

"Oh, they were rooting and tusking among the young **sal** last night, and I drove them off. Therefore I did not come to the verandah this morning. The pig should not be on this side of the rukh at all. We must keep them below the head of the Kanye river."

"If a man could herd clouds he might do that thing; but, Mowgli, if as thou sayest, thou art herder in the rukh for no gain and for no pay..."

"It is the Sahib's rukh," said Mowgli, quickly looking up. Gisborne nodded thanks and went on: "Would it not be better to work for pay from the Government? There is a **pension** at the end of long service."

"Of that I have thought," said Mowgli, "but the rangers live in huts with shut doors, and all that is all too much a trap to me. Yet I think..."

"Think well then and tell me later. Here we will stay for breakfast."

Gisborne **dismounted**, took his morning meal from his home-made **saddle-bags**, and saw the day open hot above the rukh. Mowgli lay in the grass at his side staring up to the sky.

Presently he said in a lazy whisper: "Sahib, is there any order at the bungalow to take out the white mare to-day."

"No, she is fat and old and a little lame beside. Why?"

"She is being ridden now and not slowly on the road that runs to the railway line."

sal

[sɑːl]

n. 娑罗双树

pension

['penʃ(ə)n]

n. 养老金,退休金

dismount

[dis'maunt]

v. (使)下马

saddle-bag

n. 马鞍袋

"好的,"莫格里说,"保护树苗总是有好处的。只要野兽们不糟蹋,它们就会长成一片绿阴。我们得让那些猪群挪挪地方。"

"又要他们挪地方?怎么个挪法?"吉斯博恩微笑着说。

"哦,他们昨晚在那些娑罗双树的树苗中间挖呀刨呀,闹个没完,我把他们赶跑了。所以今天早上我没到游廊那里去。这些猪根本不应该闯到森林这边来。我们得让他们待在坎叶河口的下游。"

"假如有人能够放牧天上的云,他也许可能赶走那群猪。不过,莫格里,你说过你在森林里当牧人,不是为了金钱,也不是为了工资……"

"这是先生的森林呀。"莫格里迅速地抬起头来说道。吉斯博恩点点头表示领他的情,接下去说:"如果你愿意领取工资,为政府工作,那不是更好吗?工作了一定年限之后,还可以拿到一笔养老金。"

"我也想过这件事,"莫格里说,"但是守林人全都住在关紧了门的小屋里,我觉得那里太像陷阱了。不过,我会考虑……"

"好好考虑一下吧,考虑好了告诉我。我们就在这儿吃早饭。"

吉斯博恩下了马,从家制的马鞍袋里取出早饭。这时在森林上空,炎热的白天已经降临。莫格里在他身边躺下,注视着天空。

过了一会儿,他懒洋洋地低声说道:"先生,你有没有下命令让平房里的仆人今天把那匹白色的母马牵出去?"

"没有,那匹马又肥胖又老,而且腿还有点跛。问它做什么?"

"现在正有人骑着它,而且骑的速度并不慢,他们已经走上了通到铁路线去的那条大路。"

229

"Bah, that is two koss away. It is a **woodpecker**."

Mowgli put up his forearm to keep the sun out of his eyes.

"The road curves in with a big curve from the bungalow. It is not more than a koss, at the farthest, as the kite goes; and sound flies with the birds. Shall we see?"

"What folly! To run a koss in this sun to see a noise in the forest."

"Nay, the **pony** is the Sahib's pony. I meant only to bring her here. If she is not the Sahib's pony, no matter. If she is, the Sahib can do what he wills. She is certainly being ridden hard."

"And how wilt thou bring her here, madman?"

"Has the Sahib forgotten? By the road of the nilghai and no other."

"Up then and run if thou art so full of **zeal**."

"Oh, I do not run!" He put out his hand to sign for silence, and still lying on his back called aloud thrice—with a deep **gurgling** cry that was new to Gisborne.

"She will come," he said at the end. "Let us wait in the shade." The long eyelashes **drooped** over the wild eyes as Mowgli began to doze in the morning hush. Gisborne waited patiently Mowgli was surely mad, but as **entertaining** a companion as a lonely Forest Officer could desire.

"Ho! ho!" said Mowgli lazily, with shut eyes. "He has dropped off. Well, first the mare will come and then the man." Then he yawned as Gisborne's pony stallion **neighed**. Three minutes later Gisborne's white mare, saddled, bridled, but riderless, tore into the **glade** where they were sitting, and

woodpecker
['wudpekə(r)]
n. 啄木鸟

pony
['pəuni]
n. 小型马

zeal
[zi:l]
n. 热心, 热情

gurgle
[gə:g(ə)l]
v. (流水) 作汩汩声

droop
[dru:p]
v. 低垂

entertaining
[entə'teiniŋ]
adj. 愉快的, 有趣的,
消遣的

neigh
[nei]
v. 马嘶

glade
[gleid]
n. 林间空地

"呸，那条路是在两'柯斯'外呢。那是只啄木鸟。"

莫格里抬起前臂，挡住射进眼睛的阳光。

"那条路从平房那里穿出去，然后拐了一个大弯。要是照鸢鹰的飞法，顶多只有一'柯斯'远，而且，声音是随着鸟儿传来的。我们去看一下，好吗？"

"胡说八道！在这么毒的太阳底下跑一'柯斯'的路，难道就是为了去察看森林里发出的一点声音吗？"

"不，那匹马是先生的马。我只是想把它带到这儿来。如果那匹马不是先生的，我就让它走开。如果是的，先生可以按自己的意思处理它。确实有人在骑着它拼命地跑呢。"

"你用什么办法把它带到这里来呢，疯家伙？"

"先生忘了吗？就是用赶大羚羊那样的赶法。"

"那就跑去吧，既然你有这么大的兴趣。"

"噢，我才不跑呢！"他举起手叫吉斯博恩不要出声，然后，他自己仍然仰天躺在地上，嘴里接连发出了三声高亢的呼唤——这是从喉咙深处发出的叫声，吉斯博恩从没有听见过这种声音。

"它会来的，"莫格里呼唤过后说道，"我们到树阴下去等着吧。"莫格里在清晨的寂静中打起盹来，长长的眼睫毛遮住了那充满野性的眼睛。吉斯博恩耐心地等待着。莫格里肯定是疯了，然而他却是这个孤独的林务官能够找到的最能消遣解闷的伙伴。

"嗬！嗬！"莫格里闭着眼睛懒懒地说，"他跌下马了。好吧，母马先到，然后那个人才到。"过了一会儿，他们听见吉斯博恩骑的那匹矮种公马发出了嘶叫声，莫格里打了个呵欠。三分钟以后，吉斯博恩的白色母马飞奔进了他们坐的那片林中空地，一下子就跑到它的公马伙伴身边，它鞍辔齐全，只

231

hurried to her companion.

"She is not very warm," said Mowgli, "but in this heat the sweat comes easily. Presently we shall see her rider, for a man goes more slowly than a horse—especially if he chance to be a fat man and old."

"Allah! This is the devil's work," cried Gisborne leaping to his feet, for he heard a yell in the jungle.

"Have no care, Sahib. He will not be hurt. He also will say that it is devil's work. Ah! Listen! Who is that?"

It was the voice of Abdul Gafur in an agony of terror, crying out upon unknown things to **spare** him and his gray hairs.

"Nay, I cannot move another step," he howled. "I am old and my **turban** is lost. Arré! Arré! But I will move. Indeed I will hasten. I will run! Oh, Devils of the Pit, I am a Mussulman!"

The undergrowth parted and gave up Abdul Gafur, turbanless, shoeless, with his waist-cloth unbound, mud and grass in his clutched hands, and his face purple. He saw Gisborne, yelled anew, and pitched forward, exhausted and quivering, at his feet. Mowgli watched him with a sweet smile.

"This is no joke," said Gisborne **sternly**. "The man is like to die, Mowgli."

"He will not die. He is only afraid. There was no need that he should have come out of a walk."

Abdul Gafur groaned and rose up, shaking in every limb.

"It was **witchcraft**—witchcraft and **devildom!**" he sobbed, fumbling with his hand in his breast. "Because of my sin I have been whipped through the woods by devils. It is all

是背上空空无人。

"它还不太热，"莫格里说，"不过在这样炎热的天气里，是很容易出汗的。过一会儿我们就会看见骑马的那个人了，因为人总是要比马走得慢些——尤其当这个人是个胖子，又是个老头子的时候。"

"真主啊！这是魔鬼干的事。"吉斯博恩跳起身来喊道，因为他听见丛林里传来一声狂叫。

"不用担心，先生，他不会受到伤害。他一定也会说这是魔鬼干的事。啊！听吧！那是谁？"

那是恐怖得发了狂的阿布杜尔·加福尔的声音。他在呼吁某个不可知的生灵看在他的白头发分上饶了他。

spare
[speə(r)]
v. 宽恕，饶恕

turban
['tɜːbən]
n. 穆斯林的头巾

"不行了，我一步也走不动了，"他呼天抢地地嚎叫道，"我已经老了，头帕也丢了。哎哟！哎哟！好的，我走。我一定快快地走。我跑！啊，深渊里的魔鬼，我是个穆斯林教徒啊！"

树丛分开了，从里面钻出了阿布杜尔·加福尔，他头帕丢了，鞋子也没了，围腰布也散开了，他脸色涨得通红，两只握得紧紧的拳头里尽是泥巴和草根。他一眼看见吉斯博恩，就重新嚎叫起来。他筋疲力尽，浑身颤抖，一下子扑倒在主人脚下。莫格里脸上挂着甜丝丝的微笑，注视着他。

sternly
['stɜːnli]
adv. 严厉地，坚决地

"这可不是开玩笑的，"吉斯博恩严厉地说，"这人可能会死掉的，莫格里。"

"他不会死的，他只是害怕罢了。本来他完全可以走着来的。"

witchcraft
['wɪtʃkrɑːft]
n. 魔法，魔力

devildom
['devəldəm]
n. 魔界

阿布杜尔·加福尔呻吟着站了起来，他的四肢都在颤抖。

"这是巫术——是巫术，是魔鬼的法术！"他呜咽着，伸手在胸前摸索着，"我犯了罪，所以魔鬼

finished. I **repent**. Take them, Sahib!" He held out a roll of dirty paper.

"What is the meaning of this, Abdul Gafur?" said Gisborne, already knowing what would come.

"Put me in the jail-khana—the notes are all here—but lock me up safely that no devils may follow. I have sinned against the Sahib and his salt which I have eaten; and but for those **accursed** wood-demons, I might have bought land afar off and lived in peace all my days." He beat his head upon the ground in an agony of despair and **mortification**. Gisborne turned the roll of notes over and over. It was his accumulated back-pay for the last nine months—the roll that lay in the drawer with the home-letters and the recapping machine. Mowgli watched Abdul Gafur, laughing noiselessly to himself. "There is no need to put me on the horse again. I will walk home slowly with the Sahib, and then he can send me under guard to the jail-khana. The Government gives many years for this offence," said the butler sullenly.

Loneliness in the rukh affects very many ideas about very many things. Gisborne stared at Abdul Gafur, remembering that he was a very good servant, and that a new butler must be broken into the ways of the house from the beginning, and at the best would be a new face and a new tongue.

"Listen, Abdul Gafur," he said. "Thou hast done great wrong, and altogether lost thy **izzat** and thy reputation. But I think that this came upon thee suddenly."

"Allah! I had never desired the **notes** before. The Evil took me by the throat while I looked."

"That also I can believe. Go then back to my house, and when I return I will send the notes by a runner to the Bank,

repent
[ri'pent]
v. 后悔,忏悔,悔悟

accursed
[ə'kə:sid]
adj. 被咒的,可憎的
mortification
[,mɔ:tifi'keiʃən]
n. 羞辱,羞耻

izzat
['izæt]
n.〈印地〉个人尊严,自尊心,荣誉,威望
note
[nəut]
n. 票据,纸币

们在森林里把我鞭打出来。一切都完了。我悔罪。拿去吧,先生!"他递过去一卷肮脏的纸头。

"这是怎么回事,阿布杜尔·加福尔?"吉斯博恩说。其实他已经明白对方要说些什么了。

"把我关进监牢吧——钞票全在这里——可是最好把我关得严实些,别让那些魔鬼也跟了来。我吃先生的饭,我做了对不起先生的事,要不是那些该死的林中恶魔,我本来可以跑到远远的地方,买些土地,安安静静地过一辈子的。"他在绝望和痛苦中激动地把头朝地上撞。吉斯博恩手里拿着那卷钞票翻来覆去地察看。这是最近九个月发给他的拖欠的薪金总数,这卷钞票是放在抽屉里,跟家信和换轮胎的工具放在一起的。莫格里注视着阿布杜尔·加福尔,无声无息地笑着。"不必让我上马了。我就跟在先生后面慢慢走回家去,然后你可以派人把我送到监牢去。政府对犯这类罪的人要判好多年徒刑的。"管家闷闷不乐地说道。

森林里的孤寂生活使得人们对于许多事物有了不同的看法。吉斯博恩盯着阿布杜尔·加福尔,想起了他曾经是个好佣人,再请一个管家,又得从头教会他家里的种种事情。而且,无论怎么说,总是要增加一副陌生面孔,听一种陌生语言。

"听着,阿布杜尔·加福尔,"他说,"你犯了非常严重的过失,你丢了脸,名誉扫地了。不过我认为你只是一念之差。"

"真主!我以前从来没想过要拿走这些钞票。我看着它们的时候,是恶魔扼住了我的喉咙。"

"这话我也相信。那么你回到我的住宅去吧,等我回家以后,我就派人把这些钱存到银行里去,事

235

and there shall be no more said. Thou art too old for the jail-khana. Also thy household is guiltless."

For answer Abdul Gafur sobbed between Gisborne's cowhide riding-boots.

"Is there no dismissal then?" he gulped.

"That we shall see. It hangs upon thy conduct when we return. Get upon the mare and ride slowly back."

"But the devils! The rukh is full of devils."

"No matter, my father. They will do thee no more harm unless, indeed, the Sahib's orders be not obeyed," said Mowgli. "Then, perchance, they may drive thee home—by the road of the nilghai."

Abdul Gafur's lower jaw dropped as he twisted up his waist-cloth, staring at Mowgli.

"Are they his devils? His devils! And I had thought to return and lay the blame upon this warlock!"

"That was well thought of, Huzrut; but before we make a trap we see first how big the game is that may fall into it. Now I thought no more than that a man had taken one of the Sahib's horses. I did not know that the design was to make me a thief before the Sahib, or my devils had haled thee here by the leg. It is not too late now."

Mowgli looked inquiringly at Gisborne; but Abdul Gafur waddled hastily to the white mare, scrambled on her back and fled, the woodways crashing and echoing behind him.

"That was well done," said Mowgli. "But he will fall again unless he holds by the mane."

"Now it is time to tell me what these things mean," said Gisborne a little sternly. "What is this talk of thy devils? How

情就这样了结吧。让你去坐牢，你是太老了。而且你家里的人是无辜的。"

阿布杜尔·加福尔一时没有回答，只是冲着吉斯博恩的牛皮马靴大声呜咽着。

"那么你不会解雇我了吗?"他大口地吞咽着眼泪，说道。

"那就要看情况了。这要取决于我们回去以后你的表现了。骑上母马，慢慢骑回家去。"

"可是魔鬼怎么办! 森林里到处都是魔鬼。"

"没关系的，大伯。他们不会再来伤害你，除非他们拒绝执行先生的命令，"莫格里说，"要是那样，他们也许会把你赶回家——就像赶大羚羊那样。"

阿布杜尔·加福尔愕然地张大了嘴巴，一面缠着束腰布，一面瞪着莫格里。

"他们是他的魔鬼? 他的魔鬼! 我本来还想回去以后把过错都推到这个巫师身上呢!"

"这想法挺不错呀，先生；不过我们在设下陷阱以前，先得看看落进去的猎物会有多大。其实，我只不过以为有个人拿了先生的一匹马。我还不知道你打算在先生面前把我说成是贼，不然我的魔鬼就会拖着你的腿，把你拉到这里来了。不过，现在这么干也还不晚。"

莫格里用询问的目光望着吉斯博恩，但是阿布杜尔·加福尔已经一瘸一拐地匆忙凑到白色母马身边，爬上马背逃跑了，被践踏的林间小路在他身后发出噼里啪啦的回声。

"干得不坏，"莫格里说，"不过，他要是不抓紧马鬃，还会再跌下马的。"

"好了，现在你该告诉我这是怎么回事了，"吉斯博恩有点严厉地说，"他说什么'你的魔鬼'，这

<hr>

cowhide
['kauhaid]
n. 牛皮，牛皮鞭

dismissal
[dis'misəl]
n. 免职，解雇

perchance
[pə'tʃɑːns]
adv. 也许，可能

warlock
['wɔːlɔk]
n. 术士，魔术师

hale
[heil]
v. 〈古〉强拉，硬拖

237

can men be driven up and down the rukh like cattle? Give answer."

" Is the Sahib angry because I have saved him his money?"

"No, but there is trick-work in this that does not please me."

"Very good. Now if I rose and stepped three paces into the rukh there is no one, not even the Sahib, could find me till I choose. As I would not willingly do this, so I would not willingly tell. Have patience a little, Sahib, and some day I will show thee everything, for, if thou wilt, some day we will drive the buck together. There is no devil-work in the matter at all. Only... I know the rukh as a man knows the cooking-place in his house."

Mowgli was speaking as he would speak to an impatient child. Gisborne, puzzled, **baffled**, and a great deal annoyed, said nothing, but stared on the ground and thought. When he looked up the man of the woods had gone.

"It is not good," said a level voice from the thicket, "for friends to be angry. Wait till the evening, Sahib, when the air cools."

Left to himself thus, dropped as it were in the heart of the rukh, Gisborne swore, then laughed, remounted his pony, and rode on. He visited a ranger's hut, overlooked a couple of new plantations, left some orders as to the burning of a patch of dry grass, and set out for a camping-ground of his own choice, a pile of splintered rocks roughly roofed over with branches and leaves, not far from the banks of the Kanye stream. It was twilight when he came in sight of his resting-place, and the rukh was waking to the hushed **ravenous** life of the night.

是什么意思？人怎么能像牲口一样被赶着在森林里来回跑？回答我。"

"先生是因为我帮你找回了钱，所以生我的气了吗？"

"不，可是这里面有些地方你是在玩花样，我不喜欢这个。"

"很好。只要我站起来往森林里走三步，那么不论是谁，就连先生在内，都没法找到我了，除非我自己走出来。我不愿意走出来，同样的，我也不愿意讲出来。请你稍稍忍耐一下，先生，总有一天，我会让你看到一切的。因为，只要你愿意，我们总有一天会一块儿去驱赶公鹿。在这件事上我一点没有要什么花招。只不过……我熟悉森林，就像人们熟悉他们家里的炉灶一样。"

baffle
['bæf(ə)l]
v. 困惑,不解

莫格里的态度像是在对一个不耐烦的孩子说话。吉斯博恩既觉得为难，又感到疑惑不解，同时还非常恼怒。他什么也没有说，只是眼盯着地上，思索着。等他抬起头来，林中人已经去了。

"朋友之间闹意见，"从树丛后面传来一个平静的声音，"不是一件好事。晚上再见吧，先生，等到天气凉快下来的时候再见。"

吉斯博恩就这样被独自扔在森林深处。他先是咒骂，后来大笑起来，骑上了矮种公马继续前进。他探访了一家看林人的小屋，巡视了两个新的种植场，下令烧掉一块干草地，然后出发到他早已相中了的宿营地去。那是一块儿离坎叶河岸不远的、乱石嶙峋的岩坡，坡上覆盖着树枝和叶片。当他来到休息地时已是傍晚，森林里那静悄悄的捕猎夜生活已经开始了。

ravenous
['rævənəs]
adj. 贪婪的,渴望的,
狼吞虎咽的

A camp-fire flickered on the knoll, and there was the smell of a very good dinner in the wind.

"Um," said Gisborne, "that's better than cold meat at any rate. Now the only man who'd be likely to be here'd be Muller, and, officially, he ought to be looking over the Changamanga rukh. I suppose that's why he's on my ground."

The gigantic German who was the head of the Woods and Forests of all India, Head Ranger from Burma to Bombay, had a habit of flitting batlike without warning from one place to another, and turning up exactly where he was least looked for. His theory was that sudden visitations, the discovery of shortcomings and a word-of-mouth upbraiding of a subordinate were infinitely better than the slow processes of correspondence, which might end in a written and official reprimand—a thing in after years to be counted against a Forest Officer's record. As he explained it: "If I only talk to my boys like a Dutch uncle, dey say, 'It was only dot damned old Muller,' and dey do better next dime. But if my fat-head clerk he write and say dot Muller der Inspecdor-General fail to onderstand and is much annoyed, first dot does no goot because I am not dere, and, second, der fool dot comes after me he may say to my best boys: 'Look here, you haf been wigged by my predecessor.' I tell you der big brass-hat pizness does not make der trees grow."

Muller's deep voice was coming out of the darkness behind the firelight as he bent over the shoulders of his pet cook. "Not so much sauce, you son of Belial! Worcester sauce is a gondiment and not a fluid. Ah, Gisborne, you haf come to a very bad dinner. Where is your camp?" and he

flicker

['flikə(r)]

v. 闪动,闪烁,使摇曳

knoll

[nəul]

n. 圆丘,土墩

gigantic

[dʒai'gæntik]

adj. 巨人般的,高大的

flit

[flit]

v. 调拨,搬运,搬移

visitation

[vizi'teiʃ(ə)n]

n. 访问,正式的视察

upbraiding

[ʌp'breidiŋ]

n. 批评,谴责

correspondence

[kɔri'spɔnd(ə)ns]

n. 通信联络

reprimand

['reprimɑ:nd]

n. 申斥,批评

dey

[dei]

n. 〔法国殖民者在阿尔及尔的〕总督

inspector-General

n. 检查长,监察长

小山上闪烁着一堆篝火的火焰,风儿送来一阵喷香的晚饭气味。

"嗯,"吉斯博恩说,"不论怎么说,这也比吃冷肉强。唯一会跑到这儿来的人,只可能是穆勒。可是别人还以为他这会儿正在视察钱格曼加森林呢。也许那正是他为什么要跑到我这块森林里来的缘故。"

这个高大的德国人是印度的森林部长,是从缅甸到孟买的森林总监,他常常不打招呼就像蝙蝠一样从一个地方飞到另一个地方,而且总是在人家最没有料到的地方出现。他的理论是:突然察访,发现缺点,以及对下属进行口头批评,要比一系列缓慢的通讯联络好得多;靠通讯联络的结果,往往是一份正式的书面批评——这份材料留在林务官的档案里,也许在好多年以后还会对他产生不利的影响。他解释说:"假如我像个荷兰叔叔那样跟我的小伙子们谈谈,他们会说,'那只不过是该死的老穆勒罢了',下次他们就会干得好些。但是,如果我的那个笨蛋办事员写些什么'总监穆勒对此无法解释而且很不满意'之类的话,就会一点儿好处也没有。首先,因为我并不在场,其次,因为将来接替我的那个傻瓜到职以后,也许会对我那些最优秀的小伙子们说,'瞧,你们挨过我前任的骂。'我对你讲,用官衔压人那一套是没法使树木长起来的。"

黑暗里传来了坐在火光后面的穆勒深沉的嗓音,他正弯腰站在他心爱的厨子背后。"别放那么多酱油,你这无赖!辣酱油是调料,不是汤。哦,吉斯博恩,你正好赶上了一顿非常糟糕的晚饭。你

walked up to shake hands.

"I'm the camp, sir," said Gisborne. "I didn't know you were about here."

Muller looked at the young man's trim figure. "Goot! That is very goot! One horse and some cold things to eat. When I was young I did my camp so. Now you shall dine with me. I went into Headquarters to make up my rebort last month. I haf written half—ho! ho! —and der rest I haf leaved to my glerks and come out for a walk. Der Government is mad about dose reborts. I dold der Viceroy so at Simla."

Gisborne chuckled, remembering the many tales that were told of Muller's conflicts with the Supreme Government. He was the **chartered libertine** of all the offices, for as a Forest Officer he had no equal.

"If I find you, Gisborne, sitting in your bungalow and hatching reborts to me about der blantations instead of riding der blantations, I will transfer you to der middle of der Bikaneer Desert to reforest him. I am sick of reborts and chewing paper when we should do our work."

"There's not much danger of my wasting time over my annuals. I hate them as much as you do, sir."

The talk went over at this point to professional matters. Muller had some questions to ask, and Gisborne orders and hints to receive, till dinner was ready. It was the most civilised meal Gisborne had eaten for months. No distance from the base of supplies was allowed to interfere with the work of Muller's cook; and that table spread in the wilderness began with **devilled** small fresh-water fish, and ended with coffee and **cognac**.

"Ah!" said Muller at the end, with a sigh of satisfaction

的帐篷在哪里?"他上前去和吉斯博恩握了握手。

"我自己就是帐篷,先生,"吉斯博恩说道,"我不知道你在这一带。"

穆勒看了看年轻人整洁的外表。"好的!非常好!一匹马,一点干粮。我年轻的时候也是这样宿营的。好吧,你和我一块儿吃晚饭。上个月我到总部去交报告。我只写好了报告的一半。嗨!嗨!另外一半留给我的办事员写,于是我就出来溜达溜达了。政府对那些报告可恼火了。我就是这么告诉西姆拉总督的。"

吉斯博恩抿着嘴轻声笑了,他记起了许多故事,讲的都是穆勒和最高政府之间的冲突,他是所有办公室职员公认的自由思想者,作为一位林务官,没人比他更为出色。

chartered
[ˈtʃɑːtəd]
adj. 公认的
libertine
[ˈlibətiːn]
n. 放荡不羁者,自由思想家

"吉斯博恩,如果我发现你不是骑马巡视种植园,而是坐在你的平房里向我炮制关于种植园的报告,我就要把你调到比卡内尔沙漠中心去绿化它。我非常讨厌报告和嚼舌头的公文,它们害得我们没法做自己的工作。"

"要叫我浪费时间做什么年度报告,我是不会干的。我和你一样恨它们,先生。"

谈到这里,话题转入了业务问题。穆勒想要提些问题,同时还要给吉斯博恩下达一些命令,作一些指示,他们一直谈到晚饭端上来为止。这是吉斯博恩好几个月以来吃的最文明的一顿饭。不管生活用品供应点离得多远,这也都无法妨碍穆勒的厨师的工作。在那张摆设在荒野里的餐桌上,第一道菜是辣子烤淡水鱼,最后以咖啡和法国白兰地作为结束。

devilled
[ˈdevld]
adj. 蘸了很多芥末的
cognac
[ˈkɔnjæk]
n. 白兰地酒的一种(产于法国的Cognac)

"哈!"饭后,穆勒点上一支方头雪茄烟,满意

as he lighted a **cheroot** and dropped into his much worn campchair. "When I am making reborts I am Freethinker und **Atheist**, but here in der rukh I am more than Christian. I am Bagan also." He rolled the cheroot-butt luxuriously under his tongue, dropped his hands on his knees, and stared before him into the dim shifting heart of the rukh, full of stealthy noises; the snapping of twigs like the snapping of the fire behind him; the sigh and rustle of a heat-bended branch recovering her straightness in the cool night; the incessant mutter of the Kanye stream, and the undernote of the many-peopled grass uplands out of sight beyond a swell of hill. He blew out a thick puff of smoke, and began to quote Heine to himself.

"Yes, it is very goot. Very goot. 'Yes, I work miracles, and, by Gott, dey come off too.' I remember when dere was no rukh more big than your knee, from here to der plough-lands, and in drought-time der cattle ate bones of dead cattle up und down. Now der trees haf come back. Dey were planted by a Freethinker, because he know just de cause dot made der effect. But der trees dey had der **cult** of der old gods—'und der Christian Gods howl loudly.' Dey could not live in der rukh, Gisborne."

A shadow moved in one of the bridle-paths—moved and stepped out into the starlight.

"I haf said true. Hush! Here is Faunus himself come to see der Insbector-General. Himmel, he is der god! Look!"

It was Mowgli, crowned with his wreath of white flowers

cheroot

[ʃə'ruːt]

n. 方头雪茄烟

Atheist

['eiθiist]

n. 无神论者

地松了口气，往后靠进他那张破旧的轻便折椅里。"我写报告的时候是自由思想者，是无神论者，但是到了这儿，在丛林里，我可是个大大的基督教徒。同时我又是个异教徒。"他舒舒服服地让雪茄烟头在舌头底下翻动着，双手垂在膝头上，眼睛望着前方，注视着充满隐秘响声、在幽暗中不断变化移动的丛林深处。枝条噼啪作响，就像他身后火堆的噼啪响声一样；被酷暑压弯了腰的树干在凉爽的夜晚里伸直了身子，发出窸窣的叹息声；坎叶河在无休止地喃喃低语，还有从小山头那边看不见的地方，从住着许多居民的草原那里传来低沉的响声。他喷出一口烟，自顾自地朗诵起了海涅的诗句。

"对啦，写得真了不起，真了不起。'是的，我每天显示奇迹，天哪，你看到要大为惊奇。'[①]我记得过去从这儿一直到耕地那边，这片树林子还没有你的膝盖头大，到了旱季，这一带的牲口只好啃死了的牲口的骨头。现在树木回来了，它们是一个自由思想者种的，因为他懂得这些事物的因果关系。可是那些树崇拜的还是古老的神——'基督教的神灵呜呜啜泣'。[②]这些基督教的神是没法在森林里生活的，吉斯博恩。"

cult

[kʌlt]

n. 礼拜,祭仪

在一条仅容得下马匹通过的小路上，一条黑影晃动了一下，接着黑影走动了，它走到星光下面来了。

"我说得完全对。嘘！半人半羊的农牧之神来拜访总督了。天哪，他就是神！"

来的是莫格里，他头上戴着白色花环，手里握

---

① 这句诗引自德国诗人海涅的诗集《还乡曲》（1823~1824）第 71 首。

② 这句诗引自海涅诗集《还乡曲》中的《阿尔曼梭尔》。

and walking with a half-peeled branch—Mowgli, very mistrustful of the fire-light and ready to fly back to the thicket on the least alarm.

"That's a friend of mine," said Gisborne. " He's looking for me. Ohé, Mowgli!"

Muller had barely time to gasp before the man was at Gisborne's side, crying: "I was wrong to go. I was wrong, but I did not know then that the mate of him that was killed by this river was awake looking for thee. Else I should not have gone away. She tracked thee from the back-range, Sahib."

"He is a little mad," said Gisborne, "and he speaks of all the beasts about here as if he was a friend of theirs."

"Of course—of course. If **Faunus** does not know, who should know?" said Muller gravely. "What does he say about tigers—dis god who knows you so well?"

Gisborne relighted his cheroot, and before he had finished the story of Mowgli and his exploits it was burned down to moustache-edge. Muller listened without interruption. "Dot is not madness," he said at last when Gisborne had described the driving of Abdul Gafur. "Dot is not madness at all."

"What is it, then? He left me in a temper this morning because I asked him to tell how he did it. I fancy the chap's **possessed** in some way."

"No, dere is no bossession, but it is most wonderful. Normally they die young—dese beople. Und you say now dot your thief-servant did not say what drove der poney, and of course der nilghai he could not speak."

"No, but, **confound** it, there wasn't anything. I listened, and I can hear most things. The bull and the man simply came

着一根剥去了一半树皮的枝条——这是一个对火光十分不信任的莫格里，随时准备着遇到一点儿危险就逃回树丛里去。

"那是我的一个朋友，"吉斯博恩说道，"他是在找我。喂，莫格里！"

穆勒还没有来得及透一口气，这人已经到了吉斯博恩身边，喊道："我不该走开的。我错了。但是那时我还不知道在河边被杀的那头老虎的配偶已经醒了，她正在找你。要不然我是不会走开的。她从远山区一直跟上了你，先生。"

"他有点儿疯，"吉斯博恩说，"他讲起这里所有的野兽，就好像都是他的朋友似的。"

"当然，当然。要是连农牧之神都不知道，还有谁能知道呢？"穆勒一本正经地说，"他说到老虎，究竟是怎么回事，这位和你那么熟的神？"

吉斯博恩点燃了他的方头雪茄。等他讲完了莫格里和他的种种伟绩时，雪茄烟已经烧到了他的胡须边上。穆勒一直倾听着。"那不是疯病，"当吉斯博恩描绘了阿布杜尔·加福尔是如何被驱赶的事以后，他终于说，"那完全不是疯病。"

"那么它又是什么呢？今天早晨他生气地离开了我，因为我要他告诉我，他是怎么做到这件事的。我猜这家伙在某个方面是着了魔。"

"不，那不是着魔，但是它却是一种非常美妙的东西。这类人，他们一般在很年轻的时候就死了。你刚才说你的小偷仆人没有说出是什么赶着他的马走，而大羚羊自然是不会说话的。"

"不，真该死，那儿什么动静也没有。我仔细听了，而且我是能听出大部分声音的。那头公羚羊和

Faunus
['fɔːnəs]
n. 福纳斯，自然和丰收之神

possessed
[pə'zest]
adj. 着魔的，疯狂的

confound
[kən'faund]
v. 使混淆，把…搞混

headlong—mad with fright."

For answer Muller looked Mowgli up and down from head to foot, then beckoned him nearer. He came as a buck treads a **tainted** trail.

"There is no harm," said Muller in the **vernacular**. "Hold out an arm."

He ran his hand down to the elbow, felt that, and nodded. "So I thought. Now the knee." Gisborne saw him feel the knee-cap and smile. Two or three white scars just above the ankle caught his eye.

"Those came when thou wast very young?" he said.

"Ay," Mowgli answered with a smile. "They were love-**tokens** from the little ones." Then to Gisborne over his shoulder. "This Sahib knows everything. Who is he?"

"That comes after, my friend. Now where are they?" said Muller.

Mowgli swept his hand round his head in a circle.

"So! And thou canst drive nilghai? See! There is my mare in her pickets. Canst thou bring her to me without frightening her?"

"Can I bring the mare to the Sahib without frightening her!" Mowgli repeated, raising his voice a little above its normal **pitch**. "What is more easy if the heel-ropes are loose?"

"Loosen the head and heel-pegs," shouted Muller to the groom. They were hardly out of the ground before the mare, a huge black Australian, flung up her head and **cocked** her ears.

"Careful! I do not wish her driven into the rukh," said Muller.

Mowgli stood still fronting the **blaze** of the fire—in the very form and likeness of that Greek god who is so **lavishly**

headlong

['hedlɔŋ]

adv. 头向前地

taint

[teint]

v. 感染,污染,玷污

vernacular

[vəˈnækjulə(r)]

n. 本国语,本地话,方言

token

[ˈtəukən]

n. 纪念品或留念,象征

pitch

[pitʃ]

n. 音调,音高标准

cock

[kɔk]

v. 使耸立,使竖起

blaze

[bleiz]

n. 火焰,光辉

lavishly

[ˈlæviʃli]

adv. 浪费地,淋漓尽致地

那个人简直就是猛冲过来的,他们都吓得发了疯。"

穆勒没有做声,只是从头到脚上下打量着莫格里,并且招手叫他走过来。莫格里像一头公牛踩在一条有气味的道路上那样勉强走了过来。

"不要紧的,"穆勒用当地话说道,"伸出胳膊来。"

他顺着胳膊摸到手肘弯那儿,点了点头。"正像我想的那样。把膝盖伸过来。"吉斯博恩看见他摸着膝盖骨,微笑了一下。他注意到紧挨着脚踝骨上边,有两三个发白的伤疤。

"这些是你很小时留下的吧?"他说。

"是的,"莫格里微笑着答道,"它们是小家伙们给我留下的爱的纪念。"然后他对背后的吉斯博恩说,"这位先生什么都知道。他是谁?"

"待会儿再说吧,我的朋友。他们在哪里?"

莫格里用手绕着他的头画了一个圆圈。

"是这样!你还会赶大羚羊?瞧!我的母马就拴在那儿的桩子上。你能不能把她带到我这儿来而不吓坏她?"

"我能不能把她带到先生这儿来而不吓坏她!"莫格里的声音比平时稍稍抬高了一点,重复道,"只要把拴住马后腿的绳子松开,就没有比这更容易的事了。"

"把拴住马头和马腿的尖桩拔起来。"穆勒对马夫喊道。桩子刚刚拔出,那匹高大的澳大利亚种黑色母马就抬起头,竖起耳朵来。

"小心点!我可不想把她赶进丛林里去,"穆勒说。

莫格里面对着熊熊燃烧的火堆静静地站着——他的体型、外貌跟小说里描绘得淋漓尽致的那位希腊神

described in the novels. The mare **whickered**, drew up one hind leg, found that the heel-ropes were free, and moved swiftly to her master, on whose bosom she dropped her head, sweating lightly.

"She came of her own accord. My horses will do that," cried Gisborne.

"Feel if she sweats," said Mowgli.

Gisborne laid a hand on the damp flank.

"It is enough," said Muller.

"It is enough," Mowgli repeated, and a rock behind him threw back the word.

"That's **uncanny**, isn't it?" said Gisborne.

"No, only wonderful—most wonderful. Still you do not know, Gisborne?"

"I confess I don't."

"Well then, I shall not tell. He says dot some day he will show you what it is. It would be **gruel** if I told. But why he is not dead I do not understand. Now listen thou." Muller faced Mowgli, and returned to the vernacular. "I am the head of all the rukhs in the country of India and others across the Black Water. I do not know how many men be under me—perhaps five thousand, perhaps ten. Thy business is this, —to wander no more up and down the rukh and drive beasts for sport or for show, but to take service under me, who am the Government in the matter of Woods and Forests, and to live in this rukh as a forest-guard; to drive the villagers' goats away when there is no order to feed them in the rukh; to admit them when there is an order; to keep down, as thou canst keep down, the **boar** and the nilghai when they become too many; to tell Gisborne Sahib how and where tigers move, and what

whicker
['wikə]
v. (马)嘶

uncanny
[ʌn'kæni]
adj. 神秘的,不可思议的

gruel
[gruəl]
adj. 煞风景的

boar
[bɔ:(r)]
n. 公猪,野猪

简直一模一样。马嘶叫了一声,抬了抬后腿,发现拴住后腿的绳子松开了,便迅速地向她的主人这边跑来。她把头埋进主人怀里,身上微微出了些汗。

"她是自己跑来的。我的马也会这样。"吉斯博恩喊道。

"摸摸她,看看她是不是出汗了,"莫格里说。

吉斯博恩把手放在潮湿的马肚上。

"够了。"穆勒说。

"够了。"莫格里重复道,他身后的一块岩石把声音送了回来。

"真有点不可思议,是不是?"吉斯博恩说。

"不,只不过是精彩而已。简直妙极了。你还不明白吗,吉斯博恩?"

"我承认,我确实不明白。"

"好吧,那么我就暂时不说出来。他说总有一天他会告诉你是怎么回事的。我如果说了,就太煞风景了。但是他为什么还没有死,我真不懂。喂,你听着,"穆勒转脸朝着莫格里,又说起了地方话,"我是这儿所有森林的总管,包括印度和黑水那边的国度。我不知道我手下有多少人马——也许有五千人,也许只有十个人。你该做的事就是,不要再在森林里到处游荡,不要为了好玩或是为了炫耀自己,而去驱赶野兽了。你就到我手下来工作,我就是主管森林事务的政府,你就住在这片森林里,当森林看守人。如果你没有得到让村民的山羊在林中觅食的命令,你就把他们赶走;得到了命令,就放他们来吃草;如果野猪和大羚羊繁殖得太快,就想办法使他们减少一些,这个你是有办法做到的;把老虎迁移的情况和他们迁移到了什么地方以及森林

251

game there is in the forests; and to give sure warning of all the fires in the rukh, for thou canst give warning more quickly than any other. For that work there is a payment each month in silver, and at the end, when thou hast gathered a wife and cattle and, may be, children, a pension. What answer?"

"That's just what I..." Gisborne began.

"My Sahib spoke this morning of such a service. I walked all day alone considering the matter, and my answer is ready here. I serve, if I serve in this rukh and no other; with Gisborne Sahib and with no other."

"It shall be so. In a week comes the written order that pledges the honour of the Government for the pension. After that thou wilt take up thy hut where Gisborne Sahib shall appoint."

"I was going to speak to you about it," said Gisborne.

"I did not want to be told when I saw that man. there will never be a forest-guard like him. He is a miracle. I tell you, Gisborne, some day you will find it so. Listen, he is blood-brother to every beast in the rukh!"

"I should be easier in my mind if I could understand him."

"Dot will come. Now I tell you dot only once in my service, and dot is thirty years, haf I met a boy dot began as this man began. Und he died. Sometimes you hear of dem in der census reports, but dey all die. Dis man haf lived, and he is an **anachronism**, for he is before der Iron Age, and der Stone Age. Look here, he is at der beginnings of der history of man—Adam in der Garden, and now we want only an Eva! No! He is older than dot child-tale, shust as der rukh is older dan der gods. Gisborne, I am a Bagan now, once for all."

里有哪些猎物告诉吉斯博恩先生；你还得对森林里所有的火灾发出确实的警报，因为你能够比任何人更早地发出警报。干了这些工作，你每月可以得到一些银币作为报酬。以后，你有了妻子、牲畜，或许还有孩子的时候，你就会领到一笔养老金。你的回答是什么？"

"我也正想……"吉斯博恩开口说道。

"我的先生今天早上谈到了这样一件工作。今天一整天，我一边走一边在考虑。我已经考虑好了。我如果接受这件工作，就得在这片森林里，不到别处去，我要跟着吉斯博恩先生，不跟别人。"

"就这样吧。一星期以后，政府答应付给你养老金的命令就会下达。那时你就住进吉斯博恩先生指定给你的小屋里去。"

"我正要跟你谈这件事。"吉斯博恩说道。

"我只要看见他就够了，用不着别人告诉我。无论哪个森林看守都比不上他。他是个奇迹。我告诉你，吉斯博恩，你有一天会发现这一点的。听着，森林里每一头野兽跟他都是亲兄弟。"

"我要是真正了解了他，我也就会放心一些了。"

"你会了解他的。我告诉你，我干了三十年工作，只见过一个这样的男孩，开头也是跟他一样，后来就死了。有时你在人口调查报告里会听到这类人的事，可是他们都死了。而这个人却活了下来。他是个时代错误，因为他比铁器时代还早，比石器时代还早。噢，他是人类历史的开端……是伊甸园的亚当，现在我们只缺一个夏娃了！不！他比那个幼稚的故事还要古老，正像大森林比那些神还要古老一样。吉斯博恩，现在我是个异教徒了，彻底的异教徒。"

anachronism
[ə'nækrəniz(ə)m]
n. 时代错误

253

Through the rest of the long evening Muller sat smoking and smoking, and staring and staring into the darkness, his lips moving in **multiplied quotations**, and great wonder upon his face. He went to his tent, but presently came out again in his **majestic** pink sleeping-suit, and the last words that Gisborne heard him address to the rukh through the deep hush of midnight were these, delivered with immense emphasis: —

Dough we shivt und bedeck und bedrape us,
   Dou art noble und nude und andeek;
Libidina dy moder, Briapus
   Dy fader, a God und a Greek.

"Now I know dot, Bagan or Christian, I shall nefer know der **inwardness** of der rukh!"

It was midnight in the bungalow a week later when Abdul Gafur, ashy gray with rage, stood at the foot of Gisborne's bed and whispering bade him awake.

"Up, Sahib," he **stammered**. "Up and bring thy gun. Mine honour is gone. Up and kill before any see."

The old man's face had changed, so that Gisborne stared stupidly.

"It was for this, then, that that jungle outcaste helped me to polish the Sahib's table, and drew water and plucked fowls. They have gone off together for all my beatings, and now he sits among his devils dragging her soul to the Pit. Up, Sahib, and come with me!"

He thrust a rifle into Gisborne's half-wakened hand and almost dragged him from the room on to the verandah.

multiply
['mʌltiplai]
v. 乘,增加,许多

quotation
[kwəu'teiʃ(ə)n]
n. 引用语,语录,诗句

majestic
[mə'dʒestik]
adj. 宏伟的,华丽的

那个漫长的傍晚余下的时间,穆勒一直坐在那里不停地抽着烟,呆呆地凝视着黑暗深处,嘴唇不停地嗫动,念着一行又一行的诗句,脸上露出欣喜若狂的神情。他走进自己的帐篷里,但是不久就穿着华丽的粉红色睡袍出来了,吉斯博恩听见他在午夜的深沉寂静中加重了语气,向着丛林念出了最后的诗句:

虽说我们换上衣服,着意修饰,盛装打扮,
　　你却高尚、裸体而又古老;
李比迪娜是你的母亲,布利亚帕斯
　　是你的父亲,一个是神,一个是希腊人。

inwardness
['inwədnis]
n. 内在性质,隐秘

"现在我明白了,不论是异教徒,还是基督徒,我永远也不可能真正了解森林的隐秘。"

一星期以后的一个午夜,在平房里,脸色气得发白的阿布杜尔·加福尔气急败坏地站在吉斯博恩的床脚边,压低声音把他唤醒了。

stammer
['stæmə(r)]
v. 结结巴巴地说,口吃

"起来,先生,"他结结巴巴地说,"起来,拿上你的枪。我的名誉完全扫地了。不要等别人看见,快起床去杀死他吧。"

老头的脸都变了样,弄得吉斯博恩只是看着他发呆。

"原来那个森林里的贱种就是为了这个才帮我擦亮先生的桌子,才帮我打水,帮我拔鸡毛的。我揍了多少次也不管用,他们双双逃走了,现在他正坐在他的魔鬼中间,把她的灵魂拖进地狱。起来,先生,快跟我来!"

他把一支来复枪塞进半醒半睡的吉斯博恩手里,几乎是把他从屋里拖到游廊上。

"They are there in the rukh; even within gunshot of the house. Come softly with me."

"But what is it? What is the trouble, Abdul?"

"Mowgli, and his devils. Also my own daughter," said Abdul Gafur. Gisborne whistled and followed his guide. Not for nothing, he knew, had Abdul Gafur beaten his daughter of nights, and not for nothing had Mowgli helped in the housework a man whom his own powers, whatever those were, had **convicted** of **theft**. Also, a forest wooing goes quickly.

There was the breathing of a **flute** in the rukh, as it might have been the song of some wandering wood-god, and, as they came nearer, a murmur of voices. The path ended in a little **semicircular** glade walled partly by high grass and partly by trees. In the centre, upon a fallen trunk, his back to the watchers and his arm round the neck of Abdul Gafur's daughter, sat Mowgli, newly crowned with flowers, playing upon a rude bamboo flute, to whose music four huge wolves danced solemnly on their hind legs.

"Those are his devils," Abdul Gafur whispered. He held a bunch of **cartridges** in his hand. The beasts dropped to a **longdrawn** quavering note and lay still with steady green eyes, glaring at the girl.

"Behold," said Mowgli, laying aside the flute. "Is there anything of fear in that? I told thee, little Stout-heart, that there was not, and thou didst believe. Thy father said—and oh, if thou couldst have seen thy father being driven by the road of the nilghai! —thy father said that they were devils; and by Allah, who is thy God, I do not wonder that he so believed."

The girl laughed a little rippling laugh, and Gisborne

"他们就在那儿，在森林里头，就在这所屋子的射程以内。轻轻地跟我来吧。"

"到底是什么事？出了什么事，阿布杜尔？"

"是莫格里和他的魔鬼，还有我的亲生女儿，"阿布杜尔·加福尔说。吉斯博恩吹了一声口哨，便跟着去了。他知道，阿布杜尔·加福尔有好些晚上揍他的女儿，不是没有原因的。而莫格里帮助一个他曾经用自己的力量——不管是什么力量——证明是犯了偷窃罪的人干家务活，也不是没有原因的。另一方面，森林里的求爱总是进展得非常迅速的。

森林里传来了轻幽的笛声，仿佛是哪位漫游的森林之神在歌唱。接着，一阵喃喃低语声，越来越近。一条小路通向一块小小的半圆形林中空地，空地四周长着高高的草丛和树林，形成了一道藩篱。在这块空地中间，莫格里背对着观看他的人坐在一根倒在地上的树干上，手臂挽着阿布杜尔·加福尔的女儿的脖子。他头上戴着新编的花冠，吹奏着一根粗糙的竹笛，四头硕大的狼，后腿直立，正伴随着音乐，庄严地翩翩起舞。

"那就是他的魔鬼，"阿布杜尔·加福尔轻声说道。他手里握着一把子弹。野兽们在一阵拉长了的、发出颤音的笛子声中躺下了，他们安静地躺在那里，绿眼睛毫不闪动地瞪着那位姑娘。

"看哪，"莫格里放下笛子说道，"这有什么可怕的？我告诉过你了，大胆的小人儿，没什么可怕的，你不是也相信了我的话吗？你父亲说——嗨，你要是能看见你父亲被赶着在大羚羊奔跑过的路上奔跑就好了！——你父亲说他们是魔鬼。我以你的上帝真主的名字起誓，我一点儿也不奇怪他会这么说。"

那个姑娘发出了低低的清脆笑声，吉斯博恩听

---

convict

[kən'vikt]

v. 证明…有罪，宣告…有罪

theft

[θeft]

n. 偷窃，偷窃行为

flute

[flu:t]

n. 长笛，笛状物

semicircular

[ˌsemi'sə:kjulə(r)]

adj. 半圆的

cartridge

['kɑ:tridʒ]

n. 弹药筒

longdrawn

[lɒŋ'drɔ:n]

adj. 持续很久的，久延的

heard Abdul **grind** his few remaining teeth. This was not at all the girl that Gisborne had seen with a half-eye slinking about the compound **veiled** and silent, but another—a woman full blown in a night as the **orchid** puts out in an hour's moist heat.

"But they are my playmates and my brothers, children of that mother that gave me suck, as I told thee behind the **cookhouse**," Mowgli went on. "Children of the father that lay between me and the cold at the mouth of the cave when I was a little naked child. Look" —a wolf raised his gray **jowl**, **slavering** at Mowgli's knee—"my brother knows that I speak of them. Yes, when I was a little child he was a cub rolling with me on the clay."

"But thou hast said that thou art human-born," cooed the girl, nestling closer to the shoulder. "Thou art human-born?"

"Said! Nay, I know that I am human born, because my heart is in thy hold, little one." Her head dropped under Mowgli's chin. Gisborne put up a warning hand to restrain Abdul Gafur, who was not in the least impressed by the wonder of the sight.

"But I was a wolf among wolves none the less till a time came when Those of the jungle bade me go because I was a man."

"Who bade thee go? That is not like a true man's talk."

"The very beasts themselves. Little one, thou wouldst never believe that telling, but so it was. The beasts of the jungle bade me go, but these four followed me because I was their brother. Then was I a herder of cattle among men, having learned their language. Ho! ho! The herds paid **toll** to

grind
[graind]
v. 磨(碎),碾(碎),折磨

veiled
[veild]
adj. 以面罩遮掩的,隐藏的

orchid
['ɔːkid]
n. 兰花

cookhouse
['kukhaus]
n. 户外厨房,船上厨房

jowl
[dʒaul]
n. 颚骨,面颊

slaver
['sleivə]
v. 垂涎,淌口水

toll
[təul]
n. 代价

见阿布杜尔气得直咬他剩下的为数不多的几个牙齿。这位姑娘完全不像吉斯博恩过去有时用眼角扫过去看见的那样,那时她老是蒙着面纱,沉默不语地在院子里悄悄地溜过去。如今她完全变成了另一个人——一夜之间她成了青春焕发的少女,就像兰花,在潮湿炎热的天气里,只需要几个小时就绽花吐蕾一般。

"而他们是和我一起玩耍的伙伴,是我的兄弟,是同吃一个母亲的奶长大的孩子,我在厨房后面已经告诉过你了,"莫格里继续说道,"他们就是狼爸爸的孩子,当我还是一个赤身裸体的小不点儿的婴儿时,是狼爸爸在洞口替我挡住了寒冷。你瞧,"一只狼抬起了他的灰下腭,蹭着莫格里的膝盖,"我的兄弟知道我在谈论他们呢。是的,当我是个婴儿的时候,他是只小狼,常和我一块儿在泥地上打滚。"

"可是你说你是人类父母生养的,"姑娘更紧地贴在他的肩上,温柔地说,"你是人类父母生养的吧?"

"我说过!不,我知道我是人类父母生养的,因为我的心已经被你俘虏了,小宝贝。"她的脑袋垂到了莫格里下巴底下。吉斯博恩举起一只警告的手,制止了阿布杜尔·加福尔,看来加福尔一点儿没有被眼前的美妙景象所感动。

"不过,我仍然是狼群里的一只狼,直到有一天,森林里的那些家伙让我离开,因为我是一个人。"

"谁让你离开?那可不像真正男子汉说的话。"

"是野兽们自己让我离开的,小宝贝,你永远也不会相信的。可事实就是这样。丛林里的兽类让我走,不过他们四个却跟随着我,因为我是他们的兄弟。后来我到了人们中间,学会了他们的语言,当

my brothers, till a woman, an old woman, beloved, saw me playing by night with my **brethren** in the crops. They said that I was possessed of devils, and drove me from that village with sticks and stones, and the four came with me by **stealth** and not openly. That was when I had learned to eat cooked meat and to talk boldly. From village to village I went, heart of my heart, a herder of cattle, a tender of buffaloes, a tracker of game, but there was no man that dared lift a finger against me twice." He stooped down and **patted** one of the heads. "Do thou also like this. There is neither hurt nor magic in them. See, they know thee."

"The woods are full of all manner of devils," said the girl with a **shudder**.

"A lie. A child's lie," Mowgli returned confidently. "I have lain out in the dew under the stars and in the dark night, and I know. The jungle is my house. Shall a man fear his own roof-beams or a woman her man's hearth? Stoop down and pat them."

"They are dogs and unclean," she murmured, bending forward with **averted** head.

"Having eaten the fruit, now we remember the Law!" said Abdul Gafur bitterly. "What is the need of this waiting, Sahib? Kill!"

"H'sh, thou. Let us learn what has happened," said Gisborne.

"That is well done," said Mowgli, slipping his arm round the girl again. "Dogs or no dogs, they were with me through a thousand villages."

"Ahi, and where was thy heart then? Through a thousand

brethren
['breðrən]
n. 弟兄们,同胞

stealth
[stelθ]
n. 秘密行动

pat
[pæt]
v. 轻拍

shudder
['ʃʌdə]
n. 战栗,发抖

avert
[ə'vɜːt]
v. 转移

上了放牧牲畜的人。哈！哈！畜群们在我的兄弟手里送掉了不少条性命，后来有个女人，是个老太婆，亲爱的，她在夜里看见我和兄弟们在庄稼地里玩。他们说我被魔鬼附上了身，就用棍子和石头把我赶出了那个村庄，他们四个跟着我偷偷地走了。也就是在那时，我学会了吃煮熟的肉，学会了大胆地说话。我从一个村庄走到另一个村庄，我的宝贝儿，我当过牛群的牧人，放牧过水牛，追捕过猎物，但是还从来没有人敢对我动两次手。"他蹲下拍了拍一只狼的脑袋，"你也来这样拍拍他们。他们身上没有恶意，也没有魔力。瞧，他们认识你。"

"树林里到处是各种各样的魔鬼。"姑娘颤抖了一下，说道。

"那是假话，是骗孩子的瞎话，"莫格里自信地反驳道，"我曾经餐风饮露，在月光下、在黑夜里露宿野外，所以我知道，丛林就是我的房屋。一个人难道会害怕他自己家的房梁吗？一个女人难道会害怕她丈夫的炉灶吗？蹲下身子拍拍他们吧。"

"他们是狗，不干净。"她侧过脸去，往前俯身下去，嘴里喃喃地说。

"我们已经吃下了果子，现在我们该想到法律了！"阿布杜尔•加福尔恨恨地说，"还等什么，先生！开枪吧！"

"嘘，住口。我们得了解一下发生了什么事。"吉斯博恩说。

"干得好，"莫格里说，他重新伸出手臂去拥抱姑娘。"不管他们是不是狗，他们曾经陪伴着我走过上千个村庄。"

"哎，那么你的心在哪里？上千个村庄。你一定

villages. Thou hast seen a thousand maids. I—that am—that am a maid no more, have I thy heart?"

" What shall I swear by? By Allah, of whom thou speakest?"

"Nay, by the life that is in thee, and I am well content. Where was thy heart in those days?"

Mowgli laughed a little. " In my belly, because I was young and always hungry. So I learned to track and to hunt, sending and calling my brothers back and forth as a king calls his armies. Therefore I drove the nilghai for the foolish young Sahib, and the big fat mare for the big fat Sahib, when they **questioned** my power. It were as easy to have driven the men themselves. Even now, " his voice lifted a little—"even now I know that behind me stand thy father and Gisborne Sahib. Nay, do not run, for no ten men dare move a pace forward. Remembering that thy father beat thee more than once, shall I give the word and drive him again in rings through the rukh?" A wolf stood up with bared teeth.

Gisborne felt Abdul Gafur tremble at his side. Next, his place was empty, and the fat man was **skimming** down the glade.

" Remains only Gisborne Sahib, " said Mowgli, still without turning; "but I have eaten Gisborne Sahib's bread, and presently I shall be in his service, and my brothers will be his servants to drive game and carry the news. Hide thou in the grass."

The girl fled, the tall grass closed behind her and the guardian wolf that followed, and Mowgli turning with his three **retainers** faced Gisborne as the Forest Officer came forward.

"That is all the magic, " he said, pointing to the three.

见过了上千个姑娘。我……已经……已经不再是姑娘了，你的心是属于我的吗？"

"你要我用什么发誓？用你们的真主吗？"

"不，用你的生命起誓，我就很满足了。在那些日子里，你的心在什么地方呢？"

莫格里轻轻一笑，"在我的肚子里，因为那时我还年轻，永远吃不饱。于是我学会了跟踪和狩猎，对我的兄弟们呼来唤去，差遣他们四处奔走，像国王差遣他的军队一样。因此，当他们怀疑我的力量的时候，我为这位傻呵呵的年轻先生驱赶过大羚羊，为那位高大肥胖的先生驱赶过他那匹高大肥胖的母马，其实要驱赶这些人也一样容易。就在这会儿，"他的声音高了起来——"就在这会儿，我知道你的父亲和吉斯博恩先生就站在我背后。不，别跑，就是来了十个人，他们也不敢朝前迈一步。你记得你父亲不止一次地揍你吗？要不要我下个命令，把他驱赶到森林里去跑圈子？"一头狼站立起来，露出了牙齿。

吉斯博恩感觉得出阿布杜尔·加福尔在他身边发起抖来。接着，他身边已经空无一人。那个胖子正飞快地穿过林中空地，朝山坡下面跑去。

"只剩了吉斯博恩先生了，"莫格里说，他并没有转过身来，"可是我吃过吉斯博恩先生的面包，不久以后，我还要在他手下当差，我的兄弟们也要给他干活，帮他驱赶猎物，传递消息。你躲到草丛里去吧。"

姑娘逃开了，高高的草丛合拢了，把她和跟在她身后守卫她的那只狼遮住了。莫格里和其余三个随从转身面对着走上前来的林务官吉斯博恩。

"全部魔法都在这里，"他指着三只狼说道，

question
['kwestʃ(ə)n]
v. 询问,审问,怀疑

skim
[skim]
v. 撇去

retainer
[ri'teinə(r)]
n. (旧时武将家的)家臣,扈从

"The fat Sahib knew that we who are bred among wolves run on our elbows and our knees for a season. Feeling my arms and legs, he felt the truth which thou didst not know. Is it so wonderful, Sahib?"

"Indeed it is all more wonderful than magic. These then drove the nilghai?"

"Ay, as they would drive Eblis if I gave the order. They are my eyes and feet to me."

"Look to it, then, that Eblis does not carry a double rifle. They have yet something to learn, thy devils, for they stand one behind the other, so that two shots would kill the three."

"Ah, but they know they will be thy servants as soon as I am a forest-guard."

"Guard or no guard, Mowgli, thou hast done a great shame to Abdul Gafur. Thou hast **dishonoured** his house and blackened his face."

"For that, it was blackened when he took thy money, and made blacker still when he whispered in thy ear a little while since to kill a naked man. I myself will talk to Abdul Gafur, for I am a man of the Government service, with a pension. He shall make the marriage by whatsoever **rite** he will, or he shall run once more. I will speak to him in the dawn. For the rest, the Sahib has his house and this is mine. It is time to sleep again, Sahib."

Mowgli turned on his heel and disappeared into the grass, leaving Gisborne alone. The hint of the wood-god was not to be mistaken; and Gisborne went back to the bungalow, where Abdul Gafur, torn by rage and fear, was **raving** in the verandah.

"Peace, peace," said Gisborne, shaking him, for he

"那位胖先生知道，我们这些在狼群里养大的孩子，有一段时期是用手肘和膝盖爬行的。他摸过我的手臂和腿以后，就知道了你所不知道的真相。这难道有什么奇怪的吗，先生？"

"确实如此，这一切比魔法还要奇妙。那么是这些狼赶来了大羚羊？"

"是的，只要我下命令，他们会把埃布利斯也赶来的。他们就是我的双眼和双脚。"

"那么小心点，当心埃布利斯带着一支双管步枪来。你的魔鬼们还需要学会一些本领，因为他们总是一个挨在另一个身后站着，那样只需要两枪就能把这三个都打死。"

"啊，可是他们知道，我只要当上森林看守，他们就成了你的仆人了。"

dishonour
[dis'ɔnə]
v. 玷辱，使蒙羞

"不管看守不看守，莫格里，你对阿布杜尔·加福尔干了一件很不光彩的事。你使他全家丧失了名誉。"

"什么名誉不名誉，他拿走你的钱的时候就丧失了自己的名誉，而且他刚才朝你耳边嘀咕，让你杀死一个赤身裸体的人的时候，他就把自己抹得更黑了。我会亲自去找阿布杜尔·加福尔谈，我是一个有养老金的政府雇员。他可以挑选他中意的婚礼形式，要不，他就得再被赶着跑一次。天亮以后我会找他谈的。至于别的事，先生有自己的房子，而这是我的房子。现在还可以再睡一觉，先生。"

rite
[rait]
n. 仪式，典礼

莫格里转过背去，消失在草丛中，留下吉斯博恩一个人。这位林中之神的暗示是不容忽视的，于是吉斯博恩回到他的平房去了。阿布杜尔·加福尔满肚子愤怒，同时又满肚子恐惧，正在游廊上狂呼乱叫。

rave
[reiv]
v. 咆哮，瞎说

"安静些，安静些，"吉斯博恩摇晃着他，因为

looked as though he were going to have a fit. "Muller Sahib has made the man a forest-guard, and as thou knowest there is a pension at the end of that business, and it is Government service."

"He is an outcaste—a mlech—a dog among dogs; an eater of carrion! What pension can pay for that?"

"Allah knows; and thou hast heard that the mischief is done. Wouldst thou blaze it to all the other servants? Make the shadi swiftly, and the girl will make him a Mussulman. He is very **comely**. Canst thou wonder that after thy beatings she went to him?"

"Did he say that he would chase me with his beasts?"

"So it seemed to me. If he be a wizard, he is at least a very strong one."

Abdul Gafur thought awhile, and then broke down and howled, forgetting that he was a Mussulman.

"Thou art a Brahmin. I am thy cow. Make thou the matter plain, and save my honour if it can be saved!"

A second time then Gisborne plunged into the rukh and called Mowgli. The answer came from high overhead, and in no **submissive** tones.

"Speak softly," said Gisborne, looking up. "There is yet time to strip thee of thy place and hunt thee with thy wolves. The girl must go back to her father's house tonight. To-morrow there will be the shadi, by the Mussulman law, and then thou canst take her away. Bring her to Abdul Gafur."

"I hear." There was a murmur of two voices **conferring** among the leaves. "Also, we will obey—for the last time."

A year later Muller and Gisborne were riding through the rukh together, talking of their business. They came out among

他看起来仿佛要闭过气去了。"穆勒先生已经派他当了森林看守，你也知道，他干到后来就能得一笔养老金，而且是政府雇员。"

"他是个贱种——是条狗——他是狗群里的一条狗，是吃死尸的家伙！什么样的养老金能抵得了这个！"

"只有真主知道。你也听见了，现在生米已成熟饭。你想把它张扬出去，让所有的仆人都知道吗？快点举行婚礼吧，这姑娘会使他成为一个穆斯林的。他长得非常英俊，所以你打了她以后，她马上跑去找他，这有什么奇怪的呢？"

"他说要带上他的野兽来赶着我跑吗？"

"他似乎是这么说的。假如他真是个巫师，至少也是个非常强壮的巫师。"

阿布杜尔·加福尔考虑了一会儿，然后他忘记了自己是个穆斯林，忍不住号哭起来。

"你是位婆罗门，我是你的母牛。就请你去把事情挑明，想办法挽回我的名誉吧！"

吉斯博恩第二次闯进森林，呼唤着莫格里。回答是从他头顶上传来的，声调一点也不驯服。

"别那么粗嗓门，"吉斯博恩抬头对上面说道，"现在我还来得及撤你的职，追捕你和你的狼。今晚你必须让那姑娘回到她父亲的房子里。明天按穆斯林教规举行婚礼，然后你就可以把她带走了。你现在就把她送回给阿布杜尔·加福尔。"

"我听见了，"接着，树丛中有两个声音在商议。"好的，我们服从。这是最后一次。"

一年以后，穆勒和吉斯博恩正一同策马穿过森林，谈着他们的工作。他们来到了坎叶河附近的岩

---

comely
['kʌmli]
adj. 英俊的,动人的

submissive
[səb'misiv]
adj. 顺从的

confer
[kən'fə:(r)]
v. 协商,商议

the rocks near the Kanye stream; Muller riding a little in advance. Under the shade of a thorn thicket sprawled a naked brown baby, and from the brake immediately behind him peered the head of a gray wolf. Gisborne had just time to strike up Muller's rifle, and the bullet tore spattering through the branches above.

"Are you mad?" thundered Muller. "Look!"

"I see," said Gisborne quietly. "The mother's somewhere near. You'll wake the whole pack, by Jove!"

The bushes parted once more, and a woman unveiled **snatched up** the child.

"Who fired, Sahib?" she cried to Gisborne.

"This Sahib. He had not remembered thy man's people."

"Not remembered? But indeed it may be so, for we who live with them forget that they are strangers at all. Mowgli is down the stream catching fish. Does the Sahib wish to see him? Come out, ye lacking manners. Come out of the bushes, and make your service to the Sahibs."

Muller's eyes grew rounder and rounder. He swung himself off the plunging mare and dismounted, while the jungle gave up four wolves who fawned round Gisborne. The mother stood nursing her child and **spurning** them aside as they brushed against her bare feet.

"You were quite right about Mowgli," said Gisborne. "I meant to have told you, but I've got so used to these fellows in the last twelve months that it slipped my mind."

"Oh, don't apologise," said Muller. "It's nothing. Gott in Himmel! 'Und I work miracles—und dey come off too!'"

石堆，穆勒骑在前头。在一片荆棘丛的绿阴下，躺着一个全身光溜溜的、棕色皮肤的婴儿，他背后的矮树丛中，有只灰狼的脑袋在窥视着外边。吉斯博恩一把推开了穆勒的步枪，子弹嗖地穿透了他们头顶上的树枝。

"你疯了吗?"穆勒大发雷霆，"瞧!"

"我看见了，"吉斯博恩不动声色地说，"他的母亲就在附近。天哪！你会把他们一整群都惊醒的。"

snatch up
夺取

树丛又一次被拨开了，一个没有戴面纱的女人一把抓起了婴儿。

"刚才是谁打的枪，先生?"她对吉斯博恩喊道。

"是这位先生。他忘了你男人的亲戚。"

"忘了？那倒是可能的，因为我们和他们生活在一起，有时简直忘了他们是外人。莫格里现在正在小河下游捕鱼。先生想见他吗？出来，你们这些不懂礼貌的家伙。快走出树丛，向先生们致敬。"

穆勒的眼睛越瞪越圆。他从乱跳乱冲的母马背上翻身下了马。丛林里出现了四头狼，他们围着吉斯博恩撒欢。那位妈妈站着给孩子哺乳，当那些狼蹭着她赤裸的双足时，她就用脚把他们踢开。

spurn
[spə:n]
v. 踢

"你讲的那些关于莫格里的话是完全正确的，"吉斯博恩说道，"我本来想告诉你的。但是一年来我已经习惯了这些家伙，所以我忘了告诉你。"

"噢，不用道歉，"穆勒说，"没关系。天哪！'我每天显示奇迹，你看到要大为惊奇！'"

图书在版编目（CIP）数据

丛林故事：英汉对照 /（英）吉卜林著；文美惠编译.—北京：
中国国际广播出版社，2014.5
（青少年成长励志名著精选）
ISBN 978-7-5078-3705-6

Ⅰ.①丛… Ⅱ.①吉…②文… Ⅲ.①英语－汉语－对照读物
②儿童文学－长篇小说－英国－现代 Ⅳ.①H319.4:I

中国版本图书馆CIP数据核字（2014）第037299号

丛林故事

著　　者	[英]拉迪亚德·吉卜林	
编　　译	文美惠	
责任编辑	周千红　李　卉	
版式设计	国广设计室	
责任校对	徐秀英	

出版发行	中国国际广播出版社（83139469　83139489[传真]）
社　　址	北京复兴门外大街2号（国家广电总局内）
	邮编：100866
网　　址	www.chirp.com.cn
经　　销	新华书店
印　　刷	环球印刷（北京）有限公司

开　　本	850×1168　1/32
字　　数	165千字
印　　张	9
版　　次	2014年5月 北京第一版
印　　次	2014年5月　第一次印刷
书　　号	ISBN 978-7-5078-3705-6/H·424
定　　价	24.00元